THE RHYTHM & THE TIDE

THE RHYTHM
&
THE TIDE

Liverpool, The La's
and Ever After

Mike Badger and Tim Peacock

Liverpool University Press

First published 2015 by
Liverpool University Press
4 Cambridge Street
Liverpool
L69 7ZU
UK

www.liverpooluniversitypress.co.uk
@LivUniPress

British Library Cataloguing-in-Publication data
A British Library CIP record is available

ISBN 978-1-78138-258-5 paperback

Typeset by Carnegie Book Production, Lancaster
Printed and bound by Short Run Press, Exeter

Contents

For my loving parents,
Ruth and Cliff Badger

Authors' Preface

I FIRST SAW THE NAME 'Tim Peacock' at the end of a review he had written in *Sounds*. It was a live review in which he had given my band The Onset a very favourable and considered write-up. I photocopied that cut-out many times and sent it off to get gigs and to accompany demo tapes in the years before the internet.

Later on, Tim would review the albums released on the label I started with Paul Hemmings, the Viper Label. He always seemed to 'get' them that little bit more than others – maybe because of the time he lived in Liverpool during the 1980s he had a deeper understanding of our ingredients and passion.

About 2009, Tim asked if I would like to do an interview for his online magazine, *Whisperin' & Hollerin'*, and that – I suppose – is where this all started. It ran into three long sections and I started to realize that we had opened something that was unfolding and expanding at an ever increasing rate.

I then asked Tim if he would like to work with me on a book that tried to make some sense of my life working as a creative in music and art in Liverpool. Thankfully he was up for it and now some five years down the line – with trips between Liverpool and County Cork, Ireland, where Tim lives – we have ink on paper.

It's a daunting prospect looking back on your own life. Not just because of all the deeply personal trials and tribulations, proud achievements, mountains climbed, dark nights of the soul and glorious moments in the sun. BUT where the hell do you start?

With Tim there to transcribe interviews and probe further, we endeavoured to explain what has been an incredible journey. I wanted an unbiased piece of work that told the truth as I see it, hopefully uncoloured by any partiality that lurks inside (I've done my best!).

Over the years I have done many interviews about my life in music and art, many associated with the band I started with Lee Mavers in 1984, The La's. Little did I know when I dreamt that name up on Carl Davies' couch in Kelvin Grove, Liverpool, the weight it held: not just in the history of Liverpool music but in the emergence of what would go on to be called 'Britpop' and beyond.

Though it was only essentially a few years of my life it has cast a long shadow over it; a shadow with which I have often remained concealed within. This was no bad thing though – I left the most exciting group that had happened in Liverpool for years and I wasn't going to sit pondering on the past when I could venture down new creative avenues. I have always (as long as I can remember) made art alongside music. This has sometimes been a slight quandary for me. People tend to like things to be plain and simple – 'What are you: an artist or a musician?' Whereas most creative people are exactly that – 'creative' – and it is up to us how we wish to express ourselves, it is up to someone else usually as to what puts bread on the table.

I put years into playing in a hard-working live band, The Onset, recorded albums and toured Europe and the UK and scored many triumphs and hit rock bottom more times than I care to remember, and then woke up one day making a living as a sculptor! How the hell did that happen? Well it's just one of the threads that we have woven into the fabric of this book.

I do not hold onto the past, although I cherish every experience because it has been an essential, integral part of making me who I am as a person. I am from Liverpool; we know how to survive here – it's in our DNA. I offer my sincere thanks to Tim for being such a huge part of this project and aiding me in giving clarity to what has been a great life so far. As always, though, the biggest thanks go to Family and those loved ones who give structure and purpose to our lives but so often remain behind the visible face of it all, most of all my wife and best friend, Jeanette, for her eternal love and support.

Mike Badger

'D LOVE TO SAY I saw the legendary early incarnation of The La's featuring Mike Badger, Lee Mavers and John Power. Sadly, I didn't get the chance, though I was aware of the buzz surrounding them and I'd seen what I now know were Mike's hand-drawn gig posters when I'd been shopping in Probe Records and wandering around Liverpool city centre as a teenager.

Mike and The La's have never been far away since then, though. I bought The La's' 'Way Out' single in 1987, finally saw them play live at the Royal Court (supporting Joe Strummer on his post-Clash *Rock against the Rich* tour) on the night of my twenty-first birthday in 1988, and then snapped up the original 12-inch of 'There She Goes' the week it was released. I've since written about The La's on a number of occasions, most notably in *Sounds* and – more recently – in *Record Collector*.

I've read the music press voraciously since I was thirteen. I often bought the *NME* and *Melody Maker*, but I always enjoyed *Sounds* the best. Despite what people often say, it wasn't just the 'heavy metal' paper, as it hungrily embraced everything from post-punk to Oi!, reggae, psychobilly, the early rap scene, the Paisley Underground bands and what is now usually referred to as 'Americana'. I could hardly believe it when Shaun Phillips, my first reviews editor, called me out of the blue to enthuse about a sample review of a Dinosaur Jr gig I'd sent in during the spring of 1989. I don't think I really took in what he said, but I went along to review James at the Royal Court at his request a week later. As they say, the rest is history.

I was lucky enough to be with *Sounds* in the paper's later years when Madchester, shoegazing and grunge were happening on the cusp of the 1990s. During this time, I also saw Mike's post-La's outfit, The Onset, several times. Two shows that readily spring to mind are their appearance at the 1989 Earthbeat Festival in Sefton Park and then a great show at the Hardman House, which I reviewed for *Sounds*. At this time, The Onset also featured fellow ex-La Paul Hemmings, and as a live band they were at the peak of their powers.

Post-Onset, Mike has enjoyed a singular career in both art and music. He's formed a third roots-based band, Mike Badger and The Shady Trio, designed record sleeves and enjoyed acclaim as a sculptor in recycled tin. He's also co-founded one of Liverpool's most important contemporary imprints, the Viper Label, with Paul Hemmings and amassed an enviable body of work without ever signing a major record deal. He works intuitively; always follows his heart and he's someone whose work you can just instinctively trust, which is a rare quality and something to be cherished.

The Rhythm & the Tide isn't the entire story of The La's, but it gets right into the corners of the band's crucial early days, reveals how they became such a hot property – long before Go! Discs Records came on the scene – and hopefully puts a few myths to rest along the way. It's about much more too – the Viper Label and The Onset, certainly – but also post-punk Liverpool, Britpop and a whole lotta folks whose contributions ought to be given far more kudos in histories of music on Merseyside.

Before closing, I'd like to express my most sincere thanks to Mike, our editor Anthony Cond at LUP and my wonderful partner, Ann, for their faith and belief in bringing this project to fruition. Because of you all, writing this has been a blast from stem to stern.

Tim Peacock

ONE

Huyton
(Two Dogs Fightin' –
A Black and a White'n)

B Y THE RED HOT summer of 1976 I was fourteen and going into
Liverpool to meet my friends. I was a young man and stepping out.
It didn't take me long to find the newly opened Probe Records shop on
Button Street, off Whitechapel. I can never forget seeing Jayne Casey
and Holly Johnson walking past in white boiler suits with cropped
peroxide hair. No one had seen anything like that; it had all been
patchouli oil, ex-army greatcoats, flares and long hair until then. It
was like they had just stepped off a space ship!

The sights around Probe opened your eyes. People were exclaiming
their individuality in 1976 and using their imagination. Pete Burns
would be sitting on the steps of Probe with his huge quiff, black eye
make-up, earrings and leather and was a sight to behold. Soon inside
Probe, Eric's flyers were all around advertising bands I had never heard
of like The Sex Pistols, The Damned, Elvis Costello, Deaf School, The
Buzzcocks and Magazine.

Eric's had opened the same month as Probe around the corner
in Mathew Street, right opposite the site of the Cavern, which the
Council had seen fit to turn into a plot of waste ground and to be

used as a car park. These days, people forget the diversity of youth culture of the time, but there were rockabilly gangs as well as Teds who would get their records from Probe. Another important shop from the '60s had stood opposite Probe on Whitechapel. This was NEMS, the store that had been run by the late Beatles manager, Brian Epstein. There really was a lot of history and culture down that part of town.

In 1977 I was fifteen and started to date girls, usually from Huyton College – the sister school to Liverpool College (where I attended). I was one of the first in the crowd to get a pair of tight straight-leg jeans. Hard to believe now that that could have been such a statement back then – but it was. I had also bought a pair of green baseball boots from the Probe-related Silly Billies on Whitechapel which I would wear with a blue Navy shirt from school, the CCF (Combined Cadet Force).

I was determined to have a damn good time away from the confines of school. I had developed an interest in girls quite early on. My first girlfriend was from Woolton Road, a nice Huyton College girl called Ann Haslam, and then after that fizzled out I started to see another girl from the same school, Shirley, who lived opposite Bellefield (Everton FC's training ground) in West Derby. She introduced me to pot for the first time. I had a sense of trepidation and didn't know what would happen, but my first-ever joint didn't really do anything.

She lived a few doors up from Liverpool FC's ex-manager Bill Shankly, who would play football with lads on the local field. One day leaving Shirley's I saw him walking towards me. He saw me and said, 'You al'reet?' 'Yeah', I nodded enthusiastically. He obviously had no airs and graces, a real man of the people. Even though I was a Blue he was a genuine Liverpool legend and a poet of the people. How true his words have become that 'when football is taken away from the working classes it will be the end of the game'. He also said, 'If Everton were playing in my back garden I would draw the curtains'. If he had lived on the other side of the road he would have had to!

My Dad became quite friendly with him through a mutual friend, Ian McFadyen, and ended up going to about a dozen matches with him and Bill Shankly. My Dad imitates him saying, 'When I was playing for Preston North End we'd always come to watch Everton, *The School of Science*'. This delighted my Dad no end of course.

******

Prior to Eric's, the Stadium and the Empire usually had the best shows in Liverpool. During 1977 I saw Dr. Feelgood play a gig at the Empire which literally changed my life forever, with their fist-punching, heart-pounding rhythm and blues. I had bought my first-ever record in Penny Lane Records near Whitechapel in town. It was 'Prove It' by Television on 12-inch green vinyl (after a friend of mine from school, Alan Furness, had revealed his copy to me) and it was the first of many. I remember trying to buy the single 'Tulane' by The Steve Gibbons band – unbeknownst to me it was a cover by Chuck Berry, but it had really grabbed me. I also got a treasured copy of 'Spanish Stroll' by Mink deVille, who with perfect timing had been supporting Dr. Feelgood at that Empire gig.

My Mum and Dad had a newsagent's and tobacconist shop in Cantril Farm (between Huyton and Knowsley) called Cliff's and started to sell ex-jukebox records. My Dad would let me take some home, so I would get 7-inch singles with the middle piece missing from them. Talk about a kid in a candy shop. Not only did I help myself to chocolate, I could now pick up such life-affirming treasures as 'Roadrunner' by The Modern Lovers – WOW! There's the sound of youth! Then there were all the Bob Marley singles, The Ramones – 'Sheena Is a Punk Rocker' – and more Jonathan Richman. 'The Morning of Our Lives' – that was a record to get at the age of fifteen. Then there were all the singles by The Stranglers and 'Do Anything You Wanna Do' by The Rods. That was a massive tune for me. In many ways this song set me up and confirmed for me your personal obligation to follow your instincts, as opposed to what I'd previously been told in school.

All these records were imbued with a common, yet individual identity that flew in the face of everything I had ever heard before. Actually, my sister Ros had a 7-inch single of 'I Hear You Knocking' by Dave Edmunds which I thought was fantastic! Probably my first-ever deep connection with the essential roots of rock 'n' roll, I reckon.

One great day I remember was 12 March 1977, just a week before my fifteenth birthday. Everton had reached the League Cup Final at Wembley against Aston Villa and I took the train down there with my Dad and his friend, ex-Everton and England star Brian Labone. We got loads of attention on the train because of all the fans recognizing Brian and we had a great time. (I also went to the two replays that resulted in us losing the chance of more silverware.)

In the latter part of 1977, because of constant break-ins to the family business – Cliff's Sweets and Tobacco in Cantril Farm Precinct – my Dad couldn't get insurance anymore and every time the stock went it was right out of his pocket. My Dad lost the shop and fell back on his trade as an electrician, while my Mum fell back on her profession as a secretary, working at Yorkshire Imperial Metals on the East Lancs Road, and then eventually starting to work in nursing administration at Alder Hey Hospital.

***

Back in school I was really counting the days until I could leave. My Mum and Dad had meant well in sending me there but I just wasn't cut out for toeing the line and slotting into place with everything. I was too liable to question things and saw through the futile nature of what was being thrust upon us. I had my O-Level exams coming up and found it all incredibly boring. I was expected to revise for qualifications that would have no bearing on my future – this I knew for sure. The exams were difficult. They were Oxbridge papers so the school could ingratiate itself with entries into Oxford and Cambridge.

When we got back from France after our summer holidays, it was August 1978. I knew my O-Level results would not be good as I had been far more concerned with getting with girls and partying with my mates. Still, I had hoped I would get my Art and my English Language, both of which I was considered good at. I got none. Not one – it was ridiculous. The best I had managed was an 'E' grade in Art and an 'E' grade in English Language, My Mum and Dad had worked hard and kept me there, paying my school fees for six years, and I had rewarded them with this. What actually made it far worse was that my Dad saw how upset I was and consoled me. I'd expected him to go mad, but he put his arm around me and said, 'It's all right son.'

To this day I feel it's wrong to dump all those heavy demands and responsibility onto the young, forcing them to make life-changing decisions at that time in their lives when their bodies are changing and their minds are still formulating. They are neither children nor adults at this stage and they should be allowed to learn more by experiencing from their freedom and developing social skills in a way that will help them gain confidence. Instead, I'd had one careers meeting in school and had been told to look into hotel management. Despite all this, I do have fond memories of school, my personal triumphs and friends, but I was a *mystery* to many in that school.

I always think one of the greatest things my Dad has instilled in me (albeit inadvertently) is a very healthy disrespect for false authority. I also cherish something my Mum says about life in general and our inability at times to appreciate what we have:

'Much wants more.'

******

During the summer of 1978 I decided to go to Childwall College to re-take my O-Levels and ponder what I was to do with my life. The thought of not having to wear a uniform in itself seemed like such delicious liberty. I remember my first day there sitting outside the main entrance talking to an ex-Liverpool College boy called Clive Shaw. A guy came up to us and Clive said to him, 'The mushies are out' [*magic mushrooms – Ed.*] and the man said, 'Oh, really?' while looking on the grass next to us. He picked a few and dropped them there and then, laughing as he walked off.

'Who is that?' I asked Clive. 'That's Tim Dawson the English Literature teacher', he replied. As this anecdote suggests, the contrast to school was quite profound. In fact, the whole curriculum meant a new freedom to me, to the extent of not always turning up to the classes.

******

At Childwall College, I soon hooked up with a guy called Carl Davies. He wore white deck shoes and an old suit jacket with jeans. He lived in a council house near Knotty Ash, which was just down Pilch Lane East, opposite Dovecot Baths, where I had once been a member of Everton Swimming Club. We just started talking at the bus stop one day and the subject of Jonathan Richman came up and we both enthused about his music. We hit it off and soon became good friends. I would then call over to his house – his bedroom was pasted from floor up, all over the walls and all over the ceiling with old music papers. He loved The Beach Boys and had become one of the founding members of The Beach Boys Fan Club in the UK when he was only twelve.

Carl had a huge Russian stereogram set up in the middle of his room with big old speakers and records piled everywhere. I'll never forget the time he played me 'It's as Easy as 1, 2, 3' by Jan and Dean … beautiful.

There was an unrestrained chaos to the room. I had always been quite tidy and this was refreshing. There were two beds in the room, the other one belonging to Ian, his younger brother. Ian would be at school when I would go round to Carl's to bunk off college. As I walked up the road towards his house I would know if he was in or not by the sound of the music coming down the road – 'I Think We're Alone Now' by The Rubinoos often belting out. Carl's Mum, Peggy, would open the door and before I had chance to sit down she would be handing me a cup of tea and a sandwich.

Left a single Mum with three children when Carl's Dad had gone and joined the Jehovah's Witnesses after a call at his doorstep one day, Peggy was the salt of the earth. She was a real old-school Liverpool Irish-Catholic lady from Park Road who'd moved out to the sticks with the post-war slum clearances. Peggy really would give you what she wouldn't have to give, a trait she passed on to Carl and Ian.

The song that meant the world to us on so many levels was a single I had got from my Dad's ex-jukebox rack in the shop: 'The Morning of Our Lives' by Jonathan Richman and The Modern Lovers. The lyrics from that were indelibly branded on us and always reminded us exactly where we were in our lives. In fact, there was only a week between us: Carl had turned sixteen on 11 March 1978, whereas my sixteenth birthday fell exactly a week later.

I suppose I had always felt a little different to the rest. Though I wasn't picked on by anyone, I wasn't always able to fit in because of my individuality. I always remember an incident in Bowring Park when I was about twelve, when a boy said to me, 'Ey lad, are you an American?' I was wearing red Lunes with stars on the flares, a blue vest speckled with more stars and a plastic cap (later commandeered by local boy Mark Campbell). Now at the age of sixteen I had no idea whom or what I might turn out to be. I did identify with new wave music and rock 'n' roll in general, I suppose – this was something I could aspire too. Even though I had never played a musical instrument, I liked what they were saying and the way in which they said it seemed real to me.

My new mate Carl, on the other hand, played a semi-acoustic bass guitar, knew some chords and had got as far as writing songs like 'Surfin' New Brighton' and even a tune about a young girl falling into prostitution. He was ahead of the game on so many levels, very well read and a crazy character. One verse he wrote which endeared Carl to me forever was something he had written walking home from his girlfriend's house:

Those Saturday nights were the best I've had yet,
Dancing all night with a girl I'd just met,
Walking home at night seeing beauty and trees,
Can I be sixteen forever please?

Carl had started a relationship with Gill Piggott at Childwall College. She was very attractive and hip, though a little troubled and deep. She had another friend called Jill, or 'Hippy Jill', who I'd first seen when she'd accidentally walked into one of my classes at college with a seven-foot-tall heavy-duty biker. Hippy Jill became my girlfriend for a while – probably because she wanted some action, and I was in need of some myself. It didn't last too long, though. Hippy Jill was getting a lot of grief at home. She had to leave and ended up moving in with a guy called Fred until she could find a place of her own. Fred was a bona fide punk rocker who lived in Croxteth. He was a mass of contradictions in that he was hugely into really hard, thrashy music and the whole 'punk' thing as it had become, yet he was really soft, friendly and all smiles as a bloke. Fred and I had once been in town and had ended up in the British Home Stores Café behind Probe with Lynn Burns, Paul Rutherford and a couple of other punks when out of the blue a food fight started and we all got chased out of the café onto the street. Punk was not dead yet!

******

Carl had his personal problems too. He had a fiery relationship with Gill Piggott and sometimes if he didn't phone her or go round, she'd send taxis and even – on one occasion – fire engines round to his house to get him to respond. It was all pretty extreme. Carl had his eccentricities. He always slept on the couch downstairs in the living room and would invariably still be there, fast asleep, with a cold cup of tea on the floor, when I called round at mid-day. 'He won't get up, the lazy sod!' Peggy would exclaim furiously sitting in the arm chair with a fag in the living room.

Carl, though, had his own routine. He would have been up all night reading Jack Kerouac or J.D. Salinger and writing. When he finally arose from his cocoon, he would read me pages from the books and show me his own writing. Carl rooted out great writers years before everyone else and devoured them during his all-night sessions. (I, on the other hand, have never really been much of a reader.)

Before he finally dropped off to sleep, Carl would paste the words to the songs he'd written all over the living room door next to Peggy's photograph of the Pope. I'm not sure how Peggy felt about that but she left them on the door for months – certainly the Pope's visit to Liverpool was a huge event for her.

One time Ian came in from school and something ignited a full-blown push and shove argument with Carl that ended with Ian being pushed, fully clothed in his school uniform, into a bath of cold water from the night before. Instead of anger, they both exploded with laughter. Carl, being the oldest male, wasn't exactly what you could call a typical 'man of the house'.

It was a time of personal development. I spent a lot of time decorating our attic, which my Dad had boarded out. I filled it with posters and flyers and painted band names on the floor. I had a mattress and cushions for hanging out on, smoking or entertaining – yes, a dream pad for a raver. There were Eric's date sheets across the beams and an old train set. I also hung a painting of Bob Marley smoking a joint and acquired a promotional cardboard window display of The Clash's *Give 'Em Enough Rope* and landed a radiogram that had been the family's before we got a more modern hi-fi. I had stacks of records, joss sticks, colours and words.

I was a creator in my new lair and I started to write words myself around this time. (The only academic success I had had in English at school was for my poetry as recognized by our English teacher – the American Tex Tucker. And thanks to him I had become aware that I had some talent in this area.) It was rudimentary stuff. I had written a line about a girl I had seen on the 6C bus: 'The way you sit makes my blood flow, the way you wipe the condensation from the window'.

I had made some good friends in Childwall College. There was Tracey Davies, an old family friend, and a girl I became quite close to was Suzanne Walker, who lived in nearby Menlove Gardens. One afternoon Suzanne and I went off to Kirklands in town to hang out and a sound came over the speakers that shook me to the bone – 'Peggy Sue' by Buddy Holly. The rhythm just pounded and I became a fan of Buddy that day. (Kirklands was also just a stone's throw from the Philharmonic Hall, where Holly had once played before his most untimely death.)

I started to date an Asian girl from college called Ruksanah. We got to know each other a little on a walk in the Black Woods near to Childwall Woods and made plans to meet again. It was a lovely time. We used to write to each other because she didn't have a phone, but we drifted apart as the summer approached.

******

During that summer of 1979, a group of us decided to go to the south of France in my Dad's VW camper van. There were eight of us in all. My sister Ros and her boyfriend Brendan (from St Helens Art College), their mate Richie and his girlfriend Theresa, Carl Cookson from Knowsley, Paul Clarke (an old school friend of mine) and a girl called Jeanette Handler. She was a girl Ros had befriended while working at

Top Shop in Church Street and had been set to go on holiday with her family, but her mother was now recovering from a serious operation, so Ros had asked Jeanette if she'd like to join us.

The drive went smoothly and was a lot of fun, and we found a camp site in Sainte-Maxime. One evening we were drinking and everyone was enjoying themselves. I ended up sloping off into the night with Jeanette. We just wandered around until we sat talking on the swings. I hadn't genuinely considered the prospect of starting anything with her. For one thing, I was used to the more 'bohemian' crowd. Jeanette was tall, elegant and had a naturally sophisticated manner, so that probably amounted to me feeling that she would be out of my league. Nonetheless we could feel something stirring between us and it felt wonderful. We talked for a long time and, with the small hours fast approaching, I finally plucked up the courage to kiss her.

She had been sleeping alone in a small, orange Force 10 tent next to the van and from this night on I would be graced with sharing it with her too. I'd turned seventeen in March while she had turned eighteen that same month. I couldn't have guessed what she could see in me with my dreams, musical aspirations, second-hand clothes and French cigarettes. But there it was: the onset of love and we never once left each other's side for the rest of the holiday. There was a long, stone jetty near the harbour, behind the camp site. We went there every day to sunbathe, swim and kiss. It was paradise.

On the journey home, we stopped off at a small café restaurant for a plate of *frites*. A ridiculous incident ensued with the middle-aged proprietor, I think instigated by our using the toilet before we'd sat down to eat. He'd believed we were just using the facilities and going to leave without buying anything and was very rude with us as a result. Pissed-off and hungry, we responded in kind and there was an argument. The upshot being that we left without buying any *frites* or anything else. Ros slammed the door as we left and the next thing we knew, the guy was coming after us with a handgun. We dived into our VW camper van and got the hell out of there as fast as possible leaving in a cloud of dust, just like in the movies!

Still, very little could go wrong for me at that time. Jeanette and I sat next to each other in the van, gazing into each other's eyes, having the time of our lives. Like a complete idiot, I burned a hole in her pink summer dress with my Gitane cigarette and she just smiled about it. I was so embarrassed, I embroidered an awful flower over the hole for her when we got home, but I don't really think she lost much sleep over it. We were coming back to Liverpool head over heels in love.

✶✶✶✶✶✶

On our return I started at St Helens Art College on a two-year foundation course to run between September 1979 and the summer of 1981. It was only up the railroad track from Roby. My sister Ros had gone to the same college a year before (along with Spitfire Boy and future Frankie Goes to Hollywood star Paul Rutherford – Budgie was also there too, of Big in Japan and later Siouxsie and The Banshees, Creatures and Slits).

I had a regular routine every morning. I'd get the train from Roby station with Lynn Metcalfe, who always wore her leather jacket and Siouxsie-style make-up, and I'd also see Jeanette on the train going to work at Top Shop in Liverpool in her white mac as her train pulled into the platform on the opposite line. I soon immersed myself in my art foundation course, loving the life drawing and learning about all the different mediums and approaches to art. The course convinced me to start keeping sketchbooks, although they were just as easily recognisable as scrap or notebooks as I stuck everything of interest I could find into them: something I continued doing for decades after.

I started to go out all the time too. I hardly ever stayed at home and in the evening after college I would be over at the paramount estate at Jeanette's house or calling round on Carl a lot of the time. We got our first fledgling musical thing going called Carl and The Passions with another mate, Jonee Mellor (from near Court Hey Park), on drums. In time-honoured tradition, we practised in a garage off Wheathill Road and I played percussion and sang backing vocals on Carl's songs like 'Theme from an Imaginary Rain Dance'. It was all very sketchy and formative, but it was fun and Carl enjoyed the fact he'd lifted the name Carl and The Passions from one of The Beach Boys' albums.

✶✶✶✶✶✶

New musical creativity was bubbling to the surface in Huyton. Lynn Metcalfe, the girl I got the train to St Helens with every day, introduced me to Lloyd and Sevo in the Huyton Leisure Centre Bar. They were Huyton punks from the Bluebell Estate. One day Lynn took me round to Lloyd's place on the Bluebell and he turned out to be a powerhouse, full of energy and a scarily manic laugh. On top of this he had a display case the size of the wall full of his boxing trophies. He wore black plastic kecks and a tail coat. Sevo would then turn up in tartan bondage trousers with green spiky hair and a chain and padlock around his neck. It was a twenty-four-hour appendage that was going rusty because he'd long since lost the key.

There was also a guy called Robbie and collectively the three of them were Neuklon, taken from the David Bowie track 'Neuköln' from his *'Heroes'* album, according to Lloyd. They had an unlikely musical line-up. Lloyd sang and played synthesizer. Sevo played a battered old drum kit and Robbie weighed in with more keyboards. I was intrigued enough to go and see them practise at the local community sports hall and was well impressed.

They were raw and psychotic with Lloyd hollering through lyrics like 'Someone's gotta hear me, someone's gotta run, yeah!' and following them up with hard-core riffs on the synthesizer. They had another one called 'Schizophrenic', which was a hard punk rocker and worked well despite the lack of guitars. They were striking and full of energy.

Soon, Carl would come down to practice with his old school-mate Fitzy. He had a new group called The Go-Thongs, so named because 'thongs' were the shoes surfers wore to help them stay on their boards. Initially, they'd recruited a drummer from Australia but he was an older guy and didn't really work out. Eventually, he was replaced by a primitive drum machine.

Carl had found out that the Huyton landscape was formed in the last ice age and the River Alt (a Viking name, as were Huyton and Roby) had been a great winding river. He wrote about this little stream, which was the remainder of a previous age:

Sevo, Lloyd, Robbie and Harry,
Don't you know that you're living in a
Glaciated river valley

By this time it was almost Christmas 1979, so I decided to approach Roger Eagle (manager of Eric's club) with a view to hiring the venue for our art school party. I forget exactly how much it cost, but it wasn't very much and we easily covered it from ticket sales.

It was the first time I'd spoken directly to Roger Eagle. He glared at me with a knowing, fixed expression, but he was in agreement for the night and before long Lynn Metcalfe had designed the tickets and they'd all been sold.

The party itself was a great occasion. The Go-Thongs went on first. Carl had been over to New Brighton to get real sand to throw on the stage and he'd asked me to paint a small, wooden surf board with the name 'The Go-Thongs' written vertically down it. It stood behind the drum machine between Carl and Fitzy as they performed. Their songs showed a love of The Beach Boys, Jan and Dean and the Beserkley label.

They had such songs as 'Surfin' New Brighton', with the lyrics 'Dodging oil and glass' and 'Missin' You', which started with the lines

Jim Morrison and Mama Cass are dead,
James Dean, Marc Bolan too,
Glen Miller's still missing,
And baby ... I'm missing you!

(... and then the music kicked in!)

Carl had also written a Christmas song in keeping with the occasion which went 'Yeah, it's Christmas and it's time to fall in love, a job for my Dad and peace on Earth'. It was delivered with a certain amount of irony as Margaret Thatcher had gained power earlier that year and there were dark clouds forming.

Neuklon, by comparison, were far more primal. They were great visually too. Sevo mercilessly pounded his battered, green drum kit. Robbie looked seriously cool in an old suit and trilby hat at the keyboards and Lloyd truly bawled out his lyrics like Iggy Pop. Every time he needed to twist a button on his synthesizer, his whole body needed to go with it. It was the real thing!

Overall, it had proved to be a successful night. The next time I was at Eric's I asked Roger Eagle if Neuklon could give support to a touring band at Eric's and sometime later Dave C, the lad who collected the glasses at the Grapes pub, told me that after Roger had seen Neuklon at our Christmas party he had said that they were 'the future of rock 'n' roll'.

TWO

Eric's and Post-Punk Liverpool

G OING TO TOWN ON Saturdays I would also spend time in the Tea Rooms on Mathew Street – later known as The Armadillo – and opposite that there was Eric's.

It's hard to believe it was all there, now that our lovely, dirty old town has turned into a haven for night-time revellers of a very different kind. In the late '70s, this area was awash with characters and individuals who never followed the pack but formed their own. No one looked the same; it was about freedom of expression, freedom of speech, freedom to have a good time, in fact just *freedom*.

The benevolent characters who gave us the license to express ourselves in such an exciting way formed the backbone of Liverpool's first mighty wave since the Merseybeat explosion. Probe Records shop creator Geoff Davies and Roger Eagle, DJ and founder of the legendary Eric's – the two of them, along with the Tea Rooms, were inextricably linked. The bands that played in Eric's had their records for sale in Probe, the local *misfits* and would-be *superstars* would sit for hours in the Tea Rooms opposite, planning the next revolution over pots of tea and cigarettes.

I would go to the Tea Rooms in Mathew Street and eat potato salad or delicious soup and brown bread. Older guys would sit around the tables talking about music and bands. Later I would recognize these faces to be the likes of Paul Simpson (who also worked in the Tea Rooms), Ian McCulloch, Julian Cope and Pete Wylie, to name just some of the talent that would go on to create big waves musically.

Of course, everyone who was there has his or her own particular views and memories of this essential time in not just Liverpool's evolution, but eventually its effect on a global scale. It was a time when creativity heaved and pulsed and nothing was going to halt its progress. I remember the first time I took that walk down the steps into the loud and musty depths of Eric's. I never felt intimidated in any way – I just felt at home here where people were like me, people who had no place else to go, but had no reason to go elsewhere either – it was ALL here.

Anyone who felt *different* could go to Eric's and find *unity* with everyone else. Not everyone was dressed up like dark Christmas trees either. Some were, but it was the variety of people that elevated this club from the mere status of a *Punk Club* and to something much larger and broader. You only need to look at the Eric's flyers (that I had collected for a good while before I could gain access to the club in 1978) to realize how incredibly open-minded it was. Prince Far I followed by Sonny Terry and Brownie McGee. Jonathan Richman followed by The Ramones. Rockin' Dopsie and the Cajun Twisters next to Magazine, and on it went.

One time in 1979 I went down to Eric's and Clive Langer and The Boxes were on, and during their set Roseanne Cash appeared on stage to sing with the band I thought, 'Wow – Johnny Cash's daughter!' I believe she was then in a relationship with another great songwriter, Nick Lowe, and he was also there.

I was caught up in the whole scene. I was old enough to blag my way in and I'd go with Tim Barklem from The Rooley in Huyton (he'd been Ros' friend from St Helens Art College) and we would go along wearing ripped jeans, Wrangler jackets, open-necked shirts and lots of rings on fingers.

The local music scene was starting to thrive too and I'd heard soon-to-be singles like Echo and The Bunnymen's 'Pictures on My

Wall' and The Teardrop Explodes' 'Treason' for the first time at Eric's. More Eric's sheets appeared each month, gig lists that now read like a rock 'n' roll Hall of Fame. The Cure. The Damned. Madness. Joy Division. The Pretenders. The Ruts. The Undertones. The Pop Group. Crass. Steel Pulse. Alexis Korner, and more. All of whom I saw at Eric's, quite a roll call, especially when you consider I only really caught the last eighteen months of its existence.

The Eric's DJs played heavy dub reggae alongside the latest British and American singles, while the fantastically eclectic mix of live bands was typical of Roger Eagle's across-the-board love of music. He was also very considerate in his policy making. Later he would insist the headliners play first, so you could see them and still make the last bus home.

On all the occasions I went to Eric's I never saw any trouble. There was no real drugs scene down there of any significance either; it was people who were essentially into music, who made this a safe environment. The lovely Doreen, who was usually on the door, probably knew I wasn't of a 'legal' age to enter, but thankfully turned a blind eye.

I have some childhood memories of the bands who played there, not least Steel Pulse playing 'Ku Klux Klan' in hooded white robes. Scary! I remember Ian Curtis falling into the drum kit during a possessed performance by Joy Division, resulting in him leaving the stage for half the set and Crass projecting Super-8 film onto the backdrop while playing 'Screaming Babies.'

The Cramps for me, though, figure high up on the list of occasions; their gig still stands as the dirtiest rock 'n' roll show I have witnessed, with Brian Gregory flipping cigarettes round his mouth and then spitting them into the crowd, Poison Ivy standing and twanging like a sultry New York statuette, Nick Knox pounding away on the drums, the heartbeat of rock-ability, and Lux Interior appearing on stage in black skin-tight pants, huge black quiff and gradually undressing down to a writhing, rolling mess on the stage floor in red underpants and black winkle pickers. What a night!

Myself, Sevo and Lynn Metcalfe met them all later on after the show, and they were all really accommodating. I asked for Lux's autograph and still cherish the piece of paper that Lux scrawled on the back of a Neuklon flier. It reads: 'To Mikey, who taught me everything I know, Lux Interior'.

I suppose this is the first time I was exposed to a live kind of raw pounding music that would fit into the *rockabilly* category!

Eric's was raided by the police and shut down on 30 March 1980 after a show by The Psychedelic Furs supported by Wah! Heat. I wasn't there but my friend Fred the punk from Croxteth ended up taking a swipe at someone who had decked him during the raid. It turned out to be a plain-clothes police officer and Fred got nine months inside for that moment of what he had considered to be self-defence. It was ironic that this was the only violent act I know of in the club and it had been provoked by police action.

We went on the march one sunny afternoon to protest at the shutting down of this essentially peaceful, vibrant venue, but it added up to nothing. I suppose it had served its purpose and the scene was moving on. It morphed into a kind of son of Eric's, a club called Brady's, for a while and I saw some fine live bands there too, such as The Stray Cats (more of whom later). But Brady's only lasted a short while and soon it was all gone and only Probe was left standing to man the fort.

There was never ever any mention of The Beatles at Eric's, let alone hearing any of their music. And that revolution had all started a few paces away from Eric's' doorway across Mathew Street.

THREE

The Smile that You Send Out Returns to You

ONE FREEZING WINTER DAY in 1980, Jonee Mellor called round to my house in Holly Grove. I'd known Jonee for years as he'd been a part of the Roby contingent.

Jonee had brought a guy with him who sported a huge blonde quiff and the three of us set off down Roby Road towards Huyton village. It was freezing cold and we hobbled over the frozen broken snow on the pavement. As we walked towards the village we talked and bantered. The guy with the quiff was Lee Mavers. Little did I know from that first meeting how our lives would later become entwined.

Lee had recently joined Neuklon playing bass, while Jonee had joined up on percussion with another guy called Timmo (John Timson) who now played drums because Sevo had left. Neuklon were expanding and since I'd got them their first gig at Eric's I had been placed in a tenuous managerial role. Next thing, Lynn Metcalfe and her mate had also joined as backing vocalists. Neuklon were turning into an 'electronic punk big band' and one night in Eric's Roger Eagle responded to my earlier request of a supporting slot for them asking me if they would be available to support an up-and-coming new band called Orchestral

Manoeuvres in the Dark. As it turned out their first single, 'Electricity', charted the week of the gig and Neuklon played to a packed house. I introduced them and then physically threw them on stage – 'BE IGGY POP!' That was the first time I saw Lee Mavers on stage playing bass. Great night all around.

I had started writing poems, small comments and observations in a notebook. Usually it was a case of me bitching about mediocrity or sniping at fashion victims, putting the boot in on the scallies or (worse still) the trendies. Oh, the trials of youth! I had titles like 'Pseudo Masochist', 'Jesus and Tommy', 'Parkas, Drainies and Trainies'. The last one contained the line 'all that they do and all that they know / is getting their tit at the Leisure Centre Disco'.

Dave C from the Grapes booked the bands for the post-Eric's club Brady's and gave me a slot reciting my poems with a group from Burnley called The Notsensibles, who most long-term underground heads will probably remember for their immortal tune 'I'm in Love with Margaret Thatcher'. It was my first time on stage and I was heartened because I went down really well. I exaggerated my usual persona and camped it up, spurting my words at the crowd who seemed to appreciate my disdain. Ah, teenage angst!

I'd done my first gig. A new mate of mine, Kevin Wright, who started at St Helens College in 1980, had taken to calling me Badgeroo, so I went under that name – Badgeroo and The Badgerettes, even though there weren't actually any Badgerettes. I liked the sound of it, though.

I did a few more support slots over the next few weeks and Thelma McGough, a researcher for Granada TV, saw my set at one of them. She worked on a programme called *After All That, This* presented by Nick Turnbull. Dave C introduced me to her and she told me she'd loved my performance. Would I like to appear on the show? This was an unexpected turn of events.

* * * * * *

'Dada wouldn't buy me a Bauhaus' – Adrian Henri

Aside from music and poetry, St Helens Art College proved to be something of an eye-opener for me, especially when it introduced me to the Dada and anti-art movements. Suddenly, when compared to the Dada events and bizarre words and creations being bandied around in Switzerland while World War I was raging, the whole punk thing and its aftermath seemed pretty similar.

I couldn't wait to share my excitement in discovering this new world and would go to Lloyd's or Robbie's on the Bluebell and tell them all about Dada creations – irons with spikes on them, a bike wheel on a stool, a urinal signed 'R. Mutt' and people with cones on their heads. After I'd told him all about it, Lloyd disappeared into the hall and came flying back into the living room riding a bike! What a fine Dadaist gesture. Lunatic![1]

******

Kevin Wright, my new mate from St Helens Art College, lived in Whiston and on my first visit to his place he showed me a copy of his cousin's band's 7-inch record.

It was The Teardrop Explodes' debut EP, *Sleeping Gas*, and he pointed out Paul Simpson, the band's original keyboard player, as his cousin. I was impressed, not least because Paul was a genuine style icon on the Liverpool music scene. People tried, but none quite matched his grasp of what was happening at the cutting edge of fashion and

1 Imagine how surprised I was years later to discover that one of the Dada movement's original instigators, Kurt Schwitters (and possibly another great inspiration to me, John Heartfield), had been placed in an internment camp just over the road from the Bluebell at the start of World War II – because they were Germans in England (even though they had fled the Nazi regime). Germans and other possible enemies would spend time here in Liverpool before their eventual shipment to the Isle of Man.

music at the time. He also worked, and had served Jeanette and me many times in the Armadillo Tea Room in Mathew Street.

Not long after, Kevin took me to visit Paul at his flat above a tatty antique shop in Rodney Street in town opposite the spooky church that has a pyramid in its graveyard. I took along the ukulele I had recently bought and told Paul all about my ideas for re-shaping music.

'Do you think I could get a pick-up fitted on it?' I asked earnestly.

Paul seemed pretty unfazed by my eccentric enthusiasm. He indulged us in a most magnanimous way and told us about how Will Sergeant from Echo and The Bunnymen had miked the floor to record interesting sounds. It was eye-opening and made us realize that you could do anything you wanted to do if you could channel yourself and had the conviction to follow it through. Kevin and I had formed a new band and Paul was only too happy to encourage us. We decided on the name, a Native American Indian saying, again from a Beach Boys album: The Smile that You Send Out Returns to You.

It was put onto us by Carl, and it seemed to speak volumes.

The college had advised us to visit the Wyndham Lewis exhibition in the Manchester City Art Gallery, so on Halloween 1980 Kevin and I took the train there. As we entered the gallery foyer, I saw this guy sitting in the corner. He had a big hat on and a light suit. He was drawing in his sketchbook and was swearing at his work. We could hear him muttering, 'Shit! Mother ... Fuck ... Fucker ... Shit!' It was bizarre. Who was this guy? He seemed immersed in his creative struggle, but there was something really fascinating about him. He had an aura. I went up to him and asked if I could see his work. I wondered how he'd react but he willingly obliged and flicked through the pages of his drawings. They consisted of seemingly abstract, angular lines with some strange-looking animal shapes.

'Are you an artist?' I enquired.

'Well, yeah, I do it, but I'm a musician too', he said.

'Oh, so am I', I said.

'I know', he replied enigmatically.

'How do you know?' I asked him, feeling bemused.

'I'm psychic', he said casually.

'Our band's called The Smile that You Send Out Returns to You',

I said, feeling a little more confident. 'And we don't want to have a drummer.'

He introduced himself as Don Van Vliet and called some of the guys over who had been busy buying posters of Wyndham Lewis prints from the gallery shop.

'Hey guys! These fellas are in a band called The Smile that You Send Out Returns to You', he said excitedly. 'And they haven't got a drummer!'

I was impressed. Not only did this American guy in the hat know we were musicians, but he'd just repeated the name of our band perfectly on one hearing. Any other time I'd said it to someone, they'd stumbled through it when they'd mentioned it back to me. Don was also really impressed that we didn't have drums.

'You got to get rid of that Mama Heartbeat!' he said emphatically.

'What's the name of your band?' I asked him.

'Captain Beefheart and The Magic Band.'

'I've heard your name before', I replied.

'Oh, well, we don't get too much airplay over here', said Don modestly.

'But John Peel plays you', Kevin chipped in.

'Oh what a good man', said Don. 'John has supported my work right through.'

He then must have seen how young we were and asked our age.

'Eighteen and nineteen', we replied.

'Well you gotta watch that [Ronald] Reagan guy. He's gonna be president and do you realize that you could get called up!' he said sagely. He knew the political climate the world was approaching and had also lived through Vietnam, I suppose, so he was doing his duty as a concerned gent.

I told him we were into The Cramps and Iggy Pop. He told us he'd just been with them recently, before being pulled away by the arm by John French. He was still rapping away ten to the dozen even when they finally dragged him out the main door to the gallery. They had a schedule after all.

We said goodbye and sat on the steps of the gallery, buzzing, but a little shaken and wondering what the hell that had all been about.

'He's really famous, you know', Kevin said.

Well yeah, I'd heard his name myself and if John Peel enjoyed playing his stuff... He was some character. The meeting with him had really affected us. It was like the apprentices having been shown a little of the magician's inner circle. After that, the Wyndham Lewis exhibition wasn't possible, something had just happened.

The following day, back in college, Kevin excitedly showed me the front cover of that week's *NME* and there he was again: Captain Beefheart standing in the Mojave Desert holding the same hat to his chest (a wonderful portrait taken by Anton Corbijn). I read the big feature about him with growing interest and his quotes made so much sense about music, the environment and life in general. And he was *real*! He gave two lads he didn't know the greatest thing you can give: some genuine interest and time. He lived his art 24/7 and we could vouch for that.

✶✶✶✶✶✶

Thelma McGough got in touch about the Granada TV slot. It meant that I'd have to go into Exchange Flags in town and read some of my poems for Nick Turnbull, the guy who presented the show. He liked them and I was booked to go in and be filmed reciting them the following week.

I think it was a welcome bit of acknowledgement too from my Mum and Dad. After all, I was living in a different world to the one they had grown up in, post-war, and although they let me do my thing I knew they were genuinely concerned about what the hell I was going to do with my life.

One night I was getting the train home from college and there was a crowd of Huyton scallies in the same carriage.

'It's Badgeroo!' they shouted, on seeing me.

'We saw you with Neuklon – hey, give us a poem!'

I thought I'd better do what they asked. There were a lot of them, so I went into performance mode and got my poetry book out. I ended up reading poems to some applause all the way to Huyton station. This was great fun and confirmed it for me that this was the direction I should be taking. Ha ha ha – crazy!

I had heard The Stray Cats' single 'Runaway Boys' and it really stood out from most of the things doing the rounds. To me it was what The Clash would sound like if they had a slap bass. I noticed they would shortly be playing at Brady's and they turned out to be fantastic too. All three of them had huge quiffs. Slim Jim Phantom danced on one leg around his bass drum and snare, double bassist Lee Rocker slapped and howled and singer Brian Setzer played immaculate guitar riffs on his huge Gretsch. It was the nearest thing I'd ever experienced to genuine, authentic rock 'n' roll. I went along to the show with Jonee Mellor, Gaz, Timmo, Jonner and Dyko, and one or two caught ourselves pushing our hair up into quiffs on leaving and we skitted each other about it on the way home. Rockabilly was now also a new passion.

Funny that American rock 'n' roll was still having to come over to the UK to be taken seriously. It was like back in the USA they didn't value their own heritage. This of course had been going on for some time – that's how Eddie Cochran had ended up being killed here in a car crash and a neglected Gene Vincent came over in the early 1970s (thanks to a considerate initiative by John Peel) just before his untimely death.

******

Thelma McGough had been married to the Mersey poet Roger McGough and her son Nathan asked me if I'd like to do a slot at a new venue called Plato's Ballroom. The next gig at the venue was scheduled for early in 1981 and it was to be headlined by New Order, the band who'd been formed by the three remaining members of Joy Division after their singer, Ian Curtis, had committed suicide.

I had previously seen Joy Division play at Eric's during August 1979. I loved their single 'Love Will Tear Us Apart' but I found it hard to get into that whole bleak, grey, long overcoat scene that followed them around. I respected the band, but it wasn't something that hit home personally with me. I used to call it 'getting off on being on a downer'.

Joy Division's reputation ensured there was a huge audience at Plato's the night of the show. In typical Factory Records showcase style there were several other acts on as well as New Order and me. Mike Keane's band The Royal Family and The Poor played a set, as well as a performance artist called The Box Man – Man Box. I went on and ran through a few of my poems, which were met with total indifference. Nathan had asked me to do a few poems between each act, which I proceeded to do until New Order's show time approached. This must have been one of their first shows since the suicide of Ian Curtis. I needed to know how long it would be before they would be going on, so I went to see them in the small room behind the stage and asked them. They completely ignored me. It was like I didn't exist. I asked politely again, still to no response. Factory Records boss (and Granada TV personality) Tony Wilson had appeared by the stage and – to his credit – exclaimed, 'Excuse me! This young man has just asked you a question. Would you please give him an answer?' To which they eventually did. Thanks Tony!

I got re-booked again there with A Certain Ratio and Cabaret Voltaire. I did like the way those evenings were more of an 'event' than just a gig ... but we must have been strange bedfellows!

One night Carl, Kevin, David and I all made a fire on the little island on the lake at the back of Kevin's house in Whiston. It was something to do. At about 3am in the morning I had smuggled out one of Kevin's Cabaret Voltaire records and offered it ceremoniously as a sacrifice to the fire but Kevin went mad and ordered me not to put it on, eventually seizing it back from me. I was only thinking it would have been in keeping with the band name!

During the month of May 1981, Carl committed himself to the People's March for Jobs, along with another 500 souls who endeavoured to raise the plight of the unemployed in a sterling effort, walking from Liverpool to London. His friends and family were so proud of him undertaking such a thing. Let's not forget: Unity Is Strength.

* * * * * *

Another of my hang-outs at this time was the Everyman Bistro in town. I got to know two lads there: Mick Head and Chris McCaffrey, although Chris was known as 'Biffa'. The pair of them were all smiles, had a wicked sense of humour and played music together. They had a band called The Pale Fountains and had severe haircuts, short back and sides, which they'd got cut at Victor the barber's.

Occasionally there would be an acoustic guitar knocking around at the Everyman and Mick would sing a Simon and Garfunkel song. They'd sit there the whole night, making a half of lager stretch to unimaginable lengths. They both came from Kensington, which meant they would walk home from town. They were always together and were totally into their music, Bacharach and David, but it was Arthur Lee and Love (who I had never heard of) whose *Forever Changes* album was so massively important to the young Pale Fountains.

I also met a gangly, leather-jacketed, flat-topped Hamish Cameron down in the Everyman Bistro. He was a lovely fellow and a character known by many. Sometimes he was with his girlfriend Michelle. I used to sit with my sketchbook drawing portraits of whoever was sitting round the tables – Hamish, Mick, Biffa or Jonee. I remember Hamish had once said to Jonee about 'the Palies" style when we were down there, 'Why would anyone choose to dress like a 1930s barrow boy?' They had a 'post-punk postcard look' that was shared with a few other bands from the North West and Glasgow. They had their own twist on things, though, occasionally wearing wellies, knitted fishermen's jumpers or even maybe on occasion a Boy Scout hat. We had a laugh one night when Biffa told us he and Mick had been dressed up and on their way down for their nightly visit to the Everyman Bistro, and on crossing the road in Kensington a few local girls stood on the corner just staring at them. One then said to Mick with the sarcastic concern that only a Liverpool girl could, 'Can I help you, lad?'

******

One Saturday, I went to Tuebrook and had a look around the shops there. I came across a junk shop off the main road. Inside, there were a pile of records and I looked through them. I came across a yellow label that read *Clear Spot* by Captain Beefheart and The Magic Band. Wow, that's the guy I met in Manchester.

The record had no sleeve at all, so I gave the 30p for it and took it home. I put it on and, as that *NME* interview had done, it confirmed everything I'd hoped for. There were incredible rhythms, wild man vocals and some of the most genuinely beautiful ballads I'd ever heard. These songs really hit home for me, probably because they were more accessible than some of the more raucous tracks. 'Her Eyes Are a Blue Million Miles'– what a statement? What a song! 'Too Much Time' was classic soul music and proved Beefheart could sing like Otis Redding every bit as well as he could howl like an animalistic bluesman.[2]

I soon got to hear *Safe as Milk*, The Magic Band's debut album too. Kevin had bought it and it turned out to be another really wild album. It seemed to epitomize everything the 1960s had suggested to me. The guitar playing on 'Zig Zag Wanderer' was electrifying. 'Plastic Factory' spoke of phosphorous chimneys burning. Beefheart was just amazing. He was an environmentalist, woman lover, avant-garde blues musician, an artist and an incredible songwriter. He seemed to encompass everything for me at that time.

✱✱✱✱✱✱

Back around at Carl's, new records would appear in his ever-messy bedroom. A new favourite was Aztec Camera's 'Oblivious', bought by Carl's brother Ian, who was getting into music and starting to buy records too. He had joined a drama class at the Everyman and carried a harmonica. I gave him a lift into town one evening and played him 'The Clouds Are Full of Wine Not Whiskey or Rye' by Captain Beefheart and I could tell he was intrigued by it. It was weird but wonderful. Ian was soon established as another face down at the Everyman Bistro and even with his tender years he soon ensured a place shaking the maracas in The Pale Fountains.

I spent my nineteenth birthday at Granada TV studios again when Thelma asked if I could come in to do a pilot for a new interactive game show. It was a fun day. Ted Robbins was there along with Steve Lindsay (ex-Deaf School) and Nathan McGough. But the real big news was that the host of the show was Michael Hordern, the voice of Paddington Bear and the man who had scared me as a child as the ghost of Marley in the great adaption of Dickens' *A Christmas Carol*, *Scrooge* ... what a gent.[3]

---

2 I always recommend *Clear Spot* as a perfect introduction into Captain Beefheart.

3 *Scrooge* is still shown every Christmas the message is so straight, true and honest – yet I wonder, does anything really change?

As our days at St Helen's Art College had come to an end by the summer of 1981, Carl, Kevin, David Evans (another good friend we had met there) and I made a big decision. We would get a flat together, pool our resources and form a band.

David had been a year below Kevin and me at St Helens and had initially approached us by asking if he could interview us for his fanzine. We agreed and did the interview, only to find out that David had no such fanzine at all. He just wanted to get in with us seeing as we were the guys who were always getting in trouble with the principal. Bless him, he had a wonderful naive charm that only someone from Rainford could have. He was cool, though, and I had recognized his charisma as soon as he had joined the college.

I had failed to get into Liverpool Art School to do a degree in painting and hadn't wanted to take a second choice. I was told I would have gotten into Manchester to do fine art but I hadn't wanted to, because when I looked around the painting department it had looked like all the students' work had been done by the same painter. I thought 'I'm going to be railroaded into a particular style here' and I did *not* want that. I decided firmly that I wanted to do music and no way was I leaving the city where Jeanette lived and the potential new band. In the end, we got a flat above a shop on Lawrence Road. It was as big as a house.

We started off with good intentions. We'd eat whole food, go running every morning (pinching the odd milk bottle from the doorsteps of the good people of Langton Road) and practise all day. We did it for about three days before our collective commitment started to wane.

It wasn't just a weakening of spirit, though. Something else had happened on the day we'd moved into the house which would significantly affect our plans. Gill Piggott, who lived a few streets away from our new flat, had basically moved in with Carl. He had the bedroom downstairs, I had the bedroom above his and Kev and David had the front room at the top where all the music equipment was stored.

At this stage the only musical equipment I had was a pair of bongos. It wasn't the very first instrument I'd ever owned, as I got my first ever guitar in Hessy's music shop when I was about nine years old. That was a present from my Mum and Dad and came with lessons to help get me started. It was a Spanish guitar and there is a picture of me dressed up like a rock star at home when I was about ten or eleven, wielding it high. The problem was, I lost interest in the guitar because I couldn't tune it and so it always sounded wrong when I practised (this was before the benefit of tuners), so eventually I had sold it to a school friend called Rick Zsigmond for £5.[4]

So when I'd flipped a coin in Hessy's with Carl, the decision we had to make was whether I would get a cheap bass or a pair of bongos. The coin had rolled across the floor and hit a customer's foot before coming to rest – that flip of a coin determining that I would leave the shop with a pair of sparkly green bongos, not a bass.

Nonetheless, our lifestyle and high aspirations were dealt a severe blow when our most prolific songwriter (Carl) all but disappeared for weeks. It was especially frustrating because he hadn't even left the building and was downstairs in his bedroom. It was just that Gill was a permanent fixture in there too. It was an unexpected turn of events and put paid to our grand scheme of being a working band. Eventually, we'd catch a glimpse of Carl briefly dashing to the toilet with make-up on! Then we wouldn't see him for another week.

It got weirder. Often, Carl would be on the toilet for what seemed like hours. We'd have to go to use the one outside in the yard. Then he cut all his hair off. Not that he had that much anyway, but he did it with scissors and it ended up all patchy and he just looked scary. Then we'd see him at the shops wearing a pair of white gloves for some bizarre reason. It was distressing. Sure, Carl had always been 'out there', that's where he brought all his poetic songs and ideas from, but this was something else. It seemed like he was retreating beyond reach.

Eventually, things came to a head after a few months when we had a massive bust-up with the landlady. We'd had a party one night and Neuklon had done a gig in the big top room, kicking in on full volume at around 2am. The police had come and it had got back to the neurotic landlady. She'd come round soon after that and tried to smash the record player. She'd ended up having an angina attack and we had to give her some pills to calm her down. She got some

4   Rick now has the New King's Road Vintage Guitar Emporium in London. Blimey – must have been one of his first-ever purchases!

real heavies from the letting agency and we had to call the police to protect ourselves.

Our dream of getting it together as a band had evaporated and we all moved back in with our parents. I was back in the wee box room in Holly Grove. My Mum and Dad were made up because they hadn't wanted me to move out in the first place. Still, it had been an experience, not least because the famous Toxteth riots had kicked off shortly before we'd taken the flat and the atmosphere on the streets was electric. Police from all over the north of the country were on the beat locally and walking back to Lawrence Road after we'd been out in town was always an adventure.

******

I started to hang out again with my old school mate Nick Walker. His family lived in an amazing house which his Mum and Dad had designed; it was like a collection of boxes behind a wall in Allerton. I always remember at Scout camp years before when I was at school, on parents day – when all the Mums and Dads showed up – seeing this couple and wondering who the hell they were. The lady wore a silver kind of cat suit and the man looked like Charlie Watts from the Rolling Stones. He wore a stripy blazer and had collar-length grey hair swept back. They were Nick's Mum and Dad.

Nick soon introduced me to a friend of his, Paul Hemmings – a young, debonair guitarist who lived in a beautiful house near Strawberry Field.

It must have been around this time I remember finding an old leather jacket of my Dad's and ripping the lining out. He also had an old tub of Brylcreem in the bathroom cabinet, and I took a scoop and plastered my hair back and I can remember feeling this is me and this was how I wanted to be.

******

Kevin and I decided to go to the 'Futurama' Festival held at the Queen's Hall in Leeds. Liverpool was well represented because Echo and The Bunnymen were headlining, but there were a lot of must-sees for us, including The Cramps, Burnley's great punk outfit The Notsensibles and The League of Gentlemen, featuring Robert Fripp.

The journey across the Pennines meant hitching. We started out at Windy Arbour near Kevin's place and soon got a lift up the M62 as far as a junction where we had to wait three hours to get a further ride. Typically, while we were waiting, two punk girls turned up and scored a lift in two minutes from a container driver. It was weird because The Fall had a Northern rockabilly tune called 'Container Drivers' and we were at Prestwich, where that band came from.

Eventually we secured a ride and jumped out in Leeds city centre, where our cunning plan was to find the university's student union bar, and meet some friendly students who would understand our predicament and put us up for the night.

We managed to find the student union bar and got to work. It proved a lot harder than we'd envisaged, but finally we met up with some friendly, sympathetic first-year students who took us back to their halls of residence. We grabbed a few hours' sleep on hard chairs and had Nutella on toast in the morning. We got to the massive Queen's Hall – which looked like a giant aircraft hangar – at around mid-day and wandered around, checking out the scene. There were lots and lots of Northern punks with tattooed heads and Mohicans, and lots of glue-sniffing was going on. We watched with a morbid fascination as punks breathed bags of glue and contorted their faces in looks of demented torment.

It was getting heavy. It wasn't a good vibe and with the place being entirely enclosed, the fumes from the glue lingered all around. I was *not* having a good time. I put up with it for a few hours when I looked up and saw daylight through a hole in the hall's roof and wondered what the hell the time was. I asked someone and they told me it was four o'clock. That was all I needed, another eight hours of this madness. I tracked Kev down and told him I was off. Was he coming? He'd met up with some guys from St Helens and wasn't happy with me leaving but it really wasn't my thing, so I left by myself. I couldn't handle this place. I think the fumes had got to me. I wouldn't have minded if it had been organic weed but it was just toxic to me.

I left the hall and began to randomly walk down a road. Within three hundred yards, I could see the motorway entrance. Within another five minutes, I got a ride on the back of a motorbike, getting the hell out of there. I was dropped at a roundabout, then after another five minutes a car stopped and off I went again. This was fantastic – I would be home in time for tea! The car dropped me off at another junction, which turned out to still be part of the motorway, when a police Range Rover stopped and I was reprimanded. They then took me to the next junction where I could legally hitch from.

It was all going so well until this time, but then I realized this was the same junction where Kev and I had waited at for three hours the previous day. Oh no! It was getting dark and now no one was stopping. In fact, not only did the cars make no attempt to stop, but gangs of young lads abused me on the way past. They'd drive right at me and then veer away to scare me. I felt really miserable and cold. I was wearing a T-shirt under my Dad's old leather jacket (the one that I'd ripped the lining out of). Just to add insult to injury, I had no cigarettes either, though I'd pinched a cigar of my Dad's in case of emergencies.

After what seemed like an eternity, a car finally stopped at around 9:30pm. The guy told me he was going to Preston. Not ideal, but it would do – anywhere but here! He was a weird guy, but I was grateful to get out at a junction on the M6. My torment wasn't at an end yet, however. Once again I waited and nothing happened, until I saw a light down a nearby road and made for it. It was a restaurant called the Tickled Trout.

Fortunately, Nick Walker and his girlfriend Helen were staying over at Holly Grove while my parents where away. When I got to the Tickled Trout, I called Nick and asked him to come and get me, which he very kindly did. As I waited in the restaurant's foyer, I lit the cigar I'd held back but was almost immediately thrown out by the manager of the establishment – he didn't like the cut of my jib. It really was the perfect end to a perfect day and I still had another 45 minutes to wait outside in the cold until Nick's blue Mini turned into the car park and finally put me out of my misery. Saviour!

FOUR

The Kindergarten Paint Set

THE SMILE THAT YOU Send Out Returns to You had returned to nothing more than a quote on an LP sleeve and I was looking at forming my own new musical venture.

Roger Eagle, a man who always did things for the correct reasons, had opened up a warehouse on Temple Street and had visions of it being a venue and arts establishment which would provide a creative nerve centre for musicians and artists in Liverpool. He named it Crackin' Up, after the great Bo Diddley song. Steve Hardstaff, who had designed all the Eric's and Probe artwork, had come up with a great logo for Roger's new venture that looked like a barren planet wearing a pair of shades.

Deaf School's ex-drummer Tim Whittaker had a large portion sectioned off as a studio and The Teardrop Explodes were going to do a series of gigs in the club, which had formerly been known as the Pyramid. I went to one of the shows myself and they turned in a mesmerizing performance – I remember Julian Cope had a broken foot. I was still carrying my sketchbooks with me at all times, writing down ideas for poems, thoughts and sketching people.

Roger was also looking after a band called The Frantic Elevators from Manchester. I got on well with their bassist, who played a violin bass like Paul McCartney. A guy called Dave Owens was there a lot and also seemed part of Roger's vision for the future. I arranged to have a practice up there with a guy from Huyton called Paul Green who played congas and another guy who shared my birthday. He was called Mick Mooney and he played guitar.

This was New Year's Day 1982. We were to have a practice the next Sunday but it never happened. It was a formative time for me. I had words, but not really being a musician as such, I needed melodies. I started writing 'songs' and putting them down on a tape recorder, just singing into the mic and learning as I went along. My early efforts were called things like 'I've Learnt My Lesson' and 'Staying Awake and Dreaming of You'. I also wrote a poem called 'D'You Wanna Wear My Sheepy Mitts?', which was taken directly from something a girl had said to me.

I began to do the odd day doing electrical work with my Dad and waited for things to happen. One day early in 1982, I saw Mick and Biffa and they were really chuffed because they'd been chosen as one of the *NME*'s 'Picks of 1982'. I had a bet with Biffa that I'd have a good band together by my twentieth birthday on the 18th of March.

I had really grown into a big Beefheart fan and had most of his LPs by now. I'd go to Crackin' Up and swap Beefheart quotes with Dave, stuff like 'I'm not talking about Zen – I'm talking about Zrite now!', 'Space is matter, we are matter – but it doesn't matter', 'Love over gold,' and 'All roads lead to Coca Cola'. Roger Eagle's favourite Beefheart album was *Strictly Personal* and he told me about a time he'd been in a hotel room with Beefheart, who'd told Roger he was getting some weird vibes from 'up there', pointing to the ceiling. It turned out when they were leaving the hotel that country singer Glen Campbell was staying on the floor above.

But Roger must have seen something in me and it meant a lot. This guy was a legend in Liverpool, not just because he had opened the magnificent Eric's club, but he'd had the classic northern soul club the Twisted Wheel in Manchester and after that he had put a tonne of colossal rock on at the old Stadium in Liverpool. He said to me the guys I needed to be playing with were some fellas from Manchester called The Mothmen.

I was also invited on to Janice Long's Radio Merseyside show *Streetlife* to have a chat and recite my poems. This was the first time I had appeared on the radio. I bumped into Janice a little after this in the Armadillo Tea Rooms and she informed me that one of my poems, 'Dear Dolphins', was selected to be on *Pick of the Week*.

I'd go into town and bump into Mick Head in the Armadillo or Jonee Mellor and Lee Mavers and catch up with what was happening. It was a busy time: before January ended, Jonee and I built a stage in the Pyramid Club for Dalek I Love You and I went to see a re-vamped Neuklon at Reece's café in the city.

I'd placed an advert looking for like-minded musical souls and a guy called Tom replied to it. He said he was playing with a guy called Chris Rodis and their group was called Blabber Wobble. We had a practice and it was good fun. We met up again and I brought in some of my ideas. I also said I had this name for a group: The Kindergarten Paint Set. It got the thumbs up from them. That was what our new band became, it fitted too: all youthful exuberance, rhythm and colour.

Another club, called the Warehouse, had opened on Wood Street, so despite the disappointment of losing Eric's things were looking up. I wanted to get three girl singers in and call them 'The Pallettes', and Mick Head joked that he'd thought of me when he'd been somewhere on the Dock Road and seen a sign saying 'Pallets Wanted'.

During February, I played Roger Eagle a tape of our embryonic work and he gave us a slot with the youthful Mick Hucknall's Frantic Elevators at his new venue, Adam's Club on Seel Street. The following night, we were gigging again, this time at the Warehouse to a crowd of 150 people and it went down really well. Spontaneity was a part of the KPS set-up, even though we had eight rough songs worked out at this stage. We were pleased to discover that a lot of the same people turned up on the Sunday because of the Saturday at Adam's. These shows were my first experience of being on stage in a 'group', and it was a real buzz.

A few days later I met Jonee, Mavers and Hamish at Crackin' Up. They were getting something musical thing together themselves, involving a double bass. The KPS were also gigging again, playing with The Cherry Boys and Blue Poland at the Pyramid. John Peel turned up. He said we were very new and different, but we needed to knock things together more. He was right, but it was only our third gig and we had only formed a few weeks before.

The first time I went into the recording studio was in March 1982 with The Kindergarten Paint Set. We went into a place called SOS, which was run by Alan Peters, a Huyton lad who had once lent his Gene Vincent records to The Beatles' Stuart Sutcliffe, another Huyton lad. Alan was in the band 29th and Dearborn and formed the popular Liverpool R & B band, The Lawnmower, who played regularly in the Everyman Bistro.

* * * * * *

In early April, I went to see Neuklon practise at the Bonty in town, before spending the rest of the same evening at the Mayflower Pub down by the Pier Head at a rockabilly night with Jeanette and Hamish. I had heard bits of rockabilly here and there but I was taken by the exuberance, it was like it had the energy of punk but was more polished and finished – it was the original sound of youth.

Dave C was booking the gigs at the Warehouse and he was into The Kindergarten Paint Set. He offered us the support slot with then-current pop sensations Mari Wilson and The Imaginations, whose Motown-influenced '60s pop was attracting a lot of press interest. The line-up was Tom Kemp on bass/bass drum/vocals; Helen Springer on guitar/percussion/vocals; Nicky Cullum on percussion/congas/vocals; and me on lead vocals/bongos.

* * * * * *

Dave C was trying to get a label going as an extension of the Warehouse club and offered The Kindergarten Paint Set a place on it, but despite a lot of talk and promise nothing materialized in the end. However, things were still happening with the band. A guy called Steve Grace, who I'd previously gotten to know at Crackin' Up, joined us and helped pull things together musically. Steve had been in a band called Nasty Pop during the '70s and was an accomplished guitarist, not to mention much more professional in his approach.

It was a time of creativity and I was now writing a lot. I had another song percolating called 'One Kind of Loving' and I'd go down to Crackin' Up on a regular basis, playing my bongos and enjoying the summer weather – even sunbathing out on the roof with Steve Grace and Tim Whittaker.

Meanwhile, Mick and Biffa were really making their mark with The Pale Fountains. They had been recording at S.O.S. during May and now I could buy their new single, 'Just a Girl', which sounded really great. These guys had now set a benchmark, I thought. Jonee had started driving them around, but then he was the only one of us lot with a full licence!

******

In August, I went busking with Carl. Busking was a way of getting money for cigarettes and alcohol and it would literally become a way of life for Carl. On some occasions he'd go out with Lee Mavers and the two of them would mostly play Ramones songs.

At this time I bought my first car. It was a powder blue Triumph Herald and it set me back £80 from Parkfield Motor Auctions. It came with a princely eleven-month MOT and a registration bearing the letters EMA. I hadn't passed my test but Jeanette had, so with her in the passenger seat I could drive legally.

******

Jonee was on the move as well and he got a new flat on Rodney Street, behind the tatty antique shop where Kev and I had visited Paul Simpson. He took great pride in the place and painted it in its entirety when he moved in just like the professional he was (also a qualified painter and decorator). Mick Head's brother John, though still at school, started to appear on the scene. He was a prodigious guitarist and ended up in the 'Palies' too. I met him in Jonee's new flat and gave him a plastic toy giraffe I had been keeping in my pocket. He accepted it willingly although I think he was a little bemused.

****

I'd been to visit Jonee, who he wasn't at home, but bumped into Hamish and his friends Tony Clarke and Bernie Nolan, who were in The Russian Rockabillies, on Rodney Street. They all climbed into my Triumph Herald and went to visit this guy who was a mate of Hamish's called Rogan Taylor. Rogan, who lived with his wife, Sue, intrigued me as he was writing a book about shamanism and putting it into a present-day context.

Basically, he was writing about how many rock performers – such as Jimi Hendrix, John Lennon and Bob Dylan – could be classed as 'shamen'. Some were upperworld performers and some came from the underworld. He talked with an infectious enthusiasm about it – read passages at length from his book – and I was fascinated. It seemed to make a lot of sense to me.

Hamish, Jeanette, Tony Clarke, his girlfriend Paula and I continued to go down to the Mayflower by the Pier Head on a Sunday night for their weekly rockabilly nights. The DJ, Colin Brazier, was an inspiration to me playing all this mad 1950s music that slapped you about the face and left you wanting more I'd always be going up and asking, 'Who was that?'

Standing at the bar with Alison Fay we laughed when we heard 'Ain't Nobody Here but Us Chickens' by Louis Jordan. Next up could have been 'That Certain Female' by Charlie Feathers or 'Cast Iron Arm' by Peanuts Wilson. POW!

It was great watching the girls all stroll in unison across the dance floor and I could have watched Walla and Jenny dance all night long!

******

During November 1982 I went to Chester with Carl, Jonee and drummer Alan Wills to a studio called the Chemist, which was owned by The Modernaires.

I had been talking to Alan a few weeks before about wanting to record, as he now lived in Paul Simpson's old flat above Jonee's and he had told me about his mate's place in Chester. So he sorted it out and I was very grateful to him for making the effort.

It was a three-storey terraced house on the outskirts of Chester that had an 8-track studio on the top floor. Jonee played some percussion and Alan played drums on a track – all other instruments were by the band. We ended up recording five songs, some of which I'd worked on with The KPS, during the Saturday afternoon session. These included 'Only Friends', 'I Can't Believe a Woman', 'One Kind of Loving', 'Hey Little Friend' and 'Thought Too Soon.'

The recording was a great experience for me and should have been for Carl too, but his behaviour was as unpredictable as ever. On Sunday he recorded two of his songs, including 'Tear of the Sun', but when the conscientious Dave Baynton Power (eventually to become drummer with James) had handed him the finished spool of his work, he just threw it on the floor.

The guys in the band were understandably upset about this as they'd worked hard on the recordings with him, but it explained why Carl later wouldn't give anyone a tape of his two songs. Sometimes people like to *diss* their work before anyone else does – a kind of insane 'I told you so' logic (wouldn't be the last time I came across that!).

He had us in hysterics though on the way back home singing 'Spiderman' in the car and he also commented on his own state of affairs, saying that he could 'keep twenty psychiatrists employed for years!'

I gave Geoff Davies from Probe Plus a tape of my Chester session and when I bumped into him in town sometime later I asked him what he'd made of it. He said he liked it and it sounded like some blues guy who'd killed his mother! ... 'Oh, right...'

******

This is a poem I wrote in Carl's one night:

When I've read *On the Road*,
and my quiff's developed a bit,
and I can afford a packet of cigarettes,
I'll grab Jeanette (and Carl maybe if he's good),
and one day we'll go busking in London.

(PS: Still never read *On the Road*.)

FIVE

A Secret Liverpool

IN JANUARY 1983, JANICE Long left Radio Merseyside for a job at BBC Radio 1. She phoned me up at home and asked me if I'd be interested in reading my poems on her new show. I was buzzing. Then, seemingly from nowhere, Craig Charles (with whom I had done many gigs at Phil Battle's Left Bank Bistro events on Mathew Street and other venues around town) began to read his stuff on Janice's new evening show and that was the end of that! All the same, Janice had been the first person to broadcast me on the radio a year or so before – this was now major league not just for Janice but for Craig Charles.

I'd been sending a few tapes of songs from the Chester sessions out to various labels and the quick reply I'd received from Cherry Red really heartened me, not least because they'd said the songs sounded like The Beach Boys' *Pet Sounds*! It also arrived along with a copy of Cherry Red's influential label sampler *Pillows and Prayers*, which I enjoyed.

They said they wanted to hear more, so I went back to the Chemist studio in late January to record three new songs: 'I Learnt My Lesson', 'Baby Don't Worry' and 'I Don't Like Hanging Around'. I got another note back from Cherry Red, this time saying the songs just didn't hit them in the heart. Fair enough. Looking back, these songs didn't have the simple, naïve charm that the first session had, but Cherry Red's initial enthusiasm was a real breakthrough. It gave me the incentive to keep on trying.

Jeanette discovered she could get a transfer to London with her job, so we decided to take the plunge and move down. Ros helped out by putting us up for a few weeks in her and Brendan's flat off Bell Street, near the Edgware Road, until we found a little room with a tiny kitchen at the back of a house in College Place in Camden Town NW1 above the old Greek landlady's own flat.

Our landlady had hutches full of rabbits in her back yard. We'd thought this was lovely, but then one day we heard the most horrific squealing from the yard, prompting Jeanette to see what was happening. She came back in tears, saying she'd seen the landlady wringing a rabbit's neck. They weren't pets after all, simply food and the landlady's age meant that she never had the strength to get the job done quickly! However, the atmosphere in the house was good for creativity and I'd sit in the little box kitchen and write for long periods.

I came up with 'The Time I Grew Forever'. It sounded like an American B-Movie title. It was about a young man who ate a peach and grew and grew and grew until he took off into the stars. I didn't know what to do with the story after that so I picked up a science book I had titled 'Matter' and just listed the chapters. It all worked as a story. I found that if I sped up a piece of classical music called 'The Syncopated Clock' by Leroy Anderson to 45rpm instead of 33 the lyric fit perfectly and in June 1983 I recorded it in Camden Mews off Camden Road. There was certainly nothing else like this about at the time and I had high hopes for it. Who needs drugs?

✴✴✴✴✴✴

Although Cherry Red had been less impressed with my second tape of songs, they were still interested in me. I'd had a meeting with them and they told me to call in and see them when I was in London, which I did. Mike Alway from the label said he loved my original recordings and gave me loads of records. He asked me to listen to them and tell me who I liked with a view of them playing behind me for recording purposes.

'Great!' I jumped into my imaginary bright green metallic Hot Wheels-style beach buggy and headed back to Camden Town while the horn played 'La Cucaracha'!

We arranged to meet up the following week. In the meantime, I sent them the finished version of my new track, 'The Time I Grew Forever', which I was sure they'd all love. Still confident, I went to their office the following week as expected and asked them what they thought of the new track. They had a problem. Collectively, they couldn't decide whether it was 'shit' or 'fucking shit' – their words. The beach buggy had been ditched and I rattled home on the Tube feeling very wearisome after what I'd felt had been a genuinely great start.

Some good news was lurking in the wings, though. A few weeks after the Cherry Red debacle, we moved to a nicer bedsit: the basement of a big house at 211 Camden Road (not so far from where Bob Cratchit and his family lived). It was a much bigger room, for starters, and it had a little kitchen and a small front yard. It cheered us up no end and we soon had it looking really good. I found an old typewriter and every night poured my heart out into it, getting far out and trying to understand the ways of the world. It was lovely to finally be living as a couple. Jeanette and I never argued about anything and she worked hard at her franchise in the Oxford Road Top Shop and gave me license to pursue my dreams as an artist and potential musician. Where would I be without her?

I got to know a group of people living in a big terraced house in York Way just over from where we lived. They were called David Brown (aka Dibble), Tim Higgins, Justin Bailey and Roz Mortimer. They'd all been art students who had just qualified and I got on really well with them, finding them to be very stimulating folk. Despite this, it was a frustrating time for me. A mass of questions ran through my head. Jeanette would go to work and I'd be left on my own. After a while I'd be wondering what I was doing there. I suppose the change developed into some of the darkest times I can remember, with a very real sense of alienation and depression setting in, while all the people I knew seemed so far away in Liverpool.

The York Way crowd helped me though. Talking about art and music and seeing their work was inspiring to me and I knew they liked my stuff. I would go to the Museum of Mankind and feel the power of the African sculptures and then I'd go to Camden Fruit Market at the end of the day to collect fruit wrappers off the floor. I'd take them home and stick them on to cardboard I'd found, then add strokes of oil paint and varnish them. Soon they were lined up around every wall. I would paint made-up African statues and create primitive designs to decorate the plant pots. All this helped me to keep it together in our new London life.

******

I also met a guy called Gary Hampson down at Waterloo one day with the York Way crowd. He played bass and hailed from Bolton, Lancashire. Maybe it was because he came from the north, but I seemed to have a lot in common with him. He lived in a squat in Brixton, so I would take the Routemaster bus which I had grown to love. (I actually wouldn't get on a bus in London unless it was a Routemaster.) They took the long, detailed routes around the city and I could take in all the sights from Camden through the City of London on the top deck. I often wrote about what I saw in the notebooks I took along and would scribble away until I reached Herne Hill. From there I walked through the walkway, past the old trellis and onto Railton Road. I loved these rambles and sometimes I would imagine myself in the London of the famous Ealing comedy *The Ladykillers*. I would often arrive at around mid-day, when I'd regularly get Gary up and we'd play music.

The other great thing was the Rastas outside the shops who would sell you a handful of grass. We'd get stoned and then start to play in some dark cellar somewhere. We used to play in one place where the lights would start to go on and off, but instead of looking at the terrible state of the electrics we'd think the music was causing it, pack up and then get the hell out of there thinking it was haunted. (Of course, the weed had nothing to do with it!)

I recorded some of the stuff we were putting down, sent it sponta-neously to Virgin Records and received a reply saying, 'I can honestly say this is pretentious crap!' Still, at least we hadn't succumbed to those awful synthetic sounds and haircuts you'd see clogging up *Top of the Pops* at the time.

✳✳✳✳✳✳

Another real lifeline for me was Nick Jones, who was studying in London. He had been to Liverpool College with me but he was a few years older and was an all-round good lad. I would enjoy his company and we really related to each other as we came from the same background. He lived in a flat in Lisson Grove with a couple of fellow students from his course. Caron (who later became MC Kinky) lived next door and she was friendly with the artists who lived around the corner from me in York Way and Cosway Street off Bell Street (where Sex Pistols' drummer Paul Cook also lived).

In October, Gary and I played an impromptu, two-song set with Bedlam A-Go-Go (Tim Higgins/Dibble and Caron's Band) at the City of London Poly. I played bass and Gary played guitar. It was a revelation and we knocked 'em dead. People were speechless. I don't know who was more shocked, us or them! It was a triumph of the spirit and did me the world of good. This was the first time I held a stringed instrument on stage. Up yours, Virgin!

Gary and I saw quite a lot of other bands. We went to see The Fall in Barking (we must have been), bunking in and watching from the side of the stage, getting the night bus back. I loved going over to Brixton too – seeing all the colours in the shop windows and hearing reggae pumping out and the guy who was always dancing outside the market. It was alive back then.

We made a 4-track demo with Roy, the guy from Belfast who lived behind our basement flat. He was a lovely guy and I was glad of another musical collaborator. The tape was pretty eclectic. We did a jazzy, swinging instrumental called 'Off The Rails' (featuring me on percussion and Roy adding a nice Hammond organ part), a track called 'Melody', which showed potential, and a dub instrumental with whistles and loads of bass and percussion called 'Elephant Walk' (probably inspired by African Head Charge).

I got a letter from Carl, back in Liverpool, that made me laugh. It had been scribbled on a scrap of paper and it filled me in on what he'd been up to in Liverpool in typical Carl style. 'David's group split up the day after I joined', it began. 'Caught five fish in Princes Park Lake – threw them back in. Gill might have "left" me. Went to see Kevin's group practising shite "Japan" songs. "Japan" vocals, petty bickering, etc.' He signed off with 'growing up is a killer'.

Another letter followed it in December '83. He was going to set up a record label called Davies Records and do a compilation album which would be called *A Secret Liverpool*. It was Carl's scheme to make us all a fortune and bring fame and recognition in a co-operative way. He went into a long and rambling explanation about how he was selling minutes of time to people to be included on the compilation LP and it all sounded great on paper. He wanted me to supply the artwork as well as contribute to the album itself.

****

As 1984 dawned the first thing was to sort out some sort of tangible musical direction, so I gave Gary Hampson an ultimatum. Either he was to commit to developing the music with me or simply forget it altogether. By this time, he'd taken to not turning up on time – or not turning up at all. His Brixton-style 'come day, go day, see you later' attitude was too non-committal by far for me and Carl's compilation album project was a lot more exciting, so I decided to concentrate on getting stuck into that.

I would also find time to fill an old suitcase with collages I had been making, get the bus to Pimlico and make a display of them on the railings outside the Tate Gallery on the banks of the Thames. They allowed me to lean them against the railings but not to attach them (something symbolic there, I feel). Anyway I sold a good few and the bit of money I made was very welcome.

There's always been a massive and it would appear ever-increasing gap between the haves and have nots in the 'Art' world. But who says what work is worth how much? The answer is a deeply ingrained Art Establishment that has developed over time that can elevate the price of an artist's work if it so desires on a whim. Art is subjective, what works for you might not work for someone else. Consequently this really does tend to leave the whole creative industries at the mercy of the money. Oh well, as my Grandad Fred Badger would say: 'Lucky in the Big Things'.

I'd meet Jeanette for lunch during her break from work and have cream cheese and pineapple sandwiches in Bewley's sandwich bar near Oxford Circus. I loved the Italian sandwich bars and also the barber's on Bell Street. It hadn't changed since the '50s and had a picture of David McCallum from the film *Violent Playground* on the wall outside. Ironically, the film had actually been set in Liverpool. Little things like that conspired to make London a great place to be at times. There was a recording studio above Top Shop in Oxford Circus and I would wait for Jeanette to finish work at the rear entrance. I remember Adam Faith walking past and making direct eye contact with him, like there was some connection. Another time Paul McCartney walked straight past me and got into his blue Bentley after recording upstairs.

I started a cleaning job in Finchley, organized through Chris Rodis (ex-Blabber Wobble), who was now working on the Beefheart-inspired 'Magic in the Desert' I got £10 for the Friday morning cleaning, which was most welcome. Carl's compilation album plan had begun to take shape too – literally in fact, because during March he'd had a brainwave: we'd cut out cardboard squares to make the covers for the album. They would all be recycled and so environmentally friendly and would cost us nothing!

Back up in Liverpool one weekend in March, we got stacks of boxes from the nearby supermarket and took them back to Carl's little flat on Kelvin Grove in Kensington. We started cutting with a Stanley knife and they soon began to pile up. We were really excited by the concept. It was amazing: every single copy would be unique, with the lettering disappearing off the edge, which we loved.

During this weekend, I also had a dream while sleeping on Carl's couch which would assume much greater significance later on. In this dream, a name – 'The La's' – appeared to me. I remember clear as day waking up and it being there in the forefront of my mind, written in black and white – a very simple three-letter name.

Sometimes I feel it's as if you can slip forward into what's about to happen – especially if it's related to something that has particular significance. The only way I could describe it is that it feels like the pull of the wave on the water before it's eventually drawn back to become incorporated into the wave itself – i.e., it's part of the wave but not yet.

I remember thinking to myself, 'Now *there's* a name for a band!' It was unusual too; all the other band names around were very descriptive, especially in Liverpool. It wasn't even to do with the Liverpool slang 'La' meaning 'Lad' – it was a 'less is more' thing and I thought it sounded musical, like a musical note on the scale: *la.*

Now back in London, I had my work cut out. Literally. Nick Jones had a Citroen 2 CV and the seats folded down. I got him to take me to Chinatown in Soho and we filled the car with boxes with Chinese writing on them. Nick joked that the next time he saw me my fingers would be missing a few digits. I set to work in the little front yard of 211 Camden Road with a trusty Stanley Knife once again and the cardboard cut-out 'sleeves' piled higher and higher. There were stamps on some, each one individual; some with truly bold Chinese characters, one in particular with three Chinese characters and the words 'Three Children' beneath in English.

Tracks included contributions from The Kindergarten Paint Set ('Secret Life', written by Chris Rodis), The High Five, Ella Guru (featuring Tom Kemp on bass and Paul Rhodes on drums), The Cranes and Carl's track. We mastered the first side of the album on a tape machine we'd hired from a place in London, then cut and spliced the quarter-inch tape together in my front room. Knowing the way Carl worked, it wasn't a great surprise when he decided to put his track on backwards! The curious thing was that when played backwards, the voice sounded very clearly like it said 'Please believe me' at one point, so this became the title of his song. Carl's track went out under the name The Harts because this had been his mum Peggy's maiden name. The first side concluded with 'The Time I Grew Forever', which I put out under the name Roy G. Biv, which was the spectrum abbreviated: i.e., red, orange, yellow, green, blue, indigo, and violet.

Carl decided that, to get things going, we'd release the album's first side and get 500 copies pressed up. Then, when enough had been sold, we'd press up the second side. I took the tape to get it cut at a studio in London where photos of Madness hung on the wall. The engineer seemed completely bewildered; not least with the three minutes of initial silence and the backwards tracks, but to be fair he asked no questions and just did his job.

******

A wet weekend in April proved to be important. I'd returned to Liverpool for a couple of days and I recorded a new tune called 'Throw Away World' on Kevin's porta-studio. After that, I was going to the Everyman Bistro when I bumped into Lee Mavers. He looked cool as ever: biker boots, jeans shirt and leather jacket with that all-important pompadour blonde mop on top of his head. He told me he was getting into Captain Beefheart and started quoting the tracks featured on Beefheart's legendary *Trout Mask Replica* album.

'A Hoodoo Ant Man Be'

Afterwards, I went back to Hamish's place, listened to some rockabilly and gave him a copy of the spoken-word tape of Jack Kerouac that I had played him in Camden. Hamish told me that he had played a rock 'n' roll set with Lee Mavers on guitar and he was brilliant. This coming from a musician like Hamish meant a great deal.

Listening to rockabilly music wasn't something confined to visits to Hamish's place. I came across one of the genre's great trailblazers, Marvin Rainwater, via his MGM recording 'Hot and Cold' in London around this time and it was one of the biggest catalysts for getting me more seriously into rockabilly. The lightning guitar break on that record played by the great Bill Badgett just blew my mind. It was the nearest thing I'd ever heard to a human voice coming from a stringed instrument. If that wasn't enough, also on this album was two minutes of beautiful ramblin' by Gary Williams called 'The Travellin' Blues Boy'.

I noticed in *Time Out* that the 'Mersey Poets' were performing in King's Cross. I suggested to Jeanette that we go along even though it was about to start and we were totally skint. It worked out well, though. For one thing, Camden Road was quite close to King's Cross and even though we were late for the start, we arrived to find an empty foyer and walked right through the main doors and up the stairs to find a seat without anyone stopping us. Maybe it was because I'd been in the Big Smoke for a while, but I was definitely feeling very nostalgic for Liverpool and it was good to see Henri, McGough and Patten reading. There was an after-show party downstairs and, remembering that one of Adrian Henri's poems had mentioned a Kit Kat, I bought one from the shop there and I handed it to him. Then I just walked off while he laughed.

In May, the one-sided records had been manufactured, so I went down to Mayking Records near Portobello Road in Notting Hill to pick them up. As luck would have it there was Geoff Davies from Probe Plus Records collecting copies of one of his new releases and we had a good chat. It was great to see a familiar face.

Carl came down from Liverpool and we started to put together the records with their individual cardboard sleeves. From there, we took them to a selection of record shops in Camden. At last, *A Secret Liverpool* was out and would, in our opinion, surely secure fame and fortune for all concerned.

SIX

The La's: Breakloose!

LONDON HAD BEEN STIMULATING and interesting, but I think sometimes you have to step out of something and look back at it to see it in its entirety. For example, if you are in house you can walk around the rooms, take it all in and describe each one, but you can't describe the house as a whole until you look at it from outside.

I was walking up Bold Street in Liverpool on one of our visits back home with David Evans. In the bright sunlight, I realized just how much I was missing the city. I thought, 'God, this is a beautiful place with beautiful people', and I really wanted to come back and live here again. It was our home after all, yet there we were living in London. I went to the Everyman Theatre and saw Ian Davies (now acting under the stage name of Ian Hart) in *Dream of Dreams*. David's new group, The Riotous Hues (Of Modern Colour), played and they were great too.

I talked to Jeanette about my feelings and she agreed to move back 'home'. We had both grown a lot down in London but we felt that we should now be back up in the 'Pool. I wanted to start a band in Liverpool. I would call it 'The La's' and I would get Lee Mavers in to work with (not that I had even mentioned it to him!) and there would be no turning back.

When I told Carl about our plans he decided to take our flat on in Camden Road and work the album from London. And he arrived in the van a week late! Typical.

If I had learnt anything from our stay in London amidst all that energy, writing and collaging I'd say it would be this:

Truth unto yourself.
Ignorance is innocence.
Knowledge is above belief.

On our return to Liverpool, after being collected from the coach station by my Dad, we drove through Huyton and standing there at the bus stop on Archway Road the first person I saw was Lee Mavers. Surely this was an important sign that all was in place and in order.[5]

I made a point of calling Lee the next day because I was sure he was someone who would be able to grasp what I wanted to do, especially since he'd been getting into Captain Beefheart in a big way. He said to come over to his home in Dinas Lane, Page Moss, just down the road from where I had lived in Roby. Lee had really been into The Stranglers early on and Jean Jacques Burnel had played a part in him picking up the bass.

I took with me four ideas for songs I had written. These were 'Soho Wendy', 'My Girl Sits Like a Reindeer', 'Red Deer Stalk' and 'The Time Is Right', which later evolved into 'Night Walk'. I gave the words to Lee and thought what he did with them was incredible. He'd grasped them and transposed them into riffs. It was fascinating to watch. Lee would look at my words and play on the guitar what they said to him. I suppose now I had wanted us to carry on where Captain Beefheart had left off a couple of years before with what I saw as a hard-driving, discordant rockabilly sound. I explained this to Lee, saying, 'Make it spiky and discordant. Make it rhythmical'.

---

5 They found a Viking longboat buried on Archway Road when digging for the railway there. It had been stranded on a retreating tide forever. That River Alt really had been mighty once.

Beefheart was essentially roots music ... gone West. There wasn't in fact a great deal of distance at all between his last single release in 1982, 'Ice Cream for Crow', and say the black rockabilly of 'Down Home Special' by Bo Diddley or 'Down in the Bottom' by Howlin' Wolf, or the white rockabilly of Carrie Thacquer's 'Tennessee Mama'. Move into the next decade and you've got 'Psychotic Reaction' by The Count Five and 'Rollercoaster' by The 13th Floor Elevators: like Beefheart again this music was not about the beat, it was all about the rhythm that got your heart racing.

A week later, I met Lee in Prescot and we went to practice at my Mum and Dad's new house in Burrows Lane. I gave Lee a ride down the hill on the back of my push bike while he carried his guitar with no case. We went through the material we had started and pulled it together more and later got the number 10 into town. I remember talking to Lee about the bread shop in Prescot called M. Ray and about the artist Man Ray colouring baguettes blue and how I would love to fill the M. Ray shop window with them. I also remember bringing manta rays into it. It was all very mysterious but Lee was bang onto it, in fact I can honestly say I saw a side to Lee on that bus ride into Liverpool that I loved and felt incredibly in tune with. He was totally relaxed and receptive and I had high hopes all round on our way to score some herbal remedy from Liverpool's beautiful Georgian Quarter.

By September 1984 our new project had gained some momentum. I went to the Ministry studio with Lee, who brought Timmo (a Roby lad who had played drums in Neuklon's final incarnation). We had a practice with Phil Butcher, who'd come down with a bass guitar. Kevin brought his porta-studio and we set it up and laid down about five or six tracks.

'Soho Wendy' was one – I'd got the title from a newspaper headline, 'My Shame by Soho Wendy' – and 'I Did the Painting', which was based on my time with oil paints in Camden. I liked the sound of the menacing vocals under Lee's ominous guitar riff. We also did 'Red Deer Stalk' and 'The Time Is Right' ('Night Walk'), which was about the triumph of the spirit in the face of all adversities.

✳✳✳✳✳✳

People often speak of how depressed Liverpool was during the 1980s and it was getting worse under the Thatcher government. Liverpool meant nothing to her down in Westminster, but in spite of this I had managed to make my world buzz creatively at this time. Carl settled in London and cut the second side of the *A Secret Liverpool* project. This time there would be a batch of 1,000 two-sided *A Secret Liverpool* LPs. The first track on the second side would be the first-ever release by The La's (which was effectively myself backed by The Modernaires from Chester), two minutes of ramshackle swing titled 'I Don't Like Hanging Around'.

Kevin, meanwhile, had moved into a flat on Hope Street, and he had started a relationship with Julie McGrail, a friend of David's from St Helens. Wild Swans founder Paul Simpson lived below Kevin with his girlfriend, Jan. Ian Broudie (Bunnymen producer and ex-Big in Japan/Original Mirrors) lived above them, while Mick Head and Biffa (Chris McCaffrey) stayed there a lot because Broudie had been producing The Pale Fountains.

After a short stay at our family homes Jeanette and I would also be shortly be moving into Julie McGrail's old flat in the basement of 20 Falkner Street, and not only did I have Lee Mavers to work with but Jeanette could finally stop working in Top Shop, having secured a job in the University of Liverpool's archaeological department, of all things!

In October we were back in Liverpool city centre proper. We got the Falkner Street flat, which, after the last eighteen months, was like moving into a mansion. It was situated in Liverpool's magnificent Georgian Quarter. It offered us two bedrooms, a huge living room, a bathroom and a large entrance hall, with a sweeping staircase not to mention a yard at the back where our cat, Fog, could play, safe from the attention of passing cars. Kevin's place was around the corner and Phil Butcher also lived a few doors down. Can't say we could have ever afforded anything so grandiose in London!

The address was ideal for us, but it also turned out to have a turbulent history. Much later I would discover that this address had been the centre of something that had rocked the city in another way. In Liverpool writer Tom Slemen's *Haunted Liverpool 12*, I was surprised to read a chapter called 'The Eye', dedicated to a strange case which featured our basement apartment and had seriously upset the higher echelons of Liverpool society in the 1880s.[6] In brief, this related to a series of poison pen letters (in green ink) which had been sent to various city dignitaries accusing them of various vices. Even the then Lord Mayor of Liverpool was warned he would be killed in his bed. To cut a very long story short, it seems the letters had actually been sent from what was now our new address.

******

On 3 December 1984, Lee and Timmo called round for a jam. I wrote in my diary: 'They must be The La's – they might not know it, but they are in my book!' Shortly after that session, Lee brought down Jasper (real name Jim Fearon) to play bass and now our new flat in Falkner Street was developing into a regular hang-out. I also met Roger Llewellyn, an old school friend, in town and it was great to see him. He was from 'The Park' in Huyton.

The new scene was wonderful and the early depression I had occasionally suffered in London had retreated. 'And birds have come singing out of the night – now the time is right!' I sang with some passion during 'Night Walk'. Standing at the edge of the fabled 1984 and peering into 1985, everything seemed so wonderful and possible.

The year started well too. In January I had my first exhibition in a small gallery called the Pilgrim on Pilgrim Street in Liverpool. I put posters up around the town which read simply, 'AN EXHIBITION OF MODERN ART BY MIKE BADGER'. That was what it was to me and I arranged my cardboard collages and paintings around the small gallery until I was pleased with the way they looked.

Musically, things were starting to gel. I carried on practising with Lee and Jasper and we went into the Attic Studio, a small 4-track studio on Cornwallis Street in February '85. It was a council-funded place built with the intention of giving young students musical experience. To mark the occasion, I got hold of a video camera from a hire place

6   PS: Thanks to Tom Slemen for unearthing yet another fascinating Liverpool folk tale.

on Wavertree Road and Kevin filmed the whole day as well as my exhibition at the Pilgrim.

The song ideas had been coming thick and fast. We recorded 'My Girl Sits Like a Reindeer', 'Sweet 35', 'Red Deer Stalk', 'You Blue' and an improvised instrumental we named 'Dovecot Dub', which was built around a bass riff Jasper had come up with. We all had a great time recording and it seemed so simple. We'd have a run-through of the tune and do a take. With it all going onto the Teac 4-track, mixing took no time at all and we soon had the session down. We went back to Lee's and buzzed off both the video we'd shot and the sound of the tape.

Outside of The La's, I'd see Hamish, who knew Walla (Tony Walsh), Tony Clarke and Bernie Nolan, who all played music together. Tony and Bernie had been in the Russian Rockabillies, who then evolved into another group called The Outer Limits but now played with Walla from Kirkdale. Lee knew them too. He'd previously jammed with them in a wine bar on Smithdown Road, playing rock 'n' roll stuff. They were a cool bunch of characters, dug The Clash and knew a whole lot more about '50s American rock 'n' roll sounds than me.

I'll never forget the day I called in on Hamish at his place on Croxteth Grove. He played me 'I'm So Lonesome I Could Cry' by Hank Williams for the first time and it proved to be one of those moments of true enlightenment, when I heard the lyric 'The moon just went behind the clouds, to hide its face and cry'. This was different to the highly produced 'country and western' sounds I'd associated with country music. Hank was raw, undiluted, heartfelt wonderment. I'd now even venture down to Pat and Gerry Allan's Country Music Store in Aigburth in search of the real sound of the West.

✶✶✶✶✶✶

I went to see Bernie, Tony and Walla playing with their rockabilly band at the Pyramid Club in town. Walla slapped his electric bass in fine style and Bernie sang 'Roxette' (originally by Dr. Feelgood) and played electric guitar. I'd call around to see Roger Llewellyn at his flat on Belvedere Road. He lived alone and spent a lot of his time drawing these great comic characters and distributing them to small independent shops. His record collection was a wonderfully varied and eclectic thing of wonder too, ranging from *Voodoo Voodoo* (a rockabilly compilation), through to Buddy Holly, ska, bubblegum pop compilations and Bing Crosby's 'Accentuate the Positive', which I would like to think is what I still tend to do.

The night before my twenty-third birthday, I recited some of my poems at Liverpool's famous Royal Court Theatre as a support to The Fall, thanks to Dave C, who was booking the sets. I can't remember too much about the material I recited, save for one line I remember, when I said, 'He was a member of the bourgeoisie / he was a member of the Beans on Toast football team / eleven a slice ...' And I remember reciting a poem to the sound of my foot stamping on the stage and being picked up by the PA through the microphone stands. It seemed to go OK. It was good to meet Mark E. Smith and Brix, his wife. They were great at that time, even playing 'Rollin' Danny' by Gene Vincent. He was very friendly. I chatted to him about country music and trucker songs. He seemed to admire my tenacity when I asked him for some beers from his rider: 'You're a cheeky *Get*, you – go on then!'

More poetry-related stuff came along. David Evans (who had started promoting more events) asked if I would like to support The Housemartins at the Black Bull in St Helens and it turned out to be great fun.

> I am the thirsty plant and you are my water,
> you saw me limp and sad – but now you see me tauter.
> > (From untitled poem recited at the Black Bull)

I still enjoyed the other regular things in life – like going to Aston Villa to see Everton play Luton with my Dad, and listening to a great selection of different music. Blues was big round Falkner Street around this time, not least Howlin' Wolf's 'Down in the Bottom' and a 1954 Lightnin' Slim album I had picked up in Andy Jones' new Pink Moon Records called *She's Gone*, featuring these amazing raw roots songs. It was timeless stuff and a staple for Lee and me. Another disc spun to death was the Cajun compilation I'd picked up in Probe featuring the unbridled, soaring rhythm of 'Hee Haw Breakdown' by Nolan Cormier and The LA Aces.

We'd all pile round to Rogan and Sue's and Hamish would play his fiery boogie-woogie on the piano. Roger lent me his old Spanish guitar and showed me a few chords and I got down to strumming for the first time. I had no problem with the rhythm; I just had to learn where my fingertips needed to go to form chords properly. I was keen to learn, though, and put in a lot of time strumming away. Soon after, I bumped into Lee in Sefton Park after a small break from working together. We were keen to get started again and he called round with Jasper. It was still formative and exciting and also a social thing too. We also enjoyed afternoons of poker.

I can remember Lee telling me when he was a baby he had appeared in the paper under the title 'The Blonde Beatle' because he had a blonde mop top and used to rock to the sound of Merseybeat in his pram!

I got to know Bernie Nolan well. He went out with Julie Ehlan (another familiar face from Roby) and lived in the flat on Albert Road I had visited many times before when Mark Clitheroe the biker had lived there. Bernie played double bass and most other instruments like a natural and he was just too cool for school. He was born on the day Buddy Holly had died in the plane crash. Funnily enough, another guy who also frequented the Mayflower Club's rockabilly nights in town had the same birthday and they used to argue about who was the re-incarnation of Buddy and who'd been the pilot.

SEVEN

We Have Lift Off!

TOWARDS THE END OF 1985 I bought a Burns semi-acoustic guitar and The La's began to practice much more regularly. Then, David Evans asked me if I'd like to contribute some music to a new compilation album he was putting together with the help of respected Radio Merseyside DJ Roger Hill. Everyone was given three minutes of time on the compilation but because The La's songs I was to submit were only one and a half minutes each we got to put two songs on: 'My Girl Sits Like a Reindeer' and 'Sweet 35', from the first Attic session.

The La's practised in Tony Clarke's cellar in Kensington early in 1986. Tony was occupying the La's drum stool and Bernie was on electric bass. I got a lift to rehearsals off Tony on the back of his BSA motorbike and he was a sound guy. He had decided to leave the army at his own request and was 100% committed to rock 'n' roll in the way he dressed, his love of the drums and his way of life.[7]

---

7 There's a great documentary made by Kenny Manson titled *Liverpool Rockabillies* from the 1980s available on Youtube, which centres on Tony Clarke and his girlfriend getting ready to go out for a bop in town.

Between us, Lee, Tony, Bernie Nolan and I worked up some of the first songs I'd written with the help of my trusty new accomplice: my red Burns Vibraslim semi-acoustic. I got busy writing when I acquired the guitar. My Cold War commentary 'Down at the Space Rocketry', 'The Heart Knows' and the ecologically friendly 'Trees and Plants' came tumbling out quickly, the latter inspired in tempo by a song called 'The Back Door' by D.L. Menard. We also played 'My Girl Sits Like a Reindeer', 'Red Deer Stalk' and 'Sweet 35'. With all these we pretty much managed to pull a set together in time for our first show as The La's in early 1986 at the Lamb in St Helens, where David Evans had arranged for us to support local band Benny Profane.

Whenever I phoned Lee to arrange stuff his Mum Alysia would answer the phone and then shout upstairs to his room, 'Lee! ... It's Mike Jagger on the phone!'

There was a real sense of excitement about playing for the first time. We picked up the gear in Kensington, collected Lee from his home in Dinas Lane and loaded the van and the few instruments we owned at the time. Tony Clarke was driving; his girlfriend Paula came with her mate Natalie. Bernie and his girlfriend Julie were in the back of the van too. We spent the journey to St Helens listening to 'Nuclear War' by Sun Ra and it was my first opportunity to try my big red Burns in public. Lee had already taken to calling it 'the Cowboy Boot'.

We were great that night too. I thought, 'This is what I am here to do!' I took to my newly defined vocals and guitar role like a duck to water. We opened with a Link Wray-style instrumental called 'Revamp' and we didn't put a foot wrong after that. Well, not until literally the final moment of the show when during the very last notes of the last song I hit a chord while I was walking backwards across the tiny stage and missed my footing. I fell off the back of the stage and landed on the PA, which exploded in an apocalyptic rumble of reverb springs. Typical. I spent the entire set making out I was a cool, inscrutable frontman and did all the hard work, only to expose myself as the clumsy oaf I really was. Oh well: the nuclear explosion that came out the speakers rounded the first-ever La's gig rather nicely, and might have even hinted at more seismic events up the road.

Afterwards Sniff (Phil Smith) from David's band, The Riotous Hues, told David we were the best band he'd ever seen and that we'd started something new – what a great piece of feedback! Carl Davies had attended the gig too. He was up on a visit from London and had started to drink more and more. Benny Profane also did a fine set after us; kind of cow-punk style, featuring a great take of Hank Williams' song 'I'll Never Get Out of this World Alive'.

The *Elegance, Charm and Deadly Danger* compilation LP had been released through the P.U.S.H. label. This stood for 'Promotional Umbrella for St Helens', a collective of sorts organized by David Evans. David had promised The La's two tracks and we'd duly submitted 'Sweet 35' and 'My Girl Sits Like a Reindeer' for inclusion. Sixteen local acts were featured and we got our first national press interest on the back of it, with Bill Prince from the *NME* suggesting that 'If Tom Waits had come from Widnes, he might have dreamt up The La's "Sweet 35"'.

On 17 March, the night before my twenty-fourth birthday, I put John Peel's show on, pretty much at random as I hadn't been listening to his show for ages. A track was just finishing as I tuned in, but then – to my astonishment – Peel said he was going to feature a track from the *Elegance, Charm and Deadly Danger* compilation, and in his unmistakeably droll tones, he said, 'This is The La's ... not particularly hi-fi, but worth listening to. "My Girl Sits Like a Reindeer ..."'

John Peel was right about the lo-fi performance because the song had actually been mastered onto vinyl from a cassette master, but it didn't matter in the slightest. It was a wonderful moment. Jeanette and I danced around the room and it was the perfect birthday present: for me because it was my first-ever national broadcast and for Jeanette because the song had been written about her anyway.

During April, we played our second gig as The La's. It took place out of doors in St Helens' town centre under an arch. The band was beginning to get busier. Then, that same month, we recorded with Kevin Wright on his porta-studio in Hope Street. This time, we laid down versions of 'The Heart Knows', 'Money in Your Talk' and Lee recorded a song he'd written called 'I.O.U.', which he'd played me and sounded very promising. The whole thing was again moving in the right direction and when we mixed it down at Kevin's the following day it sounded really exciting.

Can't say I was pleased to see Lee lose his quiff, though, and go for the more '60s-looking mop.

The hard-rockin' Link Wray riff-off 'Money in Your Talk' was very much my statement about the city we lived in and how money seemed to be the only thing anyone cared about. The melodic and catchy 'I.O.U.', meanwhile, pinned Lee as a real songwriting talent. Although I had reservations about that line about 'you must eat your porridge', there was no denying that the song really swung, thanks also to Tony Clarke's backbeat and my maracas to finish it off. 'The Heart Knows' was always a favourite of Lee's and has still to be released.

✶✶✶✶✶✶

We were playing live again during April, this time at the System in Liverpool as a promotional show for the *Elegance, Charm and Deadly Danger* compilation. David Evans stood in on bass as Bernie was losing interest. Once again, it went off all right and we were delighted to be back on stage once more. *Elegance* had been getting some positive press and Penny Kiley wrote an enthusiastic review of the System gig for *Melody Maker*, where she said, 'Their deadpan blues and rock 'n' roll is slightly surreal and exquisitely cool'.

Momentum was slowly building around the band and obviously Lee felt it too because it was around this time that he decided to really get stuck in with me. He wasn't just backing my ideas anymore, he was bringing in ideas of his own and we became a creative unit. Lee told me he'd been getting stoned with some mates one night in Huyton. They'd been listening to Led Zeppelin and having a laugh, when Lee put on his La's tape, a compilation of the September '84 and February '85 sessions we'd done which I had cobbled together for him. Lee had jokingly christened the tape 'Terminal Turkey' because he'd thought a lot of the stuff was crazy, but when he listened to it again it all fell into place and he thought it kicked everything into touch. Like me, he recognized there hadn't really been anything like The La's *sound* before.

From there on, things really clicked. During May, we recorded two of Lee's new ones, 'Freedom Song' and 'Son of a Gun', along with my 'Down at the Space Rocketry' and a new version of 'My Girl Sits Like a Reindeer' at Frank Sparks' studio on Duke Street in the Arena building. The engineer there was Tony Russell, who we already knew from the

Attic Studio and again things went well, but it was 'Freedom Song' from that session that had the magic. We spent some time adding 'Gregorian monk' vocals over it and it showed Lee's mesmerizing acoustic guitar work too.

Lee mentioned that we'd been offered a gig by Rogan to celebrate the first Football Supporters' Association AGM at the Triton on Paradise Street. For this show Lee and I were again joined by David Evans on bass and Tony Russell on drums and the revolving door admitting and ejecting La's rhythm sections began to turn. It was another successful gig, though, with Rogan and Sue jiving away! From the Triton, we went on to play at a party on Mossley Hill Drive near Sefton Park. Frank Sparks had arranged this and if we performed at the party he would wipe an outstanding £10 studio debt off completely. Whoa boy!

The Mossley Hill Drive party proved to be a memorable occasion. Sharing the bill were Marshmallow Overcoat, whose singer wore a beret and NHS glasses. He was a character called Barry Sutton and he soon grabbed the audience's attention, grabbing the mic and shouting, 'Right, I'm gonna pass the hat around now'. With that, he chucked his beret into the small crowd of onlookers. The whole thing was like one of those crazy '60s house parties with a psychedelic band whipping up a storm and a great scene all of its own making. We weren't as hot as we might have liked on account of playing with a day-old drummer and an equally under-rehearsed bass player, but it was still exciting. Paul Hemmings was there too, and was suitably impressed, later telling me every song that we had played was immediately memorable.

We were entering a pivotal summer with The La's and there was more and more musical activity. I wrote the song 'Breakloose' during June and I had wanted it to soar, unshackled and relentless. Lee added a more structured guitar part to what was already a strident-sounding tune. It would soon become the perfect song to open our sets with.

✳✳✳✳✳✳

One night around this time about 3am in the morning, I woke to the dreaded sound of somebody trying to enter the back door of the flat (and wasn't D.L. Menard!). Your mind starts to race, the adrenaline starts to pump and you prepare yourself for anything to happen in the next few minutes. I threw on a pair of jeans, took my life into my hands and ran into the kitchen, which had a window onto the back yard, to the sound of smashing glass. When I got there, I saw Carl chucking a brick through the kitchen window, desperately trying to gain entrance to the flat. With feelings of simultaneous relief and anger, I shouted through the glass, 'I'm gonna fuck you!'

I ran around to the door, but he'd already taken off, vaulting the gate to the yard. What a loon! He was with Paul Burns, I discovered later. He'd thought I was away and wanted somewhere after hours in town to carry on drinking.

******

Gigs were coming in regularly by this stage and what we had agreed to would take us through to the end of July. Meanwhile, on 25 June, I started on a scheme called the North Liverpool Musicians' Resource Centre in the Royal Institute, a beautiful old building on Colquitt Street.

I was signed up as both a musician and artist and was put on £2,800 per annum for attending twenty hours per week. Ironically enough, Paul Hemmings was also on the scheme. There were twenty students in all and we were asked to form three bands and start working on material. On the surface, the scheme seemed to be a great idea because it was intended to give unemployed musicians the chance to get some experience in both studio work and also gigs in the community.

On the first day, I hooked up with budding bassist John Power, a drummer called Barry Walsh and a huge guy called Danny Dean, who was already a very talented guitar player. Paul, meanwhile, joined up with the charismatic Tommy Scott and a couple more like minds, while the third band was made up of the 'cabaret' heads and more 'muso' types. Nonetheless, it was a really good bunch of fellas overall.

The fact that the scheme was, in fact, run by a single family really should have raised eyebrows at the start.

The rest of the hired, non-family staff were friendly and helpful. Especially Ted Muscatelli. We all loved Ted. He was a really decent guy who'd been there, seen it all and enjoyed showing us guitar riffs and songs in a really unaffected and genuine way. He was really funny too, confiding that he thought all the other family-connected tutor needed was 'a damn good shag' to sort him out. During the breaks on the scheme we'd go over to the little park around the bombed-out church nearby and get stoned.

Coincidently, the week I started on the scheme Jeanette and I packed up our stuff from Falkner Street and moved into a massive two-bedroom flat over a cake shop on Aigburth Road that looked down Lark Lane towards the park. Funnily enough, I had been there once before when I'd been to help my Dad on a job fixing a light in what would now become The La's' first proper rehearsal room. Weird!

The gigs kept coming. On 5 July we played at the Monro on Duke Street with The Tractors and Rawhide Chomp from St Helens and ended up going on at 2am. Lee was drunk by then and subsequently decided to temper his drinking before a show after that.

Then, on 18 July, we played with Marshmallow Overcoat again, this time at the Mardi Gras on Bold Street. Marshmallow Overcoat were getting a reputation as the loudest band around, but at the Mardi Gras they were too loud for comfort. I think they were trying to blow us off the only way they knew how – with the dial on eleven. They didn't, though – they just hurt people's ears. Shame really, as Barry Sutton had some nifty little licks on his cheap turquoise Kay guitar. The band also featured Cammy – a sound guy. Both would end up in The La's at different stages in the future.

I really got on with a young ball of energy called John Power who was starting to play bass with the band we had on the scheme now called The Zephyrs. I asked if he'd fancy coming to Aigburth to have a jam with Lee and me, as we were in need of a bass player (again!), and he was very enthusiastic about the prospect.

He was a buzz to be around as he was only eighteen years old and totally up about things in general. He fit in perfectly with us and he was the epitome of everything Lee and I needed to pull it all together. John brought some stability, a desire to be in a band and enough belief to actually turn up on time. What he lacked in experience he made up for with enthusiasm. Lee taught him all the bass lines (people forget Lee had started on bass and was very accomplished on this instrument too) and John practiced like hell to get them right – but what great bass lines he had to learn!

This was a good time, as we felt invigorated, and we spent a lot of time just laughing and having fun. Lee had always been very funny to hang with and this was one of the reasons I had so enjoyed getting to know him early on. He had a turn of phrase that was just unique – he was unaware of this too, which made it even funnier as he would say it with such a straight face. Mad stuff like 'That sounds like a three-legged donkey'.

We'd meet at the scheme and then after catch the bus to Aigburth from outside the bombed-out church. John would skin up and then when we'd go to get off the bus he'd randomly pass whatever was left of the joint to the guy sitting next to him... He was always grateful, I noticed!

I could not understand why cannabis was illegal, making criminals of people who enjoyed a simple sense of, shall we say, 'well-being'. No one had ever overdosed on cannabis in the history of the world while alcohol and tobacco, which were available on every block of shops in the country, killed tens of thousands every year.[8]

It sometimes had an amusing side to it, as well. John would borrow his Mum's car to come to work at the scheme, get stoned and take the bus back home, forgetting that he'd left the car in town. He'd end up having to get the bus back into town to bring the car home again.

I don't think John could believe what he had ended up walking into: The La's, who were rapidly becoming nothing less than the best thing to happen in Liverpool music for years.

As well as John's infectious enthusiasm, which made him great to be around, his presence in the band also helped us to pack out virtually every place we played. Being a few years younger than us he had more mates out and about and he would always invite them all down to see us play. Many times they would all converge on the flat in Aigburth before the gig. We had a great set worked up by now – starting with 'Breakloose', 'Freedom Song', 'Reindeer', 'Trees and Plants', 'Clean Prophet', 'I.O.U.', 'Get Down Over', 'Sweet 35' and 'Doledrum'.

One day, in our new practice room, I began to play a Spanish-type rhythm using bar chords I had been working on. Lee seized the

---

8 This was before the worrying proliferation of super-strong skunk weed, which can induce psychosis, especially in the young.

moment and began to sing, 'A battered street, a tattered coast' over the top, utilizing some words we'd previously been working into a ballad-type lament. This was happening, though. It was raw and suited the atmosphere of the words perfectly. It was 'Callin' All' and it was the best thing we'd written together. From then on, we would always end our set with it because nothing else could follow it.

Was this a taste of things to come? We thought we had it all at the time and we continued to work hard, practising our arses off in my spare room in Aigburth. John had really taken to the bass and by now it felt like being in a real, no-arsing-about band that was going places.

Roger Llewellyn would often attend the practice sessions. He sat silently in the corner while we played, usually working on his drawings. One day, we'd played all through our set and were having a cup of tea when John jumped out of his skin. He'd seen something move in the corner and had previously had no idea Roger was there at all. But that was Roger: always quiet, gentle and focussed on his own little world.

Barry Walsh, also from our band on the scheme (The Zephyrs) joined The La's as regular drummer as the gigs continued to increase when July turned into August. I also wrote a new song called 'Open Your Heart' that month, Lee helping with a delicate stabbing riff. It seemed to epitomize my feelings about humanity and it was highlighted by our new home and the enthusiasm building within The La's.

"We have free will, we will be free" – The La's, 'Open Your Heart'

Towards the end of August, thanks to Mick Larkin and local legend Joey Shields, we played the People's Festival in Sefton Park, which may have been literally four people playing to about fifteen, but it was still excellent. We followed this with a new recording session on 1 September at the Attic. This time, we laid down great versions of 'Breakloose', 'Son of a Gun', 'Open Your Heart', 'Doledrum' and 'Callin' All', and that was when we collectively realized we were doing something genuinely great. All the gigs and practice sessions were paying off and more of Lee's songs were coming into the set to balance out the co-written stuff.

The Monro Pub was quite a regular gig for us on Duke Street. The Monro itself was the building where the first-ever passenger tickets to America were sold – further evidence of the indelible link that Liverpool has with American culture. After all, the American Civil War technically began and ended in Liverpool. The first gun to be fired was reputedly made on Duke Street and the war ended officially when the ship the *Shenandoah* surrendered to the British, lowering the Confederate flag in the River Mersey.

The small studios and porta-studio set-ups were ideal for us. We'd just plug the guitar literally into the wall connector of the studio direct through to the desk and they'd sound great. The Attic had a simple, no-nonsense sound which gave us the perfect opportunity to get our songs down the way we wanted them to sound – and at a price we could afford. Geoff, the guy who ran the place, had been a BBC engineer, so not only did he know his stuff, but he was always a great help. The trainee engineers who worked at the Attic Studio recording receiving work experience were usually very helpful too. There was Tony Russell, who had been there the year before, Pat O'Shaughnessy and sometimes we would see later a young lad from Childwall called Edgar Jones.

These recordings started to circulate on cassette and copies of copies of copies soon started to have an impact; people started turning up to the gigs knowing the words and eventually they reached as far as Manchester.

More songs came like 'What Do You Do?' I'd come up with some words and a few basic chords and from there Lee would pick up the guitar and it would be a complete song within minutes. We had developed a special working relationship together. We continued to record songs as quickly as we were writing them. Lee started to come down with Alan Fairclough, who brought his porta-studio along.

We still suffered from a regular turnover of drummers. Barry Walsh had come and gone and, after a stand-in by John Neesham from The Walking Seeds for a couple of gigs, Timmo was back and would be the regular feature on the drum stool from then on while I was in the band. This again made us a complete and solid outfit. Timmo turned up to rehearsals in his big red American Buick Riviera and looked every inch the man for the job. Another old skinning-up buddy of Lee's, Joey Davidson, would also come along and we'd soon be seeing a lot more of him.

I was loaned a Gibson SG by a mate and it was a beast, so I was using that for live work instead of my vintage Burns semi-acoustic at this stage. When I was eventually asked to give it back, my mate confessed that it was of dubious origin and was in fact hotter than hell – and there was me playing all around town with it! I'd bought my own amp, though: a Carlsboro Scorpion with a tremolo. Lee brought in his latest new tune, the rockabilly-tinged 'Failure' and – after a bit of a struggle – I came up with a simple guitar part that sounded like a Bo Diddley riff and it fitted well with a tremolo twang.

✳✳✳✳✳✳

Back at the scheme, all the musicians got together and worked up a version of The Rolling Stones' 'Sympathy for the Devil' and I sang lead vocal. It was a great fun and we were all buzzing from it. I remember two black ladies coming to visit the scheme for some reason when all this was taking place. They were bowled over by the energy; their response meant a lot to us all and it really felt like we were bringing rock 'n' roll back into the city.

It was music full-time by now. If I wasn't practising with the lads down at the scheme, I was working with The La's at home in Aigburth and when I wasn't doing that I was filling sketchbooks and making collages. Things were rolling.

It was all a refreshing tonic and an escape from the genuine deprivation of mid-eighties Liverpool:

Caught red handed in a no go zone,
You got arrested to use the phone,
You barely hear the dialling tone,
As all around the sirens drone,

What do you do?

Jeanette and I had also been going to a meditation class for some time by now and started on a kind of spiritual self-awareness in a weekly meditation group. It was non-religious, inclusive and held in our dear friend Sandy's back room up the road towards Aigburth Vale. We both got a lot out of it.[9]

The La's had secured a residency at the Pen and Wig in Harrington Street in town and it was helping to galvanize things. In the basement of this pub just round the corner from Mathew Street we had cultivated a bona fide 'scene'. Everyone started coming down, from John's footie-fan mates, guys from the scheme like Tommy Scott and his girlfriend Jill, Paul Hemmings, Brian Hodge and Mark Hughes alongside local luminaries like John Campbell from It's Immaterial, Andy Eastwood and Echo and The Bunnymen's drummer Pete De Freitas. They were all coming to hear us play watching through a haze of Moroccan mist. We even had fire eaters down there!

Timmo changed his car and began to turn up for practice sessions in a big blue US Ford LTD, which soon had 'The La's' sprayed on one of the front wings. The band was attracting a serious following and during November we were asked to play a club called Bonaparte's by local photographer Francesco Mellina. It was in Clarence Street and we rocked the place. I remember Jonee Mellor and Bernie Connor came down to that one. We'd record the gigs and then pile back to our place, skin up and get a buzz from listening to the tapes.

However, I sensed Lee had started to become a bit more distant. He wasn't allowing me to be close anymore. Instead of things being hunky dory, the band's success (which we had worked so hard for) was making him more volatile. He would rave about stuff one day and be really excited and then the next he'd be quite dismissive about it all. Also, with our burgeoning success, Joey Davidson had begun to move into more of a 'managerial' role, helping with some organizing and so on and I sensed his influence growing within The La's.

I also had a genuine concern that the co-written material I had brought in for Lee to work on wasn't given the credence that his own songs where getting, though I was not without my contributions to his

9 I told Nigel Blackwell I had spent time meditating quite some years later, to which he said, 'Well it's better than sitting around doing nothing, isn't it?'

stuff, especially with harmonies, arrangements and little guitar licks. I did get encouragement though from Timmo, who always loved 'Trees and Plants' for instance.

After a gig at the Monro on Duke Street (another war started) we'd left our gear there overnight for convenience's sake and agreed to collect it the next afternoon. I'd forgotten to go and help load the amps and drum kit and when I arrived home from visiting my Mum and Dad's, my Carlsboro Stingray amp was lying face up in the yard with a note on the speaker weighted by a half brick. It read, 'I hope it rains, you cunt!' I couldn't believe my eyes. I was really upset about it and realized it was a direct, provocative attack on me personally by Lee.

I of course confronted Lee about it at the next practice session.

'What the fuck were you playing at, Lee? Say it had rained I can't afford another amp!' Lee dismissed what I had to say. I caught a glimpse at Joey and I could see he was smirking. With hindsight, this is the very moment that everything changed. This was the tipping point. Joey, Lee's skinning-up buddy, had assumed a managerial role and if he had been worth his salt he would have challenged Lee about this. John had also been in the room when I'd challenged Lee about this but made no comment. At the time, though, I hadn't wanted to give in to what seemed to be happening.

Because our flat was only a short walk through St Michael's to the River Mersey, I was aware of the tides and when the fog rolled in you could hear the ships horns. My mum always said my Nan could sense a change in weather when the tides changed. During November, I'd written a new song called 'Moonlight', which had been inspired by both the tides and also the moon reflecting on the dark blue Welsh slate roofs of the terraced houses at the back of our flat.

I hear howling in the midnight,
The world is all aglow,
And the ocean in the moonlight,
Aches to ebb and flow.

Next practice I played it to Lee and he added some cool, stuttering voices over the chorus. I was thrilled by his input and it gave me hope that our working relationship was still alive, but when I suggested giving it a go in the set he dismissed it outright. This was another key moment, as I had considered it to be one of the best songs I had written.[10]

There were more ominous signs. For one thing, Lee had even stopped attending practice sessions now that we had gigs all the time and an established set of songs to play and when he did turn up there was always a problem with something.

It hurt to think it was true, but I began to realize that it wasn't so much a band working together any more, but it felt like Lee wanted to have a band backing him. It seemed like he'd swallowed all the adulation we'd been getting at the gigs and was now taking singular credit for it all. As far as I was concerned we had all earned what we had achieved. It was also just so disappointing that right NOW, after we had done all this, we should have been on top of the world and enjoying the fruits of our labour, instead of getting all brooding and dark about it.

Another factor, which I can see with hindsight, was that there didn't seem to be any time to stop and try to work things out. During December the gigs were flowing like water. Every night we had a show somewhere – sometimes two in a day. From the Hillside in Huyton, to the Bow and Arrow, or the 'Blow and Arrow' as it was called locally.

We played Planet X, turning up in Timmo's Ford LTD. A bottle of amyl nitrate had been broken on the stage, so we played the entire set with thumping heads, feeling high on the fumes! I was with a band called 3 Action. I had organized a gig swap with them. They were from Hull and that brought us our first show outside Merseyside a few days later when we made the long trek across the Pennines to play at the Adelphi in their town as a double-header.[11]

I remember sitting in our living room above the cake shop before a gig when Lee started to play a new song he'd been working on called 'Looking Glass'. He was getting the words as he played, sitting on the chair in front of me. John sat at his feet, seemingly in adoration and

10 There's a practice recording of 'Moonlight' on the *Breakloose: Lost La's 1984–1986* album.

11 It would be the only time I'd play there with The La's, but they would later play there many times, as would John Power's post-La's band Cast.

I felt like my guts were being ripped apart. It was a horrible feeling and consequently I never enjoyed playing that song. The glass was smashed.

With the darker nights, a darkness too seemed to fall over the band. Reluctantly I realized that maybe Lee had his own plans. It was a terrible situation to deal with because I knew probably better than anyone what an immensely important band we had put together. I wasn't as accomplished a lead guitarist as him (very few people are), though all the songs that we played in the set seemed magical. They were our songs, it was our band and ultimately a band is only ever as good as the sum of its parts.

Still, the shows rolled on as Christmas approached. At a house party in Pelham Grove we shook off the shackles of our regular set and just got into the grooves and blew everyone away. I was getting more confident on guitar by now and at one point I knelt before my Carlsboro Stingray amp and enjoyed riding the feedback coming from the speaker.

A band had backed out of a Christmas party at Planet X, so we were asked by Kenny, the promoter, if we would like to stand in and play. I wished everyone 'Merry Christmas' after singing 'My Girl Sits Like a Reindeer'. Timmo appreciated that one!

I can remember after the gig Lee was sitting at a table by himself and I thought I would sit down and have a chat to him and try and lighten the atmosphere and bond but he seemed to be in a world of his own making. He spoke to me intensely, saying he was on a journey, connected to a thread spiralling onward through time and space. I remember thinking to myself later, 'Dear me, where does enlightenment end and psychosis begin?' It was sad: on top of everything else, I felt I was losing a friend.

Then, on 19 December, the North Liverpool Musicians' Resource Centre that John and I were attending was closed to all the students. We'd turned up to discover the doors chained and padlocked and also that we were on the local news on TV.

That same night I played what would be my last gig with The La's. It was in North Wales at the Holywell Spiritualist Church, hardly a regular rock 'n' roll venue in the obvious sense and I think it was a fundraising event. But then, Elvis was never happier than when singing in church!

That night, our set formed part of an evening's entertainment which also included some mediums giving clairvoyance. I clearly remember one of John Power's mates who'd tagged along coming into the back room where the band was and saying, 'Hey, there's a woman out there on stage rapping with the dead!'

I remember us finishing the first song in front of a completely attentive crowd and being pinned to the back wall of the stage with the applause and so it was for the entire set. Amazing!

After this triumph, however, I doubt I'll ever forget 20 December 1986. We were setting up to play a party at the Shaftesbury Hotel at the bottom of Mount Pleasant in Liverpool and Mike Fagan (Lee and Joey's mate) was helping us set up the gear. Lee was in a foul mood. He picked up a speaker cab and banged Mike on the head with it and didn't even think of apologizing. I confronted him about it and the whole thing burst into a full-blown, head to head row.

'He's helping us set up and you can't even bring yourself to apologize!' I told Lee.

'Yeah, well what's it got to do with you?' Lee retorted.

I replied, 'I'm sick of this. Are you going to be up there singing about love tonight?' I said sarcastically, in reference to Lee's words 'Love is all' from our song 'Callin' All'.

'No, and there's only you who does', he shouted back.

'Exactly!' I replied.

'Anyhow you'll be gone after the weekend', he continued.

'Forget it, I'm going now!' I replied. I got my things together and Lee, who I could tell was relieved I was going, even helped me pack my old brown case with my gear. Timmo had sat silently behind the drum kit while all this was kicking off and said nothing. John Power hadn't arrived yet. But that was it.

I had been provoked into leaving the band and from now on The La's would be a very different entity to the one that had started two and a half years before.

With hindsight, I guess it was inevitable. In terms of loyalty, I had no one in the band to back me up. Joey Davidson was Lee's mate, so was Timmo and I think John, who was very young, still couldn't believe he had walked into The La's.

It was a bitter pill to swallow. After all, we'd only really just started to take off, though the preceding six months had been incredibly prolific in terms of writing and creativity. We seemed to have got a stable band line-up at last and we had all worked so hard to get to where we were. I had wanted us to maybe define a decade or more with great albums, but the Shaftesbury incident had made it all too clear that the situation with Lee had become impossible and it certainly wasn't in my nature to resort to similar tactics just to survive.

Who was now there with any authority to confront him when he was out of order? Had he got what he wanted?

EIGHT

The Onset: A New Beginning

N OT ONE TO DWELL on what might have been, I looked forward and considered new options.

Lee and Joey called round to the flat in Aigburth to collect some of the gear which had been left in the practice room and gave me a photograph of me playing at the Monro by Glynys Jackson. It was meant to be a nice gesture but it felt like it was the retirement clock. Time to start something else.

Over the following weeks I would see Hamish, Walla and Bernie Nolan and new ideas and collaborations eventually came to pass – not least in the shape of big Danny Dean from the Scheme, who would come down to Aigburth to play music with me.

There had been talk of the music scheme re-opening, and on 23 January 1987 we were allowed back in. But all was not well. One of the family came down and became very defensive, going on to threaten us when we started asking questions. One of the other students, Mark Hughes from Park Road, had already thrown his coat to the floor and started shouting, 'Come on then – come on!' But this was how we felt, we'd been used to get funding that hadn't been spent on us! There would have been an almighty fight if I hadn't instructed Mark to 'rise above it'. Bless his cotton socks, we laughed about it later but we were all unhappy about the state of affairs. The studio the family had promised to build was nowhere near completion and rumours had begun to circulate that a whole lot of money had vanished and staff had blown the whistle to the Manpower Services Commission, so that was why the whole thing had been closed down. We'd been shafted.

It was difficult to cut either the scheme or The La's out of my life. John Power had now asked fellow student Paul Hemmings to play guitar with The La's. I remember when I saw John and Paul for the first time since I'd departed The La's – neither of them could look at me, let alone say anything, but then again, what was there to say? They were in The La's, which I'd started and was now on an upward trajectory and I wasn't in the picture. It was also hard because Paul and I went back quite a long way too. He'd been to many of The La's' gigs and his band The Twangin' Banjos had played on the same bill.

For me, the only direction was onwards and upwards. During February, I started to work with Danny Dean on a more regular basis and we arranged a recording session at Phil Butcher's studio in his Falkner Street basement. We recorded a new song, 'Rockin' Out the Depression', and two of my ex- La's songs, 'Get Down Over (With the Show You Know)' and 'The Heart Knows'.

Shortly after that first session at Phil's, Danny and I went into the Attic studio with Hamish on piano and Colin Beckett (from the scheme) playing drums. We recorded a new song called 'The Law', which had the following lyrics:

I've never been in trouble with the law,
But the law's been in trouble with me,
A force that can't release itself,
Will not be able to set me free.

We also laid down another new song of mine called 'Let's Go Home'. With the exception of 'Trees and Plants' it was my first real venture into what would now probably be called 'Americana'. It was something that was developing as a result of my growing interest in Hank Williams and – gradually – the broader country music church. Initially I'd hated anything to do with what was usually termed country music, yet the more I listened to Hank and the likes of Johnny Cash, the more I could hear it had a no-nonsense simplicity and purity that a lot of modern pop seemed to be lacking. The song itself was promising too. When aligned with Hamish's piano playing it really rocked.

In March '87 we were told that we had our jobs back at the Musicians' Resource Centre, but somehow it never materialized – again! We waited, but nothing happened. (The story of corruption and the way we had been treated was now making National Headlines.) With the re-emergence of the scheme apparently a false dawn, I went to London for a change of scene and visited Eduardo Paolozzi's beautiful 'Lost Civilisations' exhibition at one of my favourite old haunts, the Museum of Mankind.

******

Jeanette had started doing a foundation course at Mabel Fletcher College and it was a pleasure to see her discovering her creative self after years of working in other areas, and not least because of the endless support she had given to me (and The La's as a whole – we had been making a lot of noise in her home too!). She had made a great sculpture of an African American woman for her interview at Liverpool Poly, but she decided against including it in her portfolio, so instead I climbed a tree and hung it from a branch by the bandstand in Sefton Park.

A guy called Simon Cousins had joined the meditation group. Although now based in Liverpool, Simon originally hailed from a village in Wiltshire near to Chippenham. More pertinently, he played bass and was keen to make some music, so I drafted him in to practise with myself and Danny.

I hadn't seen Carl Davies for a long while – well, not since I had chased him into the night when he was breaking into our flat. It saddened me greatly when I saw Paul Burns and he told me Carl had become a full-blown alcoholic and had recently been beaten up in London. You always felt you took your life in your hands though when you went for a drink with that lad.

Before too long Jeanette got the reply from her interview with Liverpool Poly to do a BA in Fashion and Textiles. She'd got in and was to start later that year – something that I had never achieved!

I was writing a lot of new songs, many of which would later end up on The Onset's debut album. These included 'Little One', 'The Taker', 'For You' and 'Too Many People'. Working diligently with Danny and Simon, we began to work these songs up with help from the ever-versatile Bernie Nolan on drums. Kevin Wright had started to engineer at an 8-track studio down on Ullet Road and he invited me down to record some songs. As it happened, Geoff Davies from Probe Plus was also down there, doing an album with a band that had the unlikely name The Revolutionary Army of the Infant Jesus. He was interested in what I was doing, and Kevin duly gave him a tape of our new recordings.

In May 1987 The La's signed to Go! Discs after the label had attended one of the band's gigs in the third room of the Everyman Bistro that spring. Ironically, it was on that very spot that it had all started when I had met Lee on a return trip up from London and decided to work with him. It really is a funny old world!

During August I saw The La's play the Earth Beat Festival in Sefton Park. The only new song in the set was 'My Girl Sits Like a Reindeer', but re-invented with different lyrics from Lee. It was now known as 'Feelin''. I thought they played a good, tight set, but that didn't surprise me as we'd already played the socks off those songs while I was in the band the previous year. If you counted 'Feelin'' in this form, they were all Lee's songs except for 'Callin' All'. I couldn't understand how they could attempt that to be honest as my rhythm guitar part was essential to it working, so it sounded laboured to me, but despite everything I wished them well.

******

By now Jeanette had started her degree in Fashion and Textiles at the Liverpool College of Art and had arrived home with something to tell me. During our time at the Falkner Street flat, we had 'babysat' Kevin and Julie's dog Prince and I had done a painting of him in blue on a yellow armchair. It had hung in the flat, but when we left somehow it had ended up remaining there. We'd forgotten about it, but now it transpired Jeanette had been into the art school staff room and there, over the mantel piece, hung my portrait of Prince. Jeanette discovered that one of the lecturers had found it in a skip. So, while I might not have physically made it there, my presence had got into the art school after all and in the best possible way!

Then something else fantastic happened. Geoff Davies came over to our place in Aigburth to tell me he'd loved the feel of 'The Taker' and 'Down at the Space Rocketry', two songs our new band had recorded at the Sanatorium over the summer. He also liked our honky-tonk version of 'Let's Go Home' from the Attic. He said it was something that had gripped him immediately and he wanted us to do an album on his label. I was over the moon at such a prospect. Geoff had done really well during 1986. He'd released the year's most successful independent album with Half Man Half Biscuit's *Back in the DHSS* and they'd since gone on to become the undisputed league champions of caustic Mersey wit.

Until this time, Danny, Simon, Bernie and I had been calling the new band The Two-Step Angels, but Geoff had reservations. He felt it sounded too cabaret. I searched for a possible new name through my *Roget's Thesaurus* and the word 'onset' stood out in a small glow of its own on the page. From then on, we were The Onset – it was defined as 'a new beginning – a spearhead'!

The Probe Records shop was a legendary place and self-styled 'home of the Liverpool underground' since 1971. Geoff Davies had been crucial in supplying all those essential (and often eccentric) albums everyone just had to have and – along with Roger Eagle at Eric's – had inspired a major part of the last explosion in Liverpool's music scene. Geoff told me that he'd also met Captain Beefheart, who had once said to him, 'You don't put out the light'. How true!

Towards the end of 1987 The Onset played their first official gig at the System Club in Liverpool. This was the venue that had been utilized by The Teardrop Explodes for their Club Zoo events and was also previously known as the Pyramid Club. Our line-up was augmented by a conga player called Rye who I'd met at Bernie and Julie's wedding and we shared the bill with another of Geoff's acts, St Vitus Dance from Belfast, and Roger's new band, The Catfish.

******

In the New Year of 1988 I went to see an especially life-affirming gig. It was Jonathan Richman at Liverpool Poly and I was knocked out by him. All his band had was two guitars and a snare drum and yet it was magnificent.

He sang songs about UFOs, affection, chocolate drinks and ice-cream men and he could do no wrong for me. His first Modern Lovers album was a masterpiece and I had always loved him.

On 27 February we played a benefit at Liverpool's Hardman House Hotel and The La's were topping the bill. I left before they played, but Roger watched them and told me the set was exactly the same as it had been a year before. I was amazed. Why were there no new songs?

******

One afternoon in the early part of 1988 I got a visit from Paul Hemmings. He was no longer in The La's. What had happened there then? Well, it was no surprise in some ways, he was a talented guitarist but he said he'd been getting into more country/bluegrass-style music and he asked if we wanted something extra in The Onset. He'd also been nurturing his skills on mandolin and lap steel and it seemed like a great idea!

In March 1988, The Onset did their first series of shows outside Merseyside. Our Wiltshire-born bassist, Simon Cousins, had an identical twin brother called Jon who also featured in a band. They were called Ophiuchus and they were active in the West Country area on a regular basis. Through Simon and Jon, we played a series of gigs with Ophiuchus, including both Moles and The Hat and Feather in Bath, Pee Wee's Real Ale Bar in Trowbridge ('spit and sawdust') and a pub whose name escapes me in Chippenham. It was a great trip and we jammed with Ophiuchus. A friend of my sister's called Dave Bedford, who was with Fire Records, came along to see us and enjoyed the set.

In April, The Onset got a regular drummer. With the album to record and more gigs imminent, I phoned Tony Russell, who had worked as a sound engineer at the Attic and with Frank Sparks, and had played a few gigs as drummer with The La's. Tony was a good drummer and also had an additional secret weapon: a huge VW van which was ideal for The Onset. Tony was up for it. Sorted! (And he was the third ex-La to be in the band.)

I got a *King Federal's Rockabilly* compilation album from the rack at the back of Probe around this time which featured Charlie Feathers. He was amazing. He had blown me away when I'd heard him full blast at the rockabilly nights we used to go to down at the Mayflower a few years before. He didn't sing so much as hiccup, chirp, squeal and moan and soon became my new hero. Nobody extolled the rock rhythm like Charlie. His infectious, frenetic guitar hand and expressive voice were like nothing I'd heard before or since, a real live individual. He once described the sound he was aiming for by saying, 'You should be able to record the sweat of a man'. I was fired up by his music and played him in the van all the time. In fact it was to the sound of Charlie Feathers that we entered the Mersey Tunnel on our way to Oxton on the Wirral to record our first album with Geoff Davies.

We recorded the backing tracks to twelve songs in one day and still had the energy to play the Picket in Liverpool that same night. We were relaxed and confident and loved the whole thing, though we had to give into fatigue after we'd played our set and headed home instead of staying to watch Paul, who was also now playing with Tommy Scott's new band, The Australians.

Lee and John would call over on occasions to say hi, have a cuppa and smoke a joint. I think they were seeing if I was active musically and I feel they would have liked me back in The La's but I didn't want to be part of it again. Besides, I was now having a good time with The Onset and things were starting to move for us too with our debut album on Probe Plus. But I did appreciate them calling and being friendly.

We added some overdubs and extra textures to the album shortly after. Bernie played fiddle, Roger played some banjo under the name Dirk Freeman and Hamish blasted out some harmonica under the name Six-Cylinder Sid. We mixed it over the next few days. Sam Davies (formerly Eric Shark from much-loved Liverpool pre-punk group Deaf School and the other 'Bald' Brother producer with Geoff) was full of ideas and a great help with capturing the sound. With the excitement still burning brightly we went on another tour of the Wiltshire area.

Jon Cousins had arranged an itinerary for us which also included a radio interview with GWR in Chippenham.

We played a village hall in Chippenham and then Jon made the fatal mistake of asking Danny to look after the bar. Not too surprisingly, he got very drunk. As a result, some amusing things happened: not least that the guitar solo in 'Trees and Plants' went on and on and then went on a little more ... and then some more just in case. Still, it was our first night away and all that goes with it.

After the gig we went over the road to Jon Cousins' girlfriend Kerry's house. Danny walked across the road at a 45-degree angle. We went into the house for a cup of tea and a post-gig wind-down. Danny needed to pee and was shown to the outside toilet. We had been chatting for a while round the kitchen table when we realized Danny hadn't returned. We couldn't understand where he could have got to. Kerry's Dad came up with the realization that there were some trays of beer in that outside toilet. Simon went outside and there was Danny collapsed in a wheelbarrow in the back garden with an unopened four-pack in his hand. The spirit was willing, but the flesh was weak. We managed to drag him into the kitchen where he assured us he was fine before he proceeded to stick his hands into the bowl of what he assumed were nibbles and shovelled a load of them into his mouth. He then discovered it was potpourri and spat it all over the kitchen table. Goodnight Wiltshire!

The tour went really well and lasted for a fortnight, although I did hitch over to London for a day to attend the cutting of the forthcoming album. Because of its easy proximity to the shows we were playing, we found time to visit both Stonehenge and Avebury, with its mystifying earthworks and magnificent stone circles.

I did a collage cover for our new album which was titled *The Pool of Life* and took images from an old encyclopaedia. I wanted it to be empirical, illustrating the world as a whole, taking in all beliefs and influences at the time. It was a pleasure getting to know Steve Hardstaff, who worked with Geoff and Probe Plus on the covers.[12]

******

12 See the book *Cover Versions* by Steve Hardstaff.

One day I bumped into former Cavern DJ Bob Wooller on Aigburth Road. I had got to know Bob from drinking in the Grapes before Eric's shows. I remember one time we were talking about poetry. I had the impulse to scrawl a few profound lines on a piece of paper and gave it to him. Now, ten years later, he says, 'Michael, Michael come here.' He then proceeded to reach for his wallet, pull out the very piece of paper and ask me quizzically, 'But what does it mean?'

I was stunned. What a lovely, fascinating gentleman.

******

We made another trip to Wiltshire and Somerset during August 1988. We visited a great long barrow in Nettleton and we played the tiny Salamander in Bath and then headed off over to London to play our first Onset concert in the capital. The venue was the Pied Bull in Islington, where I had previously recited some of my poems to a backing tape during an evening set up by some of the York Way people called 'Workers Playtime'. On the bill this time with us was a band called The Ozric Tentacles.

This was the beginning of a new acid scene happening. The crowd were full-on psychedelic heads and I soon began to wonder what they would make of our country-based rockabilly roots sound. Illustrator Steven Appleby and a load of my sister Ros' mates had come down to support us, but as it turned out my worries were entirely unfounded. I introduced our version of Hank Williams' 'A Mansion on the Hill' as 'acid country and western' and the crowd loved us. Sure, it helped that we played a blinder that night, but I was delighted with their response because I began to realize we had the sort of eclectic sound that offered something for everyone to latch onto. I bought the new La's EP while I was still in London because it had 'Liberty Ship' and also a version of 'Freedom Song' that I'd played on.

During September, I began a part-time washing-up job at the School of Tropical Medicine, but this was rather secondary to the media interest that was beginning to grow up around The Onset. We played the World Downstairs at Liverpool's Royal Court Theatre and journalists Penny Kiley (*Melody Maker*) and John Hodgkinson (*Merseysound*) both came down to the show.

Our debut album, *The Pool of Life*, had recently been released and we'd been receiving some positive press. Penny Kiley's review in *Melody Maker* suggested, 'you can talk about variety in their songs – everything from rock 'n' roll to country – but the overall effect is a sparkling coherence full of spirit and warmth'. The *Independent*, meanwhile, had tapped into our 'tumbledown garage eclecticism', and, writing in *Sounds*, Cathi Unsworth said, '*The Pool of Life* explores the world, the Universe and everything else ... it proves to be a worldly hobos' guide to the galaxy'.

I sent a copy of *The Pool of Life* to KILI radio station on the Pine Ridge Reservation in South Dakota – I never received a playlist back from them but I like to think that our music was broadcast over there to the Lakota people. They had an eagle feather tied to the top of the mast.

******

1989: RIP Chris McCaffrey (Biffa)

******

Paul brought a copy of *Viz* magazine into a practice and said, 'Have you seen this?' *Viz* used to allow brazen adverts to be dropped into their captions and in one it stated that The La's fantastic debut album would be titled 'Callin' All' and would be out in the near future. Surprised, I thought that's the first I know about this. I thought I should cover myself here and let Go! Discs know that the 'Callin' All' title was a co-written song with Lee and myself, and I also listed other songs we had worked on together.

A week later I got a letter in reply from Go! Discs stating that Lee had written all the words and music to 'Callin' All' and said that I 'might have been in the room at the time' but that's all. This just wasn't true and we were talking about the title track of The La's debut album.

How could Lee do that to me? Bands break up and personalities clash but the music is the music ... What the fuck!

Baffled, I took advice from a local solicitor on Aigburth Road (with no expertise in copyright law at all). He asked if I had any evidence to contradict Lee's claims. I remembered Roger Llewellyn had been present on that day in the rehearsal room when 'Callin' All' had been written and when I asked him if he had any recall of the incident he said he remembered me starting the song off with my Spanish-style chord progression, and that John Power had been there too.

I hated having to immerse myself in this. However, I had a sense of duty to myself, plus there was the potential here for a large amount of revenue to be generated by this track and why the hell should I be cut out? I was still having to sign on. My solicitor sent Go! Discs a letter stating that I had an independent witness who was willing to vouch for me on this issue and in addition I also had written evidence in the form of a diary entry. It just seemed insane that I should be having to justify myself here.

Anyhow, as it transpired that was the end of it. We heard nothing back from Go! Discs. 'Callin' All' never became the title of The La's debut album and in fact never even appeared on the eventual release. Great result all round.

... Callin' No One!

******

In October we were gigging again, this time playing with The Farm and St Vitus Dance at the Hardman House Hotel. It was a benefit show for the victims of General Pinochet's deadly regime in Chile and it proved to be both a great cause and an equally great gig put on by the Latin American Solidarity Front. Pinochet was of course Thatcher's mate!

****

1988 had seen us make good progress as a band. We had played over fifty gigs, we had an album out and we'd done our first radio and TV appearances. It was all pretty positive and we saw the year out with a

Christmas bash at the Picket with The Catfish where both bands had a jam on stage as the finale to the show. It was about half full and would probably have been packed if it wasn't for The La's' sold-out show at the Hardman House in the adjacent building. Timing. C'est la vie. It seemed The La's were still on course for great things.

NINE

Tumbledown
Garage Rock Eclecticism

I NEEDED A WORKHORSE OF a guitar. The red Burns I'd been using since 1985 was a classic vintage guitar but not a gigging one, so I traded it in for a big Aria semi-acoustic called a Jazz Star. It had a sunburst finish and was great to play and suited me down to the ground.

I'd go in to see Geoff at the Probe Plus office above the Probe shop. It would always be covered in hundreds of records and tapes and Geoff would be holding court up there being very funny and provocative. I did an interview with James Scanlon from Roby for his *Blast Off* fanzine we'd had a lot of local interest with *The Pool of Life*, but national radio play had proved to be a stumbling block.

Geoff was upbeat, though. He showed me a review of the album that had recently appeared in *Folk Roots* magazine where the reviewer called us 'rednecks on speed' before going on to suggest the album was 'one of the finest things that Probe Plus had released'.

Simon had started off a little PA hire company and so we did the PA for Eugene Chadbourne's 'Shockabilly' show at Planet X in town. It proved to be a fantastic, psychedelic-tinged evening. Another of Geoff's Probe Plus bands, The Walking Seeds were on first, playing their brand of warped, '60s garage punk. Their Probe Plus album *Skullfuck* would later be cited by Nirvana's Kurt Cobain as an influence and they played a great show that night at Planet X. Another band on was Back From Nam, which featured ex-La's Tony Clarke on drums, Barry Shailes (who worked in the Probe shop) on vocals and Paul (another Probe assistant) on bass. They had a punk rock tune called 'Robocop' and kicked ass.

******

The general sense of optimism we were experiencing would be shattered by a tragedy that would resonate for decades to come. On 15 April so many Liverpool fans were crushed to death at Hillsborough, Sheffield Wednesday's football ground. What should have been an exciting Liverpool FC cup tie became one of the greatest tragedies ever suffered on Merseyside and in the UK.

The atmosphere in Liverpool was indescribable. People were shell-shocked. How could this have happened? And at a football match! The city was decimated by the disaster.

As for the *Sun* the next day and their despicable front page of lies, there was a small line under their logo – the *Sun* comment: 'Kop of Shame'. Of course we all now know it should have read 'Cop of Shame'.

I personally had not known a soul who had bought that paper before Hillsborough, let alone after. It was considered by many in Liverpool to be a right-wing rag with its support of the Thatcher regime, and I had loved seeing Holly Johnson in 1984 tearing up a copy on *Top of the Pops*.

******

The Onset were approached by a new booking agency that had set up in Liverpool. They were called D.O.A. (Dead on Arrival) and they'd already started taking bands over to play in Germany. They were all really sound, enthusiastic people and the prospect of working with them gave us all a new lift.

I got a copy of Half Man Half Biscuit's *Back Again in the DHSS* off Geoff. I'd met their frontman, Nigel Blackwell, a couple of times in the office above Probe. I loved their songs too: they brilliantly destroyed prima donnas and included in their lyrics some of the most unlikely TV and sporting personalities imaginable. If you started feeling too cool or self-important, you needed to look at the Biscuits' barometer: personally it always reminded me where your parameters in life should lie. However, they had amazed everyone by splitting up just at the time when major fame was theirs for the taking. But they didn't want it just then.

D.O.A. had been organizing our first German visit for early summer, but May still had more surprises up its sleeve. For starters, Everton lost the FA Cup Final to Liverpool, going down 3–2 in extra time. The Onset, meanwhile, were still active locally, playing a Hillsborough benefit show at a place called JD's and Paul Hemmings moved into a plush bachelor pad in Wapping Dock. I'd bump into Tommy Scott in town and we'd discuss our respective bands' prospects. 'We'll get there in the end, won't we?' he would say.

We were all really excited about D.O.A.'s involvement with the band and our first trip from Doleland to Deutschland began when we met at Paul's parents' place near the famous Strawberry Field. The Stables had been The La's' rehearsal room during Paul's tenure with the band after my departure and now we were practising for our tour there. We'd been getting more new songs up to scratch for our first European jaunt.

The journey itself was a trip. D.O.A. had an enormous white Mercedes van which was more like a house on wheels and we were buzzing all the way down to Dover, enjoying the comfort of it.

Funnily enough, as we crossed the border into Germany Julian Lennon was in the bus in front of us entering the country. Ironic – especially as his dad had once done the very same thing in the early days of The Beatles.

Our first stop was a café in Wiesbaden. I remembered that this is where Elvis had been stationed during his time as a GI in the 1950s. The town was beautiful and spotlessly clean. They had bottle banks years before recycling was the norm in the UK and paper bins at the end of each street.

Our first gig was at a club called Jukuz in Hahn, in a converted railway station. A lot of people came along to chat to us afterwards and they had really listened intently to the songs. They often wanted us to clarify what the lyrics meant and were genuinely interested in the band, I think also with us coming all the way from Liverpool.

The next night we played the first of two nights at the Goldene Krone in Darmstadt. It was quite a place. We wandered into the bar downstairs and discovered that there was cowhide stuck all over the wooden benches while a small horse was wandering around – straight up!

Upstairs there was a disco, a room that contained a giant chess set, more bars, a venue (where we were playing), a pool room, cinema and TVs. It was all housed in an old building with original Bauhaus interiors. I was in heaven. Our set lasted an hour and a half and we met a guy called Klaus Schwartze, who had written the two-volume *Scouse Phenomenon* book with family trees of Liverpool's music scene from the pre-punk mid-1970s through to 1988.

It was a great help that Barb from D.O.A. was German and knew all the best places to go so, as we had a bit of time, we headed off to a lake near Frankfurt the following day. It had bright green water and looked very inviting. We all opted to go in for a swim and it was laid-back enough for all the Germans to walk around naked. Some sights were more preferable than others! We played the Krone again that night and while it didn't hit the heights of the first show it was still enjoyable and later we laughed ourselves to sleep in our bunks up in the ancient beamed attic rooms.

The next evening we made a fire by a lake and camped out all night as we didn't have a gig to play. Amazingly, the German promoters not only paid us, but also provided crate after crate of deliciously pure beer. A far cry from what it was like in the UK! Predictably, we all got ridiculously drunk that night and – in need of a cure the following morning – I was first out of the tent. I set off to find some chocolate milk and something to eat. When I returned I discovered that a good German citizen had reported us, and the rest of the band were being rapidly shooed away by the police. We claimed we had not known that we weren't allowed to camp at that particular place. The policeman casually pointed out that we had tied one of the guy ropes of the tent to the 'Camping Verboten' sign.

******

The following night we had to go back to Wiesbaden to collect visas to travel across East Germany into Berlin, which was scheduled after the next gig. First, though, we had to drive over to a show in Hof. After the gig we were parked by a lake right up against the Iron Curtain and the border to Czechoslovakia. If that wasn't forbidding enough, an almighty thunderstorm began raging, lightning split the sky and we ended up listening to weird Eastern European radio deep into the night.

I found out the hard way that vegetarians and Germans make awkward bedfellows. I lived on cheese salad rolls and the occasional pizza if we could find an Italian place. It didn't matter, because we were having a great time regardless. We'd played three of the five scheduled stops and spent the days off enjoying the beautiful lakes and pine trees. The usually uber-cool Paul Hemmings was tearful because he was worried he was turning into a hippy with all this outdoor living.

On the journeys, the crates of beer we had acquired got steadily lighter – not least because of Danny Dean's huge appetite and frame. We'd have to pull over for a piss stop and he would stand at the side of the van pissing like a camel for what seemed like hours and, as I was in the driving seat, I couldn't resist moving the van forward slowly and exposing Danny to the road. Still in mid-flow, he shuffled sideways to get back behind it and then I'd do the same thing again. It served him right for drinking all our beer while I was driving!

The promoter at the Bahn in Hof tried several times to get me to talk publishing, but I wasn't having any of it. Besides, we all got a great surprise when my Mum and Dad turned up unannounced at the gig. They'd been on holiday in Switzerland and decided to make the trip over to Hof. It was great to see them and even better because we'd chosen that evening to play one of our most rockin' shows.

We had a real celebration after the gig, but regretted it the following morning. We all felt really rough as a result of mixing our usual intake of beer with salt, tequila and lemon. It probably wasn't the ideal condition to be in on the long journey that would take us up the autobahn into East Germany and finally to Berlin. The procession of BMWs and Mercedes we'd seen over the past few days had miraculously changed into a string of Trabants dating from the 1950s, which seemed to have shrunk in the carwash when compared with our mighty van. They only appeared to be available in one of four colours as well, and the contrast with the affluent West German lifestyle was immediately apparent. I proceeded to demonstrate my driving skills by driving into West Berlin like I was a seasoned Trabant driver and received gasps of concern from the band in the back as a result.

We had a room above the K.O.B. club, the venue we were playing that night. We found the place and dropped off the gear before we took a walk to the notorious Berlin Wall. The atmosphere was incredible and scars from the Second World War were still visible all over the place, not least the lines of bullet holes pock-marking the classically designed buildings which still stood proudly, if rather spectrally around the giant city. The gig proved to be a belter as well. It was the best we'd played on the tour and the enthusiastic crowd of rockers, punks and everyone else lapped it up.

Afterwards, we met up with two ex-squaddies from England who had spent seven years of their army lives stationed in Germany. They were called Wolfy and Russ and they said they'd been to see The Pogues the week before in Berlin and our show was better. Wow. Good feedback. We were on the lookout for some draw and Wolfy took me on a late-night journey through the streets of Berlin on a hunt for something of quality to smoke. We got the bus and chatted to two East German goth girls who had defected to the West. We got off at the same stop as the girls and Wolfy clearly fancied his chances.

'You know what would look good on her?' he leered.

'No', I replied.

'Me', he said evilly.

The search went on and on. I noticed signs for the Neukoln and it reminded me where the Huyton punk band had got it name, though swapping the L and N to Neuklon. Curiously, these streets reminded me of Huyton too.

Despite the lengthy trek, we returned to the K.O.B. empty handed. But Wolfy wasn't to be defeated. He remembered another place and though it was 3am by this time he was confident it would be fine. I was glad when Danny decided to come along with us.

'Yeah, I wanna be a Berlin Urban Street Warrior too', he said.

We walked to a biker bar called the Sexton. Chopper motorcycles were lined up outside and Guns N' Roses' hit 'Welcome to the Jungle' rumbled portentously from the speakers. But despite the macho air, the inside was a real surprise, we realized as we were being eyed-up by a number of the clientele. Wolfy was right about the draw though, and we returned spliffed up to the K.O.B.

We managed a few hours' sleep and then it was back down the autobahn through East and West Germany and then through Holland, Belgium and home. The ferry had a queasy orange and brown decor and the vegetable soup had meat in it. A ridiculously over-the-top voice over the tannoy woke us up when it announced we were approaching Dover. It had been a blast, but the thought of getting back home was blissful too.

The next day reality struck when I went to sign on. I'd come to realize by now that the only way to treat my need to sign on was to approach it as though it were *autograph practice*. Unfortunately, it was still a necessity. We'd rented a room underneath our flat as a rehearsal room for both The Onset and The Catfish and also moved our meditation night down there. When we pooled our resources, it was just about financially manageable.

✴✴✴✴✴✴

Pete De Freitas

One of the coolest dudes in town and drummer with Echo and The Bunnymen. He would come down to watch The La's from '86 onward and later offered them recording time in 1987. 2 August 1961 – 14 June 1989. Ride in Peace.

✴✴✴✴✴✴

Barb from D.O.A. got in touch again with good news. She'd received a playlist from the national German radio station Bayerischer Rundfunk in Munich and they had played eight tracks from *The Pool of Life*. It was very encouraging news and was followed by a call from Semaphore regarding licensing. It was great that things were moving in Europe but we were still operating very much at a local level in Liverpool. What was it about England? Why didn't it respect its artists? The attitude was totally different on the continent.

******

Paul decided to nail his colours to The Onset's mast full time after the German jaunt, which meant he had to leave The Australians because he couldn't juggle his commitments between the two bands. We were all pleased, but at the same time hoped it wouldn't disrupt Tommy and the band too badly.

We did a disastrous Scottish tour and then a couple of summer festival appearances. We played the Anti-Poll Tax bash in Walton Hall Park and also the Earth Beat Festival in Liverpool's Sefton Park. The whole gig was videoed and there were some great photographs taken by Mark McNulty.

By now The La's' debut album still hadn't been released – you'd hear rumours that it was going to be but then never appeared. I knew that they had recorded in what seemed like countless locations. This was all such a far cry from my days in The La's, when we were prolific and not too precious. What was going on?

Tony Russell had started to run his own little booking agency and sorted out a tour of fifteen dates for The Onset during October 1989. The first show was at the Two Pigs in Coulsham, Wiltshire, on the 5th and finished with a Halloween party in Carlisle on the 31st. The tour also swung through London, so on the 21st we played at the New Pegasus in Stoke Newington. Ros and Ben brought a big crew down with them and the show was a really good one. Despite some of the trials and tribulations, The Onset was cooking creatively and we were becoming a force to be reckoned with on the live scene.

******

The times were a-changin' around the world as the 1980s wound down. On 10 November, like most people in Europe, we watched the incredible scenes in Berlin as the Wall came tumbling down. The sheer weight and will of the people was pushing it over and it was all anyone could talk about for days. We were thrilled as we would be in Berlin again in the New Year and would be able to take it all in first hand.

All empires are destined to crumble

The Onset felt the wind of change too. CBS had been sniffing around and threatened to come and see us play in Bolton, but they never showed up. A guy called Martin Poole, who'd seen us play at The New Pegasus show in Islington, came up to see us with Dave Dixon with the view of managing us.

The music was evolving and I was listening to different things. It was still roots-y to a lot of peoples' ears, but to us it was becoming a lot more electric and broadly rock/pop. In our minds, it was a natural progression.

The band was on a roll with new material coming thick and fast. 'Endless Sun' had come into the set for the Bolton show and shortly afterwards came 'Set For Destruction', 'What Say You?' and 'The Heart Knows': the latter having been side-lined since The La's. The band liked it the first time we played it, but Paul was looking curiously at me as he'd misunderstood the title. He thought I was singing 'The Hard Nose'.

TEN

Tin Can Alley

1990. A NEW DECADE. We had a promising itinerary as we were gearing up for our second trip to Germany. In February, the sight we'd been looking forward to became a reality when the huge white Mercedes van again pulled up outside the practice room. Sadly, our excitement about making a home in the Merc again would be short-lived as it refused to go as soon as we got in it. The curse of the Scottish trip seemed to be striking again as the steering had gone. Frantically, we sorted out a covering note with the insurance people and went in Tony's Transit-sized van with no windows in the back. Because of the hassle, we'd left late and despite driving to Dover on what seemed like two wheels, we missed the ferry by about thirty seconds. And consequently the first gig of the tour.

Instead, we made straight for Darmstadt and a repeat engagement at the Goldene Krone. Once again, we got a good reception there and some of the crowd were even singing along to the songs as they'd previously taped them off the radio when played on Bayerischer Rundfunk.

Danny and Paul were becoming a double act in terms of their wicked sense of humour and Danny was turning into a real party animal on tour. On stage, he indulged in some bizarre antics. At the Goldene Krone gig, he strolled off the foot of the stage with his super-long guitar lead behind him, then skipped back up the steps slipping on the top step in the process. He lost his balance and went towards the drum kit at full tilt. Somehow, he managed to remain upright and miss Tony's drums, but then he was gone again and I'd no idea where he'd vanished to as I couldn't see him anymore. Yet he was still playing! It turned out that he'd ended up in a sitting-down position in the dressing room next to the stage but hadn't missed a note.

We had a 400-mile drive ahead of us again after that, but we did have the prospect of a gig in the new East Berlin to anticipate. We got there in good time and had a couple of hours to spare before we had to meet the promoter at the legendary Checkpoint Charlie at midnight.

We would be in the East for twenty-four hours only and couldn't return before then because of the temporary visas we had. I fancied a smoke to pass the time and we'd found an all-night café in West Berlin. I asked a couple of likely-looking guys, but they refused point blank, saying simply 'No!' when I enquired about the availability of a smoke. We had a coffee instead and were about to leave when one of the same guys came over to me and placed a block of hash on my leg. It transpired they'd thought I was police testing them out. However, one of them later confided to Danny they had seen me slump down in my chair looking totally fed up after my enquiry and had decided no one could feign that amount of disappointment.

We made the rendezvous at Checkpoint Charlie bang on time and went through into the austere East. The promoter met us as planned and asked us to follow him. He got into a white Trabant and our Transit moved in convoy behind him. He turned onto the main road and up to the traffic lights where there were another four identical white Trabants. Oh no! Which one was he? We finally realized where he was when he drove past us and – making sure we didn't lose him a second time – we followed him past the huge Fehnsehturm, the East Berlin TV tower, and pulled up outside the Knaack Club, where we were due to play the following night.

Inside, the atmosphere was electric with anticipation. The people were open and totally up for the music they were hearing. Our song 'The Taker' came on over the PA and a load of people jumped up and started dancing. I could barely contain the emotion I felt. It was like being in a film. It was hard to equate such a positive vibe with such an apparently run-down place. I then started picking up the empty ciggie packets from the floor with their amazing Eastern Bloc graphics – these would be made into a collage for sure!

Thorsten, the promoter, ran us to his girlfriend's place, where we would be staying. We backed up the van and followed him through a courtyard – followed by another courtyard – and finally we arrived outside some really old apartment blocks from the nineteenth century. We got to the stairs and walked up and up. Everywhere was really clean but it seemed like it hadn't had a coat of paint since the end of the war. It hadn't – this was the East! The flat consisted of two small rooms. One of these had a shower at one end and a kitchen at the other. The vinyl top cover of the kitchen units had a snakeskin design. There was a monolithic yellow ceramic storage heater in there too and a plastic tray from a box of chocolates was pinned to the wall. It was an empty, but potent reminder of a long gone time of luxury.

In the next room some mattresses had been pulled out for us and we said goodbye to the promoter in anticipation of the show the next day.

Before long, we pulled the black blind down, getting ready to fall asleep. I opened my eye – or half an eye at least – and one of the others must have done the same because the laughter kicked in and we rolled around the mattresses holding our stomachs because we literally could not see a bloody thing. We were in a complete void; you couldn't see anything with that blind down. It was quite literally the darkest place any of us had ever been. That blind was the original blackout blind from the war. It obviously did its job because the building was still there and, somehow, we finally got off to sleep.

I had bought some biscuits as a thank you to the promoter and when I woke up I arranged them in a fashion on the coffee table. I then proceeded to step backwards onto the tin and it flicked up and tipped all over the place, finally landing upside down on the other side of the room. Everyone creased up laughing. This was typical of me, turning into Mr Clumsy and showing just how uncool I really could be!

We got paid in advance of the gig as we would have to be leaving chronically early the following day because of our twenty-four-hour visas to enter the East. All five of us received £30-worth of Deutschmarks (or Ostmarks) apiece and were told if we didn't spend them in East Berlin we wouldn't be able to spend them at all.

At the time the exchange rate was approximately 20 marks to £1 sterling, so this provided us with a challenge. I went to a kiosk with the intention of buying some postcards and stamps and gave the lady a 20-mark note. She shook her head – she was unable to change it. It was so sad. We really struggled to spend the money as all the shops were empty. I ended up acquiring a small pocket watch, spending the equivalent of less than 80 pence in the process. We went into a nicotine-stained bar and I looked at the watch. Another guy in there noticed it and asked me if he could see it. He asked me how much I'd paid for it. I told him and he shook his head. He told me I'd been ripped off and he could have gotten it much cheaper.

We felt very awkward. We were very obviously Westerners in East Berlin and the gulf between the cultures was enormous. We all treated ourselves to a three-course meal for the equivalent of £1, and I noticed all the apples in the bowl on the counter were bruised, something you'd never see in the West. The gig that night was a great success and we were filmed by a West German TV crew for a documentary about the East. We were treated really well by the people at the Knaack and we gave away a load of T-shirts, badges and records after the show.

We left East Berlin early the next morning and were allowed to stop and chip away at the remains of the Berlin Wall when we stopped at Checkpoint Charlie. We were all determined to leave with a small bit of it. It was history, after all. We had a long drive ahead of us, as the road down to Eberbach near Stuttgart was a full-on twelve-hour affair. And it had been snowing. During a traffic standstill on the autobahn we had the time to get out of the van and build a snowman in the central reservation. It was a huge relief to stretch our legs and also avoid the dreadful US forces radio station we were force-fed when we tried to listen to music along the way.

The hold-up lengthened and we ended up arriving horribly late for the gig. We were hungry, tired and anything but ready to jump on stage and give it 110%, but we tried anyway. It was already 11pm by the time we launched into the set and a lot of people had left or were drifting away, but it proved a surreal experience regardless.

A strange-looking guy in a red shell suit bounced up and down during the set on a little trampoline in front of the stage and the band ate sandwiches during breaks between songs. Danny had found a huge lemon in the dressing room and came out on stage with it on his head. We were so tired afterwards and the walk to the promoter's flat nearly killed us. Once again, we had to walk up five sets of stairs with our bags and by the time we finally got to his flat we literally collapsed inside and slept the sleep of the just.

Mercifully, we had the next day off, so Paul and I went shopping and returned with some fascinating tin toys. That evening the guys who owned the flat went to see a show by They Might Be Giants, so we had the whole place to ourselves. Those guys were so decent and trusting and even gave us a block of hash to enjoy. I also had about 100 magic mushrooms with me and we put them in a pot to boil and make some tea. There was enough for six cups when we'd brewed up and we drank it all. Nothing happened at first but then it really kicked in big time. There was an acoustic guitar in the flat and Danny began playing David Bowie's song 'Andy Warhol'. I realized this was all related to a dream I'd had a few weeks before. I even remembered the date of the dream. I was frozen to the bone.

In my heightened state, I didn't know how the guys would take to me explaining this dream I'd had, but I put it to them anyway. Paul was especially intrigued and encouraged me to tell all while placing his arm under Danny's and contributing to the playing of the guitar. Danny added his fingers to the fretboard and, as the two of them played the same guitar, I related my dream over the top.

In the dream I was standing on the steps of a theatre. Outside, Mick Jagger was playing a slot machine and Brian Jones was there too. Then Mick Jagger spoke to me about the mushrooms that grew on the steps. He asked if they were psilocybin. I said, 'Yeah', then said, 'You've blown my mind – you talked to me about these mushrooms ages ago in a dream I had'. He'd broken my dream. Then, there was a call and everyone went inside the theatre. People sat on the floor but there was no show. On the stairs on the way in I asked Brian Jones what he thought of the Stones documentary which had been on recently. He said they were all pleased with it. In it, a Liverpool girl was getting married. She'd spoken of a farm in Oregon then a man at the back played 'Andy Warhol' on a ten-string guitar … the tune that Danny had been playing originally moments before with Paul chipping in on the fretboard. Ten fingers – this could well be interpreted as a ten-string guitar in anyone's book. It's funny how dreams can sometimes replay the future. This was all heightened, of course, because of the stirring effects the mushrooms were about to have on us.

From then on it was a spectacular evening. Andy Harding (the tour manager) enthused, 'Hey Mike, good mushroom tea!'

'Boiled 'em myself', I replied, beaming.

Everyone had a fantastic time, even Tony, who had never even smoked a cigarette. Andy took us into the kitchen and started pointing: 'Come quick, look, look!' he urged.

He showed us the view out of the window and we all saw … houses. What had he expected us to see?

He looked bewildered. He told us we weren't getting what he saw at all, which just set us off laughing uncontrollably. We talked incessantly and the medicine dream added to a sense of unity we all shared.

The next day we bade farewell to the guys at the apartment. We'd had a blast and we had all shared a positive bonding experience, and our hosts had been generous to a fault. After all, in the cold light of day, would I have given over my apartment to five complete strangers to party in? It was only on the way out that I noticed a name on the mailbox in that block was Dr Mesmer, which only added to the weirdness.

We left town at mid-day feeling peaceful and mellow. I had a great feeling. We loaded the van and Paul called me Dr Alimantado. As we entered Austria the snow began to fall and the scenery got better and better, with pine trees everywhere and scenic, winding roads leading us into the darkness of the evening. We arrived at the next stop on the tour: a club called Vakanz in a tiny town called Bezau. It was basically a house in a valley in the snow with fields all around it. Who the hell was going to come out here for an evening's entertainment?

We loaded our equipment onto the small stage at the end of the room and went for something to eat at the 'hotel' we were staying at in the nearby village. Expecting nothing, we returned to the venue to discover it was packed with people. We were a huge hit from the first song we launched into, and the manager put a crate of beer on the stage to encourage us. We tore through the set and made to leave the stage, but the exit was through the crowd and they were having none of it. 'No way out! No way out!' they chanted in unison. OK. So we plugged in again and played a couple more. Once again, we made to leave the building and the people closed around us. 'No way out! No way out!' rang in our ears a second time and once again a crate of beer arrived on the stage. We played the entire set again and they were still up for more! We finally backed out the door feeling shattered, flattered and battered.

We had a quick skin-up in the dressing room and went back down. Some of the crowd were still there and one guy explained to me what he felt whenever he heard music from Liverpool. He said it always had its own identity and spirit and I felt on top of the world on hearing this. The gig had been the mother of all gigs, best one ever. I walked outside into the freshest air I had ever had the pleasure of breathing and walked across the field in the snow before turning to look back at this magical little house in the dark valley. It was a moment to savour.

The next day, the view from the hotel window was phenomenal, so we borrowed a sledge from the hotel proprietor and went up in the slopes to play in the snow and shoot some Super-8 film. It was a drag to have to leave, but we still had another show left, which meant heading back into Germany, this time to Reutlingen and a club called the Zelle. Although it couldn't quite hit the heights of the previous show, it was another stunning gig with lots of encores. And we made a live recording of a new song, 'What Say You?', through the PA desk. There was a totally crazy girl in the audience who jumped onto the stage, sidled up to me and put her hands in my pockets! After the show, she flirted outrageously and sat on my knee. She said her name was Cobra and she was quite clearly off her head. We had a narrow escape when her Irish boyfriend turned up, forcing us to make a sharp exit.

Then it was back to old Blighty, with warm beer you had to pay for and back to getting a pittance for your shows.

Back in England, we played at a college in High Wycombe. Our co-manager, Dave Dixon, brought Dave Dix down to see us with a view to producing a four-track EP we were hoping to release on Furious Fish, Martin Poole's little label. That was fine, as Geoff hadn't intended to release anything else by The Onset, at least at this time.

Dave Dix had been in the band Black, who had had a big hit with 'Wonderful Life', and I had actually been filmed for the video of the song outside an old butcher's shop on Aigburth Road, but it had been edited out of the video. Dave said he was very enthusiastic about The Onset. He enjoyed our set and our overall sound. He told Danny he was the only guy he'd ever known who could sing and smoke at the same time.

The whole Manchester scene was kicking off around this time. The Stone Roses and Happy Mondays were getting into producing tunes with dance-y grooves and baggy beats and what became known as the 'Madchester' scene was about to go off the scale. Before long, people would again be wearing flares without fear of reprisal and people would start calling each other 'man' without a hint of irony. This was a long way from our own *roots revival* –trippy beats and ecstasy was not our thing and so probably helped to isolate us further as a going commercial concern within the industry. We weren't going to jump on any bandwagon, either.

During April 1990 we went to Square One Studios in Bury, outside Manchester, a favourite haunt of The Fall. We recorded 'What Say You?', 'First I Feel You', 'Two-Step Angels' and a different version of 'Precious Love'. Danny suggested we slow down 'What Say You?' and it became a big grooving, looming thing that rocked out in style during the middle section. 'First I Feel You', though, developed into a great pop song. Despite the frustration of the recording methods, it was more than worthwhile when we heard the sound coming together and the fruits of our labour taking shape.

There was still room for fun and surrealism in the studio. At one stage Danny donned a pair of shades and started walking his legs while still sitting in one of the studio chairs. The chair moved freely on casters across the wooden studio floor, so Danny began swerving around holding an imaginary steering wheel of an imaginary sports car. He 'drove' behind the desk and drank from an imaginary bottle of Jack Daniel's, before pulling out and swerving around some more. He proceeded to hail some 'friends' he'd seen and waved them over to jump in the back – he was on his way to the beach! This was all as a result of the inevitable newfound stardom we were all about to obtain from what we were listening to on the speakers.

******

During July 1990 I did something I'd done many times before but this time ended up having a much greater significance. It was the simple act of throwing away an empty tin can. It was hardly an important event, in that I was hungry and wanted to eat the beans. I'd done it probably hundreds of times. On this occasion, though, I'd noticed the can sitting there in the bin. For some reason, the metal intrigued me. I fished it back out of the bin, washed the can and removed the label. Something clicked with me and I decided to cut it open with a big pair of scissors. I went on to make a car out of the metal around a wooden frame. It was an open top, with front and back seats, a windscreen and fenders. Feeling inspired, I made another one the following day and another one the day after that. I got a pair of tin snips from a local shop called Rapid Hardware and I also started making soap dishes and baskets out of fencing wire. It was fascinating and addictive.

******

I had taken a kitchen job at the School of Tropical Medicine. I would be paid £12 for four hours' work but the food was amazing, made by the Belgian Chef Benoit. It was a job for other Liverpool singers too, as Dave Jackson from Benny Profane would put a shift in, as would Frank Martin, singer in The Walking Seeds.

Back in Liverpool we had a string of visitors call at our rehearsal room. Paul Hemmings' friend Henry Epstein came to see us practising. He was an old neighbour of Paul's and had been involved to some degree with The La's after my departure, resulting in his friend Rob Swerdlow managing them. Katrine and Kate from Dresden (who we had met in Edinburgh) also called in to Liverpool, enjoying their tour of Europe.

My new interest in tin sculpting was developing nicely. I had made my first tin robot and I also acquired a rubber stamp saying 'Tin Top Designs' to help keep track of the continuing array of tin cars I had been making. (I numbered each one.)

During September we did another gig for the Latin American Solidarity Front at the Hardman House and raised a lot of money for that very just cause. The same day, Paul played us The La's' eponymous debut album, which had finally seen the light of day a full three years after they'd signed to Go! Discs. Lee has famously dissed the album ever since, but I enjoyed the record and noticed that my harmonies, guitar parts and arrangements had been included. I was actually very pleased about this, but still didn't think it sounded as good as the demos we'd done four years earlier.

The Onset's second release, the *What Say You?* EP, was released on Martin Poole's Furious Fish label. Writing in *Shout* magazine, John Hodgkinson had described 'First I Feel You' as 'a glorious slice of chiming, jangling pop that storms the brain and lays siege to the memory cells' and went on to call 'What Say You?' as 'literal rockabilly'.

In celebration, Ros, Ben, Jeanette and I all went out with actors Iain Glen and Suzi Harker in London. We ended up back at Iain and Suzi's place in Greenwich, where I played songs all night on Iain's guitar. One of them nights you remember!

Leaving Martin Poole's flat in Hackney that weekend, his girlfriend Louise said, 'Mike – try on this leather jacket, it's been here ages'. There was a beautiful heavy black biker jacket hanging on the peg next to the door. I put it on and it fitted me perfectly. Quality!

'Don't you think Mike should take it, Martin?' asked Louise.

'Whose is it?' I asked.

'It was Jean-Jacques Burnel's', I was told. The Stranglers' bassist had left it a long time ago and it was just hanging there. It was a beautiful jacket but I felt that if I had taken it, it wouldn't have been right, it was like it was his *buffalo robe* – not mine. Besides which, I'd just gotten a genuine TT fringed biker jacket from a car boot sale in Anglesey.

ELEVEN

It's a Long Way Back to Germany

DJ MARK RADCLIFFE WAS presenting his popular *Hit the North* show on BBC Radio 5 during the early 1990s and he became the only mainstream DJ to give the *What Say You?* EP any national airtime. He also invited us onto his show in Manchester to be interviewed.

During this chat, I had a moan about the media focussing on Manchester and ignoring Liverpool in the process. But Mark really knew his onions and we were very grateful for the airing he gave us. He even knew that it had been Fairground Attraction's Graham Henderson who had played accordion on our track 'Two Step Angel'. He knew about me being founder of The La's and some of the other band members also having spent time in that band. I was surprised. He played 'First I Feel You' off the EP and the opening track off *The Pool of Life*, 'Rakin' Em Down' – all fifteen seconds of it!

The Onset started playing a string of support shows with Half Man Half Biscuit, who were back performing after their self-imposed break. Nigel and the boys were still on top form too. They were determined not to 'tour' in the traditional sense – it was more like two gigs a week at most – but there were some fantastic shows and the majority of them were packed to the rafters.

I took ten *What Say You* 12-inch EPs into Probe and left them on a sale or return basis in June 1991; around the same time as we went into the Pink studio in Liverpool to record 'First I Feel You' for a slot on *Granada Reports*. These were still times when local unsigned bands could get a slot to showcase themselves on regional TV. Remember those days? Bring it back!

From the Pink we were taken to an old abandoned warehouse down at the docks near the Pier Head to perform the song for the TV cameras. I recognized the place instantly: it was the same setting *Rapido* had used for The La's' slot on their programme ... even more synchronicity! It was a great experience and we felt a lot of much-deserved energy from the excitement of our momentary delivery to sure-fire fame and recognition on screen. That night, Paul and I celebrated by travelling to Stoke to play half a dozen tunes acoustically on mandolin and twelve-string guitar with the lads from Furious Fish's other band, Fishmonkeyman.

We hadn't finished with Granada yet either. The following Monday, we were down at the Albert Dock to perform 'First I Feel You' once again, this time for the *Celebration* programme. It was a good experience again, and to our total delight we spent two hours chatting with the legendary Michael Bentine (from the Goons, *Potty Time*, etc.) in the studio's green room. The conversation was fascinating, taking in everything from religious fundamentalists and nationalism through to flying saucers and crop circles. I've always thought you don't have to be religious to live a spiritual life.

✶✶✶✶✶✶

Martin Poole had some news for us. French Radio station France INPER had been playing the *What Say You?* EP on *La Session Noire* and they had contacted him because of the numerous requests they were receiving for copies of the EP from La FNAC, the equivalent of HMV in France.

As a result, Martin had been in touch with Virgin Publishing and they offered a deal with Circa in France. But guess what? Our man inside Virgin had got the boot the very morning we were supposed to sign, when Virgin were taken over by EMI. All you can surmise is that that wasn't meant to be. If it had been the day before, however, the whole history of The Onset might have been very different.

******

The cheque for £400 from Granada TV, which we needed to help fund the German tour, hadn't arrived. Consequently, I made a frantic call to Granada to find out what had happened when there was ring at the doorbell. I asked Granada to hold and went to answer it. When I opened the door, there was a policeman standing there. He told me they'd found a cheque addressed to me in a flat in Toxteth – on a bed in some guy's flat I'd never even heard of. I didn't ask what that had been in connection with, and with a mixture of shock and relief I went back up to the flat, picked the phone up and told Granada about it. They cancelled the original cheque and sent us a new one. It turned out the guy who'd stolen the cheque was a corrupt postman.

Simon told us that he was going to leave the band after the German tour. Oh dear, this was going to seriously change things as he was a great bass player and also a fine singer and both his playing and harmonies were an important element of The Onset. You gotta do what you gotta do, I suppose.

We played a couple of warm-up gigs for the German tour, supporting Half Man Half Biscuit at the Citadel in St Helens and also in Wolverhampton. As D.O.A.'s beautiful Mercedes van was beyond our use, we'd borrowed Nick Walker's classic VW campervan to do the tour. It was bigger than Tony's Transit and that was good enough. Katrine, our medical student friend we'd met in Edinburgh, had moved to Liverpool permanently and became Tony's partner. She came with us on the German tour.

******

The World May Change but
It Will Always Be Filled with Goths, Vandals
and Philistines

As we'd done the previous time, we kicked our third German tour off with a return visit to that palace of hedonistic delight known as the Goldene Krone in Darmstadt. We'd brought our cover of Willie Dixon's 'Spoonful' into the set after loving The Shadows of Knights' version and, while we knew we had to face up to Simon leaving the band at the end of the tour, we were determined to have the time of our lives regardless.

As expected, Danny got horrendously drunk that first night. Up in the rafters of the beautiful, ancient building, the five of us were in the three large bunks waiting for him to return from the bar. You could hear him coming well before he appeared as we heard a regular 'boom ... boom ... boom' from his giant footsteps as he made his way down the corridor towards the room. Katrine and Tony had one of the bunks, but Katrine (whose English wasn't quite up to scratch) made a bit of a verbal faux pas. She'd meant to say, 'Danny, go to bed' – or basically, 'Shut up and go to bed' – but she actually said, 'Danny, come to bed, come to bed'. 'Mmm', Danny exclaimed sarcastically. We all howled laughing.

We all thought he'd drifted off in his bunk, when he muttered, 'Danny no mates!' before finally going off to sleep.

Then, like the hero he was, the next morning Danny threw up out of the skylight and then took a huge swig from the half bottle of wine he'd opened the night before as though nothing had happened.

We played a place called the Picaboo Club in Russelsheim the following night. It didn't exactly provide an audience tailor-made for The Onset. We'd noticed a crowd of goth-y punks outside when we arrived, but took no notice. After all, there always seemed to be goths when we were in Germany, so we got on with the job of sound checking and went to hang out in the dressing room. Sometime later, a concerned Paul came in to tell us there was a big crowd sitting around in the dark out there ... with fangs!

Danny went out there and, when he returned, confirmed that yes there were indeed a huge crowd of goths in the club – and heavy-duty goths at that. Before long, heavy, industrial sounds came booming from the PA like sledge hammers hitting iron girders. I nervously took a look out into the club. There were frilly sleeves and collars and blackness galore. Needless to say, our brand of upbeat, Hank Williams, roots-influenced rock didn't exactly go down too well with them and it must have come as quite a shock to the system for this pale-faced crowd.

After our set, the music got even heavier. The darkness out there was truly scary and by the look of this ominous gathering, it seemed the natives might not be happy. However, my visions of them sacrificing us began to fade when a guy in leathers and a top hat put his arm in the air and started to … what, move to the music? Then, someone joined him in a similar action. The dark crowd made a semi-circle in front of the stage and watched on like some sinister ritualistic event was about to occur.

Then I noticed the stage curtains twitching a little and, scarcely able to believe what I was seeing, a rolled-up trouser leg appeared from a gap in the curtains and started to swing about from side to side. I laughed my head off! I mean, who would have thought of Eric Morecambe at a time like this? Danny Dean, of course. No band should be without one!

After our pleasant surprise at getting out alive, we spent the next day on an eight-hour drive to Dresden where we had a gap between scheduled gigs. We stayed at Katrine's mate Kate's flat in the only old part of Dresden that survived the Allied bombing campaign during WW2. Green gaslights shone on cobbled streets, trams on cables rumbled past and there was an amazing old cigarette factory with a glass, Islamic-style dome that shone across the city like the tip of a burning cigarette in the dark of night.

Despite the length of the journey, we played a semi-acoustic set at an all-night café that first night in the city. It was so real and life-affirming after the madness of the Russelsheim date and everyone loved the music. Well, apart from one guy who was dressed like he was in The Village People and stood alone at the front of the stage. Oh well: as we'd long since discovered, you can't please all the people all the time in this game.

Dresden was an incredible city. Over 25,000 people had lost their lives during WW2 when the Allied Forces dropped nearly 4,000 tonnes of bombs on the city that held so many refugees. We wandered around the ruins that had been left as a memorial to them. Awful! These days, Dresden was packed with a new breed of refugees now that the Cold War was drawing to a close and it made for an interesting cultural melting pot. S.H.A.R.P. (Skinheads Against Racial Prejudice) stencils with the Trojan helmet to symbolize the Jamaican ska movement adorned walls, while hundreds of Trabants puttered around, emitting their two-stroke fumes, reminding us of our time in East Berlin the previous year.

Miles of Russian trucks with red stars on their doors pulled up at traffic lights when we crossed the road on their retreat to the East. Occasionally the odd Mercedes full of property developers and assorted business people from the West could be seen gliding by looking to invest in property left in the vacuum. Dresden had a soul of its own and a history of art and culture that no bombs could ever successfully destroy.

We went to the local fairground and nearly died on the roller coaster's gravity-defying loops. We also enjoyed riding the bumper cars and firing rifles at moving targets on the bank of the River Elbe. Back at Kate's flat, we drank Hel beer and the close proximity of the Czechoslovakia border meant a day trip to Prague was possible. The landscape was fascinating and we drove miles along cobbled roads lined with tall pines, although when we crossed the border we noticed acid rain had destroyed a lot of the trees.

Prague itself was beautiful and steeped in history. I bought some typical items: pre-Revolution packaged sweets and a bottle of fierce-looking red liquor with a horned man on the label. On the way back, big bright neon signs lit up the countryside and we stopped to spend what Czechoslovak currency remained in a restaurant. All six of us had a delicious three-course meal with wine because money was no problem. It had echoes of the situation we'd experienced in East Berlin and while we thoroughly enjoyed the food and drink, it was strange to suddenly feel so affluent in such a poor country.

As we approached the East Germany border, what seemed like dozens of young girls lined the trees and streets looking for trade with the drivers of the cars and trucks. At one point, a Mercedes with West German number plates darted in front of our VW van and halted suddenly, almost causing us to run into the back of him. He'd obviously seen a girl who'd taken his fancy and was one of the many West Germans who came over the border for cheap sex with the poor Eastern European girls whose pimps stood in the shadows. It was really heart-breaking to witness the whole thing. Some of the girls looked so terribly young. Absolutely awful!

We left the honest and sincere people of Dresden and travelled to our next date, which was in Dachau, scene of one of the Nazis' most notorious concentration camps. The day after the gig, we visited the site and it proved to be another unforgettable experience. Despite the clear, blue sky and sunshine, there's no way to deny the horror of seeing the gas chambers and incinerators – and no birds sang while we were there. It's impossible not to feel the weight of history in a place like Dachau. The events in such places have left an indelible stain on that ground and humanity forever.

At the gig, which was in an old railway station, the stage actually backed onto the platform where many Jews would have been transported to the concentration camp. It was truly shocking and unimaginable to believe what had happened on that very spot just fifty years before.

We played at Wunsdorf near Hannover. Our engagement was at a small club called Wohnwelt and we totally ripped the place up. At one point the power went off, except for the mics, so I improvized by singing my a capella number 'Simple Little Barbarian'. It went like this:

As they erase all the cultures,
Bastardize the stars,
Apply logic to life,
And travel in cars,
I'm just a little barbarian,
But I know I'm going to go far.

It was a little ditty Danny later took to calling 'I'm an Indian, so give me a spliff', but it went down well that night.

From there we made for Hamburg. We loaded the gear into the dirty little club where we were due to play and Danny asked the promoter where we were staying.

'I don't know', he said blankly. He wasn't interested either.

That was enough. We decided to leave Hamburg. No accommodation – no gig – read the feckin' contract next time! We had a very different experience in that city compared to The Beatles! We headed to Berlin a night ahead of schedule. We began to question the wisdom of this decision as the heater packed up in the van and it was painfully cold driving down the autobahn through the night. We finally made it to Katrine's brother's place in the former East Berlin at a ghostly 2am and quickly got the schnapps out. It was more than welcome.

The Knaack Club gig had nearly brought me to tears on our first visit as it had been so wonderful. This time round it prompted a similar response but for entirely different reasons. Since our first gig, a shit-load of money had been thrown at the place, but with disappointing results. The live room had been totally deadened with sound-proofing and it sounded horribly dull. It didn't bode well for the show, but we blagged a second night's accommodation in the East with another of Katrine's friends and were looking forward to another great Berlin experience. Katrine was proving an invaluable lifesaver and we greatly appreciated her help.

The next day we drove into the former West Berlin and got quite a shock. Since the fall of the Wall it had changed enormously and after the incredible place we'd experienced twice it could have been any city now. It was very disappointing and typically Westernized now – more than just the physical presence of the Wall was missing.

We drove back to the East and went to the venue to eat. I lost my rag when they served me 'vegetarian' food full of meat. I thumped and kicked the bar. It felt like the last straw at the time because I was tired and hungry after two nights of being messed around with people not reading contracts properly regarding our accommodation and catering. We'd very clearly stated that there were two vegetarians in the band. I was getting literally sick to the stomach with the 'wing and a prayer' promoters we were dealing with. Thankfully, the guy behind the bar was very good about it, in fact he was probably very scared of what I was going to do next. He cooked me some cheese on toast, tomatoes and eggs instead. It restored my blood sugar and I wasn't an animal anymore.

The accommodation provided for the band was only a tiny room and it was actually over the door of the club. You could actually see people coming and going through the boards beneath. It was somewhere to lie flat and that was all. What's more, every time someone entered through the door of the club, it swung back and slammed in the frame, rattling our room above. It really wasn't somewhere you could hope to relax properly so we stayed up and drank as we obviously weren't going to get any sleep until after the club closed. Fortunately, the music was great: lots of Sex Pistols, Ramones and Doors. We found a box of records upstairs – albums by a communist-era East German rock 'n' roll band called Puhdys. There was a picture of the band on the sleeve and they all had moustaches and seriously dodgy haircuts. Brilliant!

We thought we'd finally got some rest sorted later when – at around 4:30am – some guy, speeding off his head, broke into the club and started calling a girl's name and disturbing the hell out of us. We told him to fuck off or we'd get the Polizei so he left – headfirst through the window he'd appeared from. I now needed a piss, so I shuffled off to the dirty club toilets in a daze wearing a pair of underpants, a dirty T-shirt and my low-heeled brown-suede Spanish cowboy boots. How glamorous the rock 'n' roll life can be.

The cleaner woke us up at 8:30am and Sabine the promoter turned up to ask us, brightly, if we'd all had a good night's sleep. We were all fazed as hell, but Sabine was so pretty we just smiled politely and said:

'Yes, thanks – it was great!'

******

We blew out the next gig because it meant undertaking another 800-kilometre-round drive and we just collectively thought 'nah' – not least because we had the use of Katrine's auntie's luxurious apartment that overlooked Marburg, where we were due to play the following night. Katrine had enjoyed her time in Liverpool, but she had to stay in Germany after the tour and go back to medical school and we would really miss her. What a sweetheart. Tony was a lucky man and he knew it ... We owed her a hell of a lot as she had saved our arses on numerous occasions during this tour.

The gig in Marburg was in a huge hall that formed part of the university. Clearly, the promoter there was used to bands with bigger budgets than The Onset's, because when we pulled up in Nick's blue and white VW camper van he asked us when the gear would be arriving. Ha! We were sitting on it.

It proved to be another eventful evening. We were given what worked out at about £35 to go and get some food and we found a Greek restaurant. I ate *garten teller,* which included feta cheese and a green bean salad, and I was very grateful. It was probably more nourishing than the rest of the food I'd had on that tour put together and the rest of the band ate well too. We arrived back at the hall ready to ROCK in no uncertain terms.

For a change we got to enjoy a good support act, as it was Edward II and The Red Hot Polkas, who played a cool blend of reggae and folk. After that, we returned to our dressing room for the usual pre-gig warm-up of relaxation and a few beers. The only trouble was that the stuff that had been provided on our rider was way stronger than the usual beer we drank and I ended up mutating into Iggy Pop during 'Spoonful'.

Still, despite my 'Wild Man of Rock' antics, we'd played to 400 students who even knew the songs, so it had been quite a triumph. Afterwards, the promoter – who was even more pissed than anyone in the band – gave me our food money a second time and I kept it for the band. I wouldn't normally have done this, but a lot of stuff had gone wrong of late and it didn't seem unfair at the time. There again, I had also previously slipped the Puhdys rock 'n' roll album into my bag even though I would probably never play it! My moral compass was starting to spin after all the twists and turns of this tour.

With hindsight, three weeks of sleeping in different beds every night was starting to corrode my moral fibre. We stayed in a place above a political bookshop that night and while it was small compared to Katrine's auntie's place, it was OK. It was situated next to the river and had the advantage of being above a café, where I ate two breakfasts the next morning. The band were taking the piss out of me because I had gotten so fearfully drunk the night before.

Carl Davies, Anglesey, 1981
(photo by Gill Piggot)

Kevin Wright,
Anglesey

Ian Davies, Radio
Merseyside, 1980

A Secret Liverpool LP,
recycled cardboard
covers, 1984

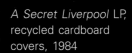

David Evans (with Tractors), St Helens, 1986

Mike Badger, St Helens Art College, 1980

Lee Mavers, Falkner Street, 1985 (photo by Jeanette Badger)

Mike and Jeanette, Paris, 1985

The La's: Lee Mavers, Mike Badger, Bernie Nolan (bass) and Tony Clarke (hidden, on drums), the Lamb in St Helens, February 1986

The La's: Mike Badger, Barry Walsh, John Power and Lee Mavers, Aigburth, September 1986 (photo by Nicholas Jones)

Mike Badger and John 'Timmo' Timson (drums), the Monro, 1986 (photo by Glynys Jackson)

John Power and Mike Badger, Bold Street, Liverpool, July 1986

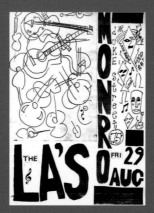

La's posters designed by Mike Badger, 1986

Receipt for recording session at Attic Studio, September 1986

MP demands inquiry into pop 'school'

Probe Plus

Recording Company
12 Buckingham Avenue

aber sonst immer ganz locker

Konzert von „The Onset" aus Liverpool im „Vakanz" – ungreifbar viele musikalische Einflüsse verarbeitet

Space's ship in your neighbourhood

SEEN here outside Gosport Museum is Mike Badger, with his spaceship entirely made from... The spaceship was... ly pop group Space with Female of the bourhood and Dark launch of their albu... Along with a big f... of the Lost and Foun play by the Liverpoo port's Connections b... This weekend new Show at the RN Sub...

Wirklich Ungewöhnliches barg das Konzert von „The Onset" am Donnerstag in der Geborgenheit des Vakanz, des verpönten Independet-Treffs im Bregenzerwald.

Show by ex-rocker

THE artist who designed the album cover for top band Space, who is a former rocker himself, is to

What new commercial canker lies beneath those hallowed streets where name like John, Paul, Echo and Frankie once walked (and now drive round in limousines)? . . . Find out with this week's fab album.

'THE SECRET LIVERPOOL'

A collection of 15 tracks from bands so secret that their names are not listed on the album. With a little bit of investigative nouse Backhanders has discovered 25 copies that have not been snapped up by greedy record executives or mega chainstores and we are giving them away to you.

Angelic subject for show

YOU'VE heard the song, watched the video, now see the original Avenging Angel sung about by Liverpool band Space.

The angel, cunningly disguised as a cheese grater, features in the latest exhibition at Harrogate's Tubal Cain Contemporary Arts Foundation of works by Liverpool sculptor Mike Badger.

All aboard for a ferry Art attack

ourneys have become an different artist every month as they constructed entirely from re...

Expedition to Mucky Mountains Halted by Fence

Mikes referring to the new E.P. :What Say You", just released on Furious Fish Records. The Title track is literate rockabilly and synchronistic lyrical pointers to Mandela and Hendrix, and "First I Feel You" a glorious slice if chiming, jangling pop, that storms the brain and lays siege to the memory cells. Dave Dix's production retains the energy and vitality of The Onset, whilst bringing out the subtleties of the instrumentation, dnd the band become more aware of what they can achieve. Mike is a passionate believer in the emotional power of music, honesty being the key word, forsake that, and as he would say, you're just wheat before the sickle.

John D. Hodgkinson

THE INDEPE...
● THE ONSET
The Pool Of Life
Probe Plus Probe 19
TUMBLEDOWN garage eclecticism from this Liverpudlian band, released under the imprint of their home city's premier left field record shop,

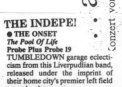

MUCKY MOUNTAINS
WELCOME TO MUCKY MOUNTAINS

Silent Secrets (from Viper LP 'Volume')

The La's founder and sculptor to Space releases a low-key acoustic LP. Sounding like the theme to '70s kids show *Magpie* and the La's rocking out in a taverna, Lee Mavers clearly wasn't the sole custodian of songwriting gold.

Elegance: straighten your face for the Las who sing "My girl sits like a reindeer" without smiling. Their deadpan blues/rock'n'roll songs are slightly surreal and exquisitely

Thank heaven, then, for The Onset, who boast two former members of the notorious La's: guitarist Paul Hemmings, who also doubles on mandolin, and singer Mike, the owner of the biggest Gretsch since Brian Setzer. sidled up to succinct rockers 'Let's Go Home' and 'Rockin' Out The Depression', and they all possessed a knowing, human touch. Marvellous.

TIM PEACOCK SOUNDS

Danny Dean (no band should leave the garage without one) on Paul's BSA, 1990

Geoff Davies, founder of Liverpool's Probe record shop and the Probe Plus label

The Onset, Otterspool, 1989 (photo by Brian Morow)

The Onset at the Berlin Wall: Simon Cousins, Paul Hemmings, Tony Russell, Mike Badger and Danny Dean, 1990 (photo by Andrew Harding)

Jeanette, Aigburth, 1990

The Lightning Seeds: Martyn Campbell, Chris Sharrock, Mike Badger and Ian Broudie (Bunnymen's rehearsal room, 1995)

Jonathan Richman 'making way' out of the Glastonbury Festival, 1992

Mike washing dishes in the School of Tropical Medicine, Liverpool, 1991 (photo by Benoit)

Giant Tin Fish (commissioned by Manchester City Council), Albert Dock, Liverpool, 2000

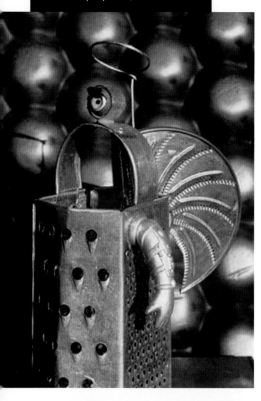

Avenging Angel (commissioned by Space), 1998

Paul Hemmings, Strawberry Fields, 1998

Tommy Scott backstage, Blackburn, 1998

Tin Planet Robot, animated TV advert for Space's *Tin Planet* album, 1998

Lost and Found
exhibition flyer,
Warrington
Museum, 1997

WARRINGTON MUSEUM PRESENTS

LOST AND FOUND

STARRING MIKE BADGER'S
TIN SCULPTURES · COLLAGE · FOUND OBJECTS

WARRINGTON MUSEUM & ART GALLERY
BOLD STREET · WARRINGTON
TELEPHONE : 01925 442392

28TH JUNE – 30TH AUGUST 1997
OPEN MON-FR1 10.00-5.30 SAT 10.00-5.00
CLOSED SUNDAYS & BANK HOLIDAYS

Lee Mavers, Silbury
Hill, 1999

Mike Badger and Adrian
Henri, Gostin's Gallery, 2000

Recording with
Yungchen Lhamo,
Queens, New York,
2003 (photo by
Ernie Paniccioli)

Robby Stevenson and
Danny Roberts (The
Hokum Clones), the
Viper Studio, Penny
Lane, 2003

Afrika Bambaataa,
Mike Badger and Ernie
Paniccioli (photo by
Mark McNulty)

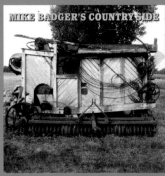

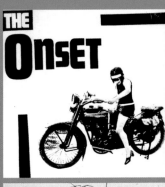

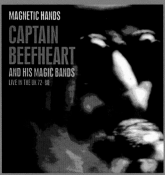

Mike Badger's Country Side (Gen 12)
Badger Tracks compilation (Gen 14)
The Onset – The Onset (Gen 10)
Captain Beefheart – Magic Hands Live In The UK
    1972–80 (VIP 11)
The La's – Breakloose: The La's 1984–1986 (VIP 52)
The La's – Callin' All: The La's
    1986–1987 (VIP 62)

Edgar Jones – More Than You've Ever Had (VIP 37)
Various Artists – The Great Liverpool Acoustic
    Experiment (VIP 10)
Various Artists – The Song Before The Song (VIP 39)
Various Artists – Unearthed (Liverpool Cult Classics
    Vol.3) (VIP 23)
Various Artists – Unearthed Merseybeat Vol.1 (VIP 16)
Mike Badger – Rogue State (VIP 83)

From there, we set off for the final gig of the tour in a place called Langenburg in the very south of Germany. Bill from D.O.A. had pointedly referred to it as 'Mental Land', which sounded ominous, but then life on the road was beginning to take its toll on all of us by now. I sat in the front of the van while Simon drove and found a pair of black leather gloves sitting there on the dashboard. I put them on my feet and pretended to be a chimpanzee. It seemed perfectly normal to me at the time, although Paul did deliver a gentle warning.

'Jeanette's gonna say "get that mad man out of my house" when you get back, y'know.'

It was true that this tour was by some way the weirdest yet – however, we hadn't finished yet. A black cat ran across the road in front of us on the way to the autobahn. I noticed Simon change into third gear, yet we were going down a hill. I just couldn't fathom it.

'How come you've gone into third, yet we're going down a hill?' I said, confused.

'We're not going downhill, we're going uphill', Simon replied, trying to cling to normality in the midst of the lunacy.

I looked out the back window of the van and we were going uphill, then when I looked out of the front window … yeah, we were definitely going downhill. The rest of the band had heard me question Simon and I sparked off an argument in the van. Some were convinced we were going uphill and more disagreed. We couldn't reach a consensus.

But the weirdness had only just begun. As we came off the autobahn we travelled for miles over sweeping fields before dusk began to fall. The only sight breaking up the monotony was the occasional dark crucifix against the sky. As we approached Langenburg there was an orange hue above the valley where the place was nestled. We pulled into the little village that might have served well as a scene from a Hammer movie. The atmosphere was fraught in the van – this was a very strange-looking place. It wasn't like anywhere we'd previously visited in Germany. 'Mental Land' for sure, Bill.

We parked in an empty street and went to look at the instructions we had written down on our itinerary. Suddenly, there was a piercing yell from the back of the van. Disoriented, I looked out of my window and nearly jumped out of my skin. A woman's face with red spiky hair had appeared looking in (which was why Danny of all people had screamed in first place – he's only six-foot-three-inches tall!), but it was a real start. Now we could all see her peering into the van. Trembling, I wound down the window ... to find out it was the promoter introducing herself.

We were stunned. She calmly requested we follow her, but we couldn't understand it. There hadn't been a soul around. Where the hell did she come from? Where did her car come from? There was nothing in front of the van when we had arrived, was there? Fucking hell, we were spooked. Definitely no one had seen her car there when we'd pulled in. Oh well – let's just follow it as requested.

We travelled down the road into a wooded area and pulled into a car park that had a sports hall at one end. This was on the edge of the town and it was to be the setting for the tour's final show. Inside, the stage was raised about a foot from the floor in the middle of the hall and it had a huge, red pentacle drawn in the centre of it. Weirder and weirder.

Seriously spooked out, but attempting to remain calm, we set the gear up and concentrated on the normality of sound checking. Bill had told us this was a strange place and he wasn't wrong. He also told us they all come out of the woods to see the bands here, which must also have been correct because one minute the place was empty and the next it was rammed, just like it had been at the Vakanz show in Austria. We'd previously believed *that* show to be the mother of all gigs, but, if anything, the show in Langenburg surpassed it.

Of course, the fact it was Simon's last show with The Onset ensured it was an emotional affair from the off. We'd been saving a bottle of champagne for the occasion and I opened it on stage. I gave each member of the band a drink while they were still playing and then passed it out to the audience. It was like communion. We played for an hour and forty minutes and the audience loved it.

There was a 'social club' arranged upstairs for after show parties and a wild night was had by all. I'd gone out into the car park to see if there was a joint going and someone eagerly pressed a block into my hand. He was even apologetic that it was all he could get! It was more than sufficient. When I got back to the club, I heard this fantastic sound. I walked upstairs to discover there was a drum kit up there and Tony was behind it. Danny had joined him on electric guitar and they'd already got a group of people completely mesmerized with the spontaneous, free jam they were playing.

In a separate room, a German guy brought three girls to meet me. 'Oh hi!' I said, now starting to feel rather embarrassed by all this attention, I really wasn't used to this. Then I bumped into a blissful-looking Paul. He was waxing lyrical about the 'good wine' and exclaiming we were now folk heroes in this town. He was right! Despite the eerie start to the evening, that's how they were in Langenburg. We were made to feel like gods that night.

We finally got back to our accommodation well into the next morning. It was over an antique shop and the owner very graciously opened another expensive bottle of wine in our honour. It was ironic that I'd kicked off about the lack of organization a few days before, because during the last two gigs we had been privy to both wonderful organization and great courtesy and had been given an insight to the real, hospitable Germany at its very best.

Simon's last hurrah with The Onset had been a blast, though of course we still faced the long drive back to Zeebrugge with very fragile heads. 'Long' became 'overwhelming' when Danny missed the turn at Cologne, which sent us back around the autobahn encircling the city. Oh well, we casually said, never mind, Dan. We'll have to go around again. As the exit approached again half an hour later, I said to him:

'OK, Danny, it's this one … It's this one Danny … It's FUCKING THIS ONE DANNY! NOOOOOOOOO!!'

He'd missed the damn thing a second time, only this time we knew too well how long it was going to take before we had the chance to leave the seemingly inescapable vortex that existed around Cologne.

By the time we pulled into the port of Zeebrugge we'd travelled thousands of miles and we had barely two hours to eat and sleep before we boarded the ferry. A coach then proceeded to pull up next to the van and threw out a crowd of German school kids. They chattered incessantly and way too loudly for what felt like an eternity. Danny responded as only he could: by writing 'FUCK OFF BITTE' in reverse writing in the condensation clouding the van's window.

✶✶✶✶✶✶

After decompression back in Liverpool and after waking up next to Jeanette asking sincerely, 'Who are you?' (I really was still that disorientated and luckily she never took it the wrong way!), my first port of call was Probe Records shop the following day.

It had been a while since I'd taken the ten *What Say You?* EPs into the shop and I wanted to know if they might need any more. I called in and asked the assistant, Mick Aslanian, to see how they were fixed. He checked the stock at the back of the shop, then came back and smiled apologetically:

'It's OK, we've still got eleven.'

TWELVE

Seeds

STILL, WE HADN'T DONE too badly in Germany. We'd each come back with £200 from the tour, which enabled me to trade in my Antaria Jazz Star for a black, Johnny Cash-style Fender La Brea acoustic at Hessy's music store. It was time for a change. I liked the new guitar immediately.

The most pressing issue was Simon's departure, so I asked Bernie Nolan if he'd like to join the band on bass. Bernie was an incredibly versatile musician and I always remembered him telling me about how he'd heard rock 'n' roll music for the first time. He was just a young kid at a fairground and 'Jungle Rock' by Hank Mizell was pumping out from the waltzers. It was an image I'd never been able to forget. Then before we knew it Paul decided to disappear into the woodwork.

Away from the band, I continued to make my tin cars and began branching out into trains, boats, robots and planes. My artistic endeavours had begun to get some recognition, as I did my first exhibition with the 'Merseyside Unknowns' at a venue at the back of the Philharmonic Hall in town and it went down great guns. I made more money in a few days than I had ever done with the band. I suppose lots of people in Liverpool were playing guitars but no one was making robots and Cadillacs out of tin cans!

Nonetheless, business continued as usual with The Onset. We played a few gigs before Christmas with Bernie debuting on bass. One was a Greenpeace benefit I had organized at the Liverpool Poly Student Union titled 'I'm Dreaming of a Green Christmas'. Another one of these shows was with Half Man Half Biscuit at the Leadmill in Sheffield, where I saw Lee's mate Joey Davidson for the first time in ages. He'd had his problems and was on a rehab programme as a result of heroin use. It had been rife in parts of Merseyside during the '80s, filling the gap for the disillusioned who had no prospects in a society that counted them void of purpose – indeed, you could say in certain parts:

Opiates had become the religion of the people.

******

During the summer Jeanette had gone down to Glastonbury with friends, so I was spending my thirtieth birthday alone. Suddenly, a call came in from The Lightning Seeds' management company. They asked me if I would be available to perform on *Top of the Pops* with Ian Broudie and the band as their new single, 'Life of Riley', had charted high enough to get on the programme that week. I was gobsmacked. This had come right out of the blue, not least because I had only ever met Ian once when I went round to his house on Beaconsfield Road with Kevin, Julie and Jeanette, although I knew Kevin had passed on a copy of our EP to him.

Anyway, I shook myself out of my stupor and agreed to do the TV slot. I had it all planned. I'd go to London, see Ros and Ben, get some money and no doubt some 'personal glory'. But it never happened in the end because 'Life of Riley' didn't chart high enough to quite make the top 20. However, it turned out that it wouldn't be the last time I'd hear from Ian Broudie.

Around this same time, Paul Simpson had the idea of animating my tin sculptures on Super-8 film and he built a fantastic space scene in his cellar, with planets made from Christmas balls hanging against a black sheet and a ball in the foreground with a joss stick burning behind it. It looked amazing and I even came up with the name *Tin Planet* for the concept.

Then, after I'd forgotten about The Lightning Seeds again, Ian Broudie rang me himself. This time he asked if I would appear in the video for the new Lightning Seeds' single called 'Sense'. I would be playing guitar and he'd call round to the flat to play me the song the following day.

That next day proved to be a phenomenal one. Jeanette went to have a pregnancy test at the chemist on Lark Lane. I waited outside and she came out smiling – well, it's positive, we're going to have a baby! The emotions welled up inside me and I smiled the Smile of Life. This had come totally out of the blue. Jeanette's first fear was losing the baby, while my first was the thought of the new responsibilities this brought. The hopes and dreams for the future. The state of the world. Being a parent. But mostly we just felt so incredibly honoured to be in such a position.

The news was so seismic that I'd almost forgotten about Ian Broudie, but he was as good as his word and came round to show me the chords to the new single as planned. I gave the impression I was there, but really I was on the ceiling. Ian's request was timely, though, because I'd have some much-needed money coming in thanks to this video.

The video shoot was a total trip. Jonee Mellor drove us down to London in a people carrier along with bassist Lloyd and Kevin, whom Ian had gotten to play keyboards. It was great to see Jonee again after all these years and we got to stay at the notorious Columbia Hotel at Hyde Park Corner. In true 'Colombia' tradition, we scored some oil, got very high and I talked excitedly with Kev about impending fatherhood.

We shot the video the following day in a studio in Acton. The set comprised a giant radio which we were filmed playing inside. We got the full industry works, getting pampered by make-up artists. Former Specials and Fun Boy Three frontman Terry Hall, who'd co-written the song with Ian, was there too. I went up to him in excitement and said that The Specials' 'Gangsters' had changed my life. With hindsight, it was the corniest thing I could possibly have said to him, but he was very decent about it.

'It changed my life too', he replied.

Afterwards, the rest of the lads left for Liverpool, but I stayed on in London, and as if by perfect timing I went to Dan Greaves' party at Tandem. The animated film he'd shown us at New Year called *Manipulation* had only gone on to win an Oscar! It was great to see his lovely wife Em too and the Oscar stood on the shelf looking resplendent and weighed a ton.

✶✶✶✶✶✶

I thought that would be the only taste of London I'd get, but not so. I was soon back in the capital, and flying down no less. This time I was doing a kids TV show with The Lightning Seeds at the famous Pinewood Studios, though funnily enough I remember very little about being there. I remember listening to The Cure's 'Friday I'm in Love' on the way down there a lot more than the shoot itself, though I do recall being flown back to Liverpool and, in great contrast, spending much of the same afternoon sitting in Kieran and Dave's full-size tepee which had been erected in our allotment so Dave could waterproof it.

Then Paul reappeared and generously set up a recording session at Spirit Studio in Manchester (where we recorded 'Underworld' and 'Around the World in a Haizy Daze'). Then it was off to do a TV appearance and a trip to Ebbw Vale in Wales to do a further TV show with The Lightning Seeds. It was another memorable experience, travelling over the moon-style landscape and listening to The Modern Lovers' songs 'Astral Plane' and 'Pablo Picasso'.

The exciting times we'd been experiencing continued on our return to Liverpool. David Evans got in touch and asked me if The Onset would like to support Jonathan Richman when he played the Citadel in St Helens. Was the Pope Polish? Yes, of course we'd be over the moon to support Jonathan.

While we were waiting for the St Helens show to come around we played another show with Half Man Half Biscuit, this time at the Derby Wherehouse, where the show was videoed by a TV company. The Biscuits' set would later be released as a live concert on VHS by Probe Plus. Our set was really good that night, especially 'Down at the Space Rocketry' and 'Spoonful', the old Willie Dixon blues number we'd been featuring for the past twelve months or so.

We were already vibed up about the St Helens gig with Jonathan Richman when things got even better. David Evans called again, this time to ask if we'd like to take Jonathan to Glastonbury, as his next show after St Helens was the festival. And from Glastonbury could we then take him on to London? It was magnificent and he'd even pay all our expenses too! I figured that if we were taking him to Glastonbury the following day, he may as well stay at our flat in Aigburth the night after the show at the St Helens Citadel as we would have to be getting off early the following morning.

The St Helens gig took place on 27 June 1992. We did a good sound check and Bernie was now playing double bass on some of the songs, like 'Precious Love', which gave the band a new dimension.

Jonathan turned up a little later and I explained my plan about him staying at our flat because of the early date in the morning. He was very enthusiastic about the idea and proved to be great fun to be around.

Jonathan toured with simply a haversack and his guitar. His philosophy was the less you ask of a venue, the less that can go wrong. All he asked for was the use of a Fender Twin Reverb amp and his fee. It was very refreshing, not to mention self-contained. Jonathan was anything but a pampered rock 'n' roller. We piled into the car and drove to Aigburth after the gig. He scoffed nuts from a little packet, and when I asked what they were he said, 'Oh, it's health food. Lou Reed got me into it.' I replied, 'I thought that Lou Reed was into his drugs?' 'Yeah', replied Jonathan, 'good clean food and good clean drugs.' I laughed.

When we got back to our flat in Aigburth he insisted on helping us load the gear into the practice room before I could even show him his bedroom. Then, to my delight, he came rushing out asking who had made the tin can sculptures. I told him I had and felt full to the brim with joy that he was so excited about them.

It was incredible to think that Jonathan was asleep in the next room! His song 'Morning of Our Lives' had been the soundtrack to my teenage years, hanging with Carl and Ian and Kevin and David when we were growing up. His uniquely uninhibited songs had been a huge influence on me. What a dude. I noticed that he slept on the floor next to the bed we had made up for him with the door wide open.

The next morning Jonathan was already up; in fact, he was smiling at me from the bedroom door, glad to see I was awake. Jeanette thought he was a little crazy doing his yoga in our tiny kitchen on that bright summer morning, but he was great. His agent had told me no one had ever seen Jonathan eat anything, but he had a croissant with us for his breakfast and asked if he could feel Jeanette's bump that held our new addition.

We didn't have much time, so we set off in Danny's car right after breakfast. Tony came along for the ride as well, so Jonathan and I sat in the back. He had absolutely no inhibitions at all and by the time we'd gotten onto the motorway he had his head on my shoulder and was having a nap. At this point, I was saying repeatedly to myself, 'That's *Jonathan Richman's head* on my shoulder having a nap!' Damn, I would have felt weird doing that with one of the lads in the van who I'd known for years … but not Jonathan.

We stopped at a service station and told jokes and then back in the car chatted about music for ages. I asked Jonathan what music he enjoyed and it was, 'Oh, well it's just like straight rock 'n' roll, shaboom shaboom'. He also said he liked Van Morrison and Rod Stewart's 'Maggie May' along with Paul McCartney's 'The Long and Winding Road'.

Jonathan went on to reveal that he felt the best audience he could have would be one that cried, so I told him I had felt that way when I heard him play his song 'Affection'. He listened intently as I told him about Glastonbury and its relation to William Blake's 'Jerusalem', the mythology surrounding the place and about it being the hub of the 'old ways' of life. He was fascinated.

As we approached the festival site we were overtaken by an open-topped sports car full of people with dreadlocks. With just two words, Danny made us crack up with his observation: 'Designer crusties!'

We spent the best part of the afternoon at the festival. It was baking hot and an experience in itself. We went to see Jonathan play in the acoustic tent and the place was packed. It was hilarious to watch the ravers off their heads on God knows what trying to move and swing to Jonathan playing his song 'UFO Man'. After he'd finished that, he went straight into 'Affection' and I knew he was playing it because I had told him how much it meant to me in the car. I felt really touched that he played it and it just made my day.[13]

Just trying to leave the festival looked like it would be a Herculean task because the track leading to the exit was swamped with people. We made very slow progress until Jonathan had an idea. He got out of the car and started to jog in front of it, shouting, 'Make way! Make way!' while waving his arms around and looking back at us in the car, laughing. It worked a dream too. It seemed unreal, but it did the trick and people kept stepping out of the way of the car. We travelled at least half a mile this way and when he finally got back in the car at the exit, he was laughing his head off and you could tell he'd loved every moment of the experience.

We stopped off at Stonehenge on the way to London, but missed the chance to look around the stones by minutes as it was being cordoned off for the night. We settled for looking at the stones from the road instead. Then we got back on the road for London. Jonathan gave us our petrol money and expenses at the gig that night and even rang for an Indian takeaway for us. Carl Davies was promoting the gig that night (David had kept that quiet!) and he was very pleased when we showed up, as we had been delayed. I was delighted to see him too, despite everything. He was sober but it was obvious that his drinking had taken its toll on him. He looked rather battered by it all.

Frank Sidebottom was supporting. Jonathan was so excited about the prospect of seeing him and Frank was absolutely brilliant. We had to go shortly after that, but I spoke to Jonathan again just before he went on stage, telling him there would always be a triangle between

13 I saw this review somehow years later: 'Who can forget Glastonbury 1992, Jonathan sings "People all over the world are starving for affection" and within two minutes, the entire audience are swapping addresses and resolving to phone their mothers' (Peter Paphides, *Time Out*).

the Eiffel Tower, Liverpool and him, in reference to Jonathan previously telling us about mythological triangles. We bid him a fond farewell, watched his first few numbers and went to leave.

The exit was via the dressing room and we found Frank Sidebottom sitting all alone in there. He was still wearing his huge papier-mâché head, which amazed us as we thought the first thing he'd want to do would be to take it off in all that heat. It must have been at least twenty minutes since he'd come off stage. What's more, he was holding his giant head in his hands in a gesture of sorrow. It was like the lines between fiction and reality had become entwined in a very unnerving way, I thought I'd better see if he was ok.

'Are you alright Frank?' I asked quietly.

'No', replied a melancholy Frank.

'Why? What's the matter?'

'Oh, it's Little Frank [*Frank's smaller puppet pal – Ed.*], he's let me down again'.

'Nah, no way', I replied. 'I thought he was really good.' I thought this would cheer him up, but it had the opposite effect.

'That's what I mean', Frank moaned. 'He stole the show!'

This was getting too surreal for Danny, Tony and me. We left quickly, feeling like we'd just been in a scene from the old classic horror film *Dead of Night*.

******

I began to feel my artwork would take me somewhere. I worked more and more on my tin sculptures, creating some medicine shields from tin lids. I also began to take French GCSE at Riversdale Tech and my dreams became fuller and more detailed. I filled pages of notebooks with them.

The Onset remained a going concern of sorts, but extracurricular projects held sway at this time. Paul was helping former *Sounds* journalist/ writer and Membranes frontman John Robb with his ambient/dance music project Sensurround. He put some bass and lap steel on a track called 'Deep Inside Your Love', while I contributed some backing vocals. Elsewhere, Ros' fella Ben became a villain on the TV series *Eldorado*. Ben had been cast as the murderer and I got to keep the boots he had been wearing. I loved those boots: they were really hard-wearing. For several years I walked around in a pair of murderer's boots.

The end of 1992 was celebrated with the birth of our first child. The day was 22 December. Jeanette's plans of a home birth went out the window and she had to have a caesarean while under a general anaesthetic after a long and exhausting labour. This had meant that when the baby was delivered, she was handed to me first. I stood in the corridor of Oxford Street Maternity Hospital (with Sandy, who had been Jeanette's birthing partner). In an unexplainable event, as our baby was placed into my arms, all the fire alarms went off in the hospital. Crazy, overwhelming and beautiful.

'Welcome to the world, Amber', I said.

THIRTEEN

The Pool of Life Revisited

M Y NEXT LIVE APPEARANCE wasn't an Onset gig, but was with Paul and John Robb.

We went over to Manchester during the afternoon and had a jam at John's and some food. We went directly to the venue, an upstairs pub, and sound checked. There was a good vibe in the place. The overall idea was that we wanted to do something like Tom Waits. It ended up being a very punky Tom Waits, but pretty great for all that.

Pete Wylie was on the same bill, and he was as passionate as ever, although he was dead nervous before he went on. It was his first-ever solo gig. I recall him playing a song called 'Forever Disneyland' about the Guildford Four.

Before John, Paul and I went on, this bloke called Mike (from a local band called The Man from Del Monte) came on to do a set. He had a lady singer called Sheila Seal performing with him. I was really taken with her. She was a Scot with a discernible Celtic lilt in her voice which really impressed me, and later on I called her up. She would later appear on two Onset sessions: the first was for *The Pool of Life*

Revisited and the second was for the unreleased *Stone* album, which we would record at Ian Broudie's during 1994–95.

John, Paul and I were very well received. We used a minimal amount of equipment – marimba, Casio, two guitars and voices and it was fun. Mark Radcliffe and Marc Riley were compèring the evening and they had enjoyed our set. Mark Radcliffe remembered having featured The Onset on his *Hit the North* programme and said that he had enjoyed our album.

✳✳✳✳✳✳

Our good friend Henry Epstein had introduced me to an old family friend, John Rubin, who had recently had a freak hit with a singer called Rozalla. He managed artists and Henry had introduced him to me thinking he might be able to help. Thanks to this, John Rubin committed to helping out financially with a new album that would appear on Probe Plus, an expanded CD reissue of our debut album with additional new tracks to be called *The Pool of Life Revisited*.

Geoff Davies had come to some of the practices to hear the new songs. He brought a Kinder Egg with him and said, 'This is your advance'. But he insisted on keeping the toy in the middle for his young son, Zach! He'd always offered lots of support over the years and again we were indebted to Geoff. I loved the time when I first got to know him, buying records in Probe. He used to discuss the album tracks with you as he was so passionate about music. He might have even gotten involved with The La's early on too, I think, but he could remember chasing Lee out of the shop when he was seen robbing records.

When the album eventually surfaced, maybe I was naive, but I was disappointed when both John Peel and Andy Kershaw failed to pick up on it for their Radio 1 shows. No doubt they got a lot of material to wade through, but in my view there was just too many of what seemed like miles and miles of widdly-widdly African guitar solos echoing out from their shows. But then again they owed me nothing.

While the album missed out on airplay, it did at least attract a couple of rave reviews. Writing in *Groove* magazine, Billy Doherty said, "Unlike most country/rockabilly you think you've heard a million times before, The Onset's humour and deep, heartfelt compassion creates an original vibe, anointing whosoever feels utterly languid with a new knowledge'. Journalist Jonathan Street was even more hip to it with his review for *Shout* magazine, writing, 'The album oozes with a mixture of styles and textures to appeal to all emotions; guaranteed to make you want to stamp your feet, slap your thighs, smile and sigh all at the same time. For blues and country freaks, it's an absolute must. For any other freaks ... you'll probably enjoy it too!'

Reviews of that nature were often the things that helped to keep me going when I doubted the wisdom of continuing with The Onset. During 1994 I was again writing a lot of new songs for a fresh onslaught on our elusive public and at least our Heineken Live Festival went well. We rose to the occasion and played a well-received show on the same bill as local stars The Christians.

******

During July, a simple trip to take Amber to playgroup ended with me checking the answering machine to discover Ian Broudie had left me a message. He wanted to know if I'd like to appear in the video for his new single, 'Lucky You'. I was excited, not least because it was pencilled-in to be shot in London on Thursday and Friday the following week and – at £180 per day – it was great money. I was still having to sign on, and times were hard with a little bundle of joy to provide for.

Ian called round the same evening to show me the song on guitar and fill me in about the video shoot.

I was soon heading to London via coach on Wednesday. I had good company as Andy Eastwood and Martyn Campbell (formerly from Rain, but now The Lightning Seeds' new bassist) were also on board. We chatted for ages, mostly about the changing fortunes of the Liverpool scene.

Martyn and I arrived at a posh hotel and a man in a top hat opened our cab door on arrival: just the kind of treatment The Onset got whenever we stayed down in the Smoke! We took a long walk to Regent Street and then enjoyed a lovely Greek salad and a cappuccino in a Soho restaurant. We met up with Ian Broudie and Chris Sharrock (by this time another ex-La and The Lightning Seeds' current drummer) a little later on and had a few drinks in a couple of Soho hangouts.

The downside was that I woke up with a sizeable hangover the next morning. It probably wasn't the ideal way to feel on the way to a video shoot, but before I could begin to dwell on it I was being whisked away to a studio in Bow in the East End with Ian.

A lot of thought, preparation and money had gone into the shoot. The camera crew filmed us in a re-created practice room that looked very authentic, while at the other end of the studio the place had been decked out to look like a Las Vegas revue. There were dancing girls in feathers everywhere, whom we hung out with, and Manchester comedian John Thomson (as in 'Smokin' Guy' from the *Fast Show*), who played a great role in the video as an ageing rock 'n' roll/country singer based on Dennis Hopper in Blue Velvet.

Ian asked me to play some of The Onset's new stuff on the way home. I stuck the CD in the player and he asked me how we'd managed to get such an authentic old sound on 'Starlight Tuneful 9', especially as it had been recorded at his studio! I replied that it was simply a case of sticking everything through a guitar amp and sending it back into the mixing desk. The whole trip to London had been a real buzz and I'd even been paid decently. So this was what it felt like when a record company was involved.

******

That same July, the *Liverpool Echo* ran a big piece about The Onset just missing out on the Woodstock twenty-fifth anniversary gig organized by Sid Bernstein, which John Rubin had tried to get us onto. The piece in the *Echo* was total class, including stuff like 'they may not be at Woodstock '94, but you can see them in Falkner Square this coming Sunday!' It was very funny.

The Falkner Square Festival had been organized by the wonderful Joe Farrag, but we even had to blow that one out because I had been bitten by a horsefly on the foot and it had swelled up like I had elephantiasis. Discussing the *Echo* article, Danny said we should have been photographed outside the timber shop on Park Road called Woodstock with the caption 'From Stardust to Sawdust!'

Bernie Nolan told us he wanted to leave but Simon Cousins was on hand to join up again and take over his old spot as Onset bassist. When he came back, Simon felt he didn't really know why he'd left The Onset in the first place, but then Bernie never really explained why he wanted to leave either. I just accepted it and felt glad I was still mates with them both.

******

While we were on a break in the Lake District I read an *NME* article about The La's and was pleasantly surprised. Admittedly, it was an article titled 'Where are they now?', but I was happy because I actually got a mention in it.

When we got home I discovered a letter from Fred Dellar from the *NME* apologizing for the briefness of the article. He had very kindly included a copy of the original piece he'd submitted, but to be honest I'd been happy with the way the published article had come across. It was a fine, balanced piece, even when edited.

******

14 February: Valentine's Day. Nettee went to the chemist for a pregnancy test. Amber and I had been to the launderette and Tesco and had arranged to meet her there. As we walked in, The Lightning Seeds' single 'Sense' was being played on the radio and I think then I knew for sure what the result of the test would be. Sure enough, there was a tick on positive and we soared with happiness. Both conceptions were linked with The Lightning Seeds. Seeds: and again a very welcome source of some income!

******

On the way back from London, after the 'Lucky You' video shoot, Ian Broudie and mentioned that he needed a full-time guitarist to join The Lightning Seeds. I don't know if he was seeing if I might have been interested or not, but I immediately thought of Paul Hemmings for him. What's more, at the time Paul was living over the road from Ian and Becky on Beaconsfield Road. Anyhow, they met up and it worked out and next thing Paul was soon about to tour both England and the US with The Lightning Seeds and he showed me an extensive list of the gigs on the itinerary. The US dates were especially impressive, taking in cities from coast to coast and lasting most of October. I would have loved to have been doing those dates, but only with my own band – I am a singer-songwriter after all.

Ian Broudie had also mentioned that while they were on tour we could use his studio in town. Don't mind if we do – thank you.

✻✻✻✻✻✻

During the summer of 1995, The Onset played what would be the band's last regular run of gigs at a venue called Sunnyland Slim's in Liverpool. Because it was a tequila bar with an almost Southern rock mentality and a lot of Cajun music being played, our roots-y rock sound was ideal for them. They offered us a residency of sorts and it seemed like a good idea. We'd often done fruitless tours slogging around the UK to little overall effect, but this way at least we could play and get paid regularly and still go home to our beds every night. Plus, we didn't even need to play covers.

We did some good gigs there, brought in a lot of regulars and enjoyed playing the new songs, but the story of The Onset at Sunnyland Slim's isn't half as interesting as the story of the venue itself. Best known as a soul club named the Sink, the basement venue was first opened in 1963, although the street-level bar on top of it (known as Rumblin' Tums) was established in 1958. Situated on Hardman Street, a stone's throw from Liverpool's famous Philharmonic Hall, the Sink was also a popular venue for up-and-coming bands cutting their teeth on the national circuit. The club's regular DJ was Norman Killon, later a staff member at Probe Records and the equally legendary Eric's DJ. After its time as Sunnyland Slim's the venue closed for a while, until my old mate Jonee Mellor returned to Liverpool, teamed up with Eddie O'Callaghan and refurbished the club, re-opening it as the Magnet in 1998.

It might have been different for The Onset had a label stepped in to help out, but even allowing for John Rubin's sterling efforts and Geoff helping out again, it just never happened. In that sense, The Onset had one of the gentlest deaths in rock 'n' roll. In fact, as I recall, we never really officially split up. We even played a few more gigs around the city before 1995 ended, but there was just this … understanding that it was over.

FOURTEEN

One Man's Fish
Is a French Man's Poisson

'D INTENDED TO MAKE up a booklet to showcase my tin creations for a while and in June 1995 I finally got around to it, heading into Liverpool to purchase some slide films to photograph everything I'd made that was still in the house. It proved to be great fun to photograph and compile and I was very proud of the end result. I didn't know it at the time, but the booklet would end up playing a big part in getting me my first one-man show at Warrington Museum in 1997.

My fledgling sculpting career suddenly got a welcome boost when, from nowhere, the British Craft Room at Liberty of London got in touch asking me to make them a tin clock. Well, maybe it wasn't entirely out of the blue. A while before, a friend of ours, Joanne Irvine, asked me if I'd sent any slides of my tinwork to Liberty. She'd told me that if they accepted you then it could open doors, so I sent Liberty a brochure I'd had made of my sculptures at local design company Nonconform. To my surprise, they not only got back in touch, but asked me to make the clock for a show they were doing based around the concept of 'time'.

It was an interesting project, so I headed into Liverpool in search of the right metal for the job. After a bit of searching, I found a perfect old tin in Quiggins and went home. I completed the clock by adding a found clock face I'd had for a while onto the hinged lid of the tin, then stuck the mechanism through and attached the fingers. It looked like a mantelpiece clock, but I was happy with it, even if it did have a surreal presence of its own. It looked like it was from *Alice in Wonderland* to me.

In Oct 1995 we rented a house in Addingham Road, Allerton. I'd managed to keep on the room below our flat on Aigburth Road, ostensibly as a studio for my art and sculpture, but also for its qualities as a potential rehearsal space. That space in Aigburth had been our home for years and a hotbed of creativity for both The La's and The Onset.

Then just two weeks later, with so much stuff yet to unpack, our lives were blessed once more with the birth of our son Ray on 29 Oct, another caesarean but at least this time Jeanette was conscious, and you'll never guess what song was playing on the little transistor radio in the theatre as he was being delivered: 'Lucky You' by The Lightning Seeds. Lucky us!

******

Danny Dean, Roger Llewellyn and I formed a fledgling band called The Kachinas. I gave a tape of new stuff to ex-Room/Wild Swans drummer Alan Wills, who was getting a new label off the ground. He phoned me up soon after and told me he loved it.

'It's really brightened up the afternoon for me and the missus', Alan enthused. But then he added, 'But how old are you guys?'

I told him I was thirty-five. Sweet thirty-five.

'I'm thirty-six myself', he said, 'but these guys I'm working with, they're only eighteen, they're happening and they're unbelievable!'

He was referring to the band that would later be taken to the nation's heart as The Coral and I understood exactly. It felt sad in a way though – I had never tried to compete with the kids even when I was one. Maybe that was the problem!

I went on to mention Neil Young and Captain Beefheart as influences, and they went on to make some of their best music when they'd reached middle age but ultimately you do what you do, no matter what age you are, that was what I firmly believed and continue to do so. If it's in you, then you have a responsibility to honour it or I believe it can become destructive.

All the same I was glad Alan had responded so positively to The Kachinas' songs. That gave me a lot of heart. I'd respected Alan ever since he'd been so instrumental in me recording my first solo material at The Chemist in Chester all those years ago.

In the autumn of 1996 we were invited by Paul and Jan Simpson to stay in their cottage up in the Highlands of Scotland near to a beautiful little fishing village called Plockton, famous for the opening scenes in the classic movie *The Wicker Man*. We had three days of unbroken sunshine in a land that could have been drawn by the *Rupert Bear* artist, Bestall. Jan was working on the *Hamish Macbeth* TV drama and they had relocated up there for the shoot. I remember us going down Loch Corran on a boat trip looking back at the Cullins of Skye with a low sun beaming over them. Paul saw me gasp in awe and just mouthed, 'Heaven'.

This would later become an annual occasion and welcome retreat from city life.

On the way back we called to see my cousin David Kenwright, who lived in Aberdeenshire, via Loch Ness, an eerie and forbidding place. We got an ordnance survey map and visited the local stone circles, many covered in pictograms.

✱✱✱✱✱✱

My sculpting was very rewarding. I loved – and continue to love – the spontaneous aspect of it. I suppose I didn't (and still don't) like to think too much about the creative process. I liked it just to happen and fall into place in its own time. I felt I was giving license for the event to take place. I always enjoyed the crafting of my work, but in many ways the less I had to do with analyzing the creative process the better it would turn out. It might sound daft, but the best ones just seemed to create themselves. I felt that if something called to me, I'd receive its signal and then bring it to life. Like in my collage work, an image I might have cut out from a page might land on a background and then a new world or situation would arise from that.

Alternatively, I could just as easily be inspired to create a sculpture because the old indicator from my car looked like it could be a robot's head! And so it went and still goes on. Inspiration observed no clock and when the world spoke to me (at whatever time that might be in 'real' terms) I felt it was up to me to reply.

Although I wasn't yet able to say sculpting was my 'profession', it began to open doors for me during 1996 and '97. The Liberty show was followed by a small exhibition at London's Hackney Museum and during June I got a message from *Homes and Gardens* magazine. They wanted to include me in their July issue because of the Hackney show.

******

I was aware Tommy Scott was doing something with his new band, Space, but I hadn't really paid much attention to what was going on until listening to Mark Radcliffe's programme on BBC Radio 2 when he played their track 'Money' and it really made my ears prick up. Over the next few months they began to cultivate a big following and became hit makers with 'Female of the Species' climbing the charts.

I hadn't actually seen Tommy for ages, though Paul Hemmings (who had featured in The Australians) had kept in touch with him. Then Paul got me on the guest list with him to see Space play with Welsh popsters Catatonia and it was a great night. I saw Tommy after the show and he was really warm, made up to see me. He even told me 'Precious Love' was one of his favourite songs ever. Great to hear him say that.

******

Art was taking precedence over music at this time. The booklets I'd compiled as a portfolio for my tin sculptures had turned into a real asset and I found myself sending around forty of them off in the post. One or two went to animators who had contacted me with a view to animating my work, but mainly to museums and galleries. I was pleasantly astonished to discover my work seemed to be finding a market. In the wake of being part of the British Craft Room at Liberty, I had begun to sell quite a few pieces – to places as widespread as the Reclamations Gallery in Lavenham (Suffolk), the Greenwich Woodlands Gallery in London, Ambleside's Old Court House Gallery in Cumbria, and the Bunhoga Gallery in Shetland. I was amazed to discover interest from further afield, with brochures also going off to parts of Europe.

Fred Dellar, who had been the first writer to acknowledge my contribution to the early La's in the *NME* back in '94, was now working for *MOJO* magazine. He called me around this time to ask me about The La's' early recordings. He ran a readers' query page at the back of the magazine and responded to questions. He had run a piece on the 1986 *Elegance, Charm and Deadly Danger* compilation LP featuring what he thought were the earliest La's releases: 'My Girl Sits Like a Reindeer' and 'Sweet 35'. A guy called Terry Banks from Sydney, Australia, had been in touch with Fred informing him that there was actually an earlier release by The La's on side two of the *A Secret Liverpool* LP from 1984.

Fred had got in touch with Go! Discs to ask them about these recordings and they had said The La's had not released anything before signing to Go! Discs. This had agitated Fred and he had told them, 'Well, what's this album I've got here in my hand then?'

His job was to get facts right and he resented being told something that wasn't factually correct and consequently printed a second follow-up in *MOJO* after interviewing me on the phone. I was able to tell him also about Ian (Hart) Davies' involvement with *A Secret Liverpool*, funding it with his brother Carl. In fact, the very first release under the name The La's was 'I Don't Like Hanging Around', which was in fact myself with backing band The Modernaires from the Chemist Studio in Chester in 1983.

FIFTEEN

Tin Planet

DURING JANUARY 1997 THE most exciting development on the art front was a call I got from a lady called Cherry Gray from Warrington Museum and Art Gallery. I had sent her the booklet of my sculptures I'd compiled with Nonconform during 1996 and she wanted to meet me. Intriguingly, her husband, Richard Gray, was the head of Manchester's City Art Gallery – where I had met Captain Beefheart sixteen years earlier. Through Cherry I was offered my first 'one-man exhibition' at the Warrington Museum and Art Gallery during the summer of 1997.

I was still working with Dan, Roger and Tony Mac as The Kachinas at this stage. We needed to re-mix some of the recordings we had made in Lori's studio in Bethesda, North Wales. I had bumped into Ian Broudie and he said if we needed some studio time his new studio on a barge on the Thames down in Richmond was available. All we needed to do was box off Kenny the engineer.

The studio on the river barge had belonged to Pete Townshend and was near to Townshend's Eel Pie Studios. To give him his due, Ian had again come through for us at a crucial time.

Down in Richmond, an A&R woman called Charlie turned up to hear the songs. Mick Moss had gotten her over from, of all people, Go! Discs. She listened with interest and seemed to like the songs, and after we'd chatted for a while she promised she'd play them for label boss Andy MacDonald. I was hopeful to a point, but it was hard not to feel cynical considering all they'd endured with The La's, not least the seemingly endless rejected studio sessions for their album. Would Go! Discs really want to touch an ex-La's 'barge mixes' with a barge pole? I didn't think so.

******

The Warrington exhibition kept getting closer to being realized. On 26 February, I met with Jon Barraclough for lunch and talked about the forthcoming exhibition which I wanted to call *Lost and Found*. The name had come to me instantaneously when Cherry Gray had begun to set the wheels in motion. I liked it immediately and knew I shouldn't question it or consider alternative names.

I was glad I'd kept up with Jon. He'd been a good friend of Ros' and Ben's and had moved from London up to Liverpool to work in the graphics department at Liverpool Art School. He'd been a good mate for years and took many photos of The Onset along the way before he'd become head of the college in its entirety. He'd even employed The Onset to play in the corner while the college had been enrolling new students.

Jon had ended up working with Nonconform and over lunch we discussed their involvement with publicity and colour enlargements for *Lost and Found*. Jon was very positive about the whole thing and also spoke of the possibility of housing the exhibition at Liverpool John Moores University after its run in Warrington.

During April, Henry Epstein got in touch again. In typical fashion, I hadn't heard from him for a while and then he popped up out of the blue, asking me if I'd like to go and see John Power's band Cast playing in Manchester on the Sunday. I said I was up for it.

It was the first time I'd seen Cast. They had already had a few top 10 hits and the show was really good. We bumped into Alan Wills there and it was good to see John's wife Belinda (who was pregnant) at the after show. I could tell John was really happy I had come along and we shared a bottle of champagne to celebrate his success.

I remember taking Ray to play-group the next day on Lark Lane, chatting to Bernie Connor in there with his little son Buddy and feeling pretty rough ...

******

19 May 1997 was an historic day. The Tories lost power for the first time since 1979.

******

Survivalist Junkyard Fetishism

I'd been looking forward to it for what seemed like forever, but finally my first major exhibition, *Lost and Found*, opened at the Warrington Museum and Art Gallery on 30 June and ran for just over two months. Admission was free and the flyers billed it as starring 'Mike Badger's Tin Sculptures, Collage and Found Objects'. The flyer also had a mini-bio that revealed a little about my modus operandi when it came to art:

> The images are drawn from popular culture and reflect Mike's fascination with the Sci-Fi B-movie genre and the Merseyside music scene. The central focus of the exhibition is a large-scale interactive automaton based on a fairground ride, created from found objects. Also included are decorative sculptures and original collages.

Thanks to Cherry Gray's seemingly bottomless enthusiasm, *Lost and Found* was a spectacular show. The gallery spent a lot of money on painting all the walls and panels and framing dozens of my collages. They also wanted it to be as interactive as possible, so I crafted sculptures like one called *Rocket to the Moon*, where you hit a lever that sent a rocket up to hit a tin can like a strength test at the fair. Paul Hemmings had put together an ambient sound collage of clockwork toys – African and Indian chanting and space-age sounds that echoed the visual subject matter over the PA – and it complemented the exhibition beautifully. The opening was well attended and it really did feel like the first day of the rest of my life.

I was elated about the exhibition, but an incident which occurred while it was running reminded me I was still learning my craft when it came to tin sculpting. I was busily making a biplane one day in July and drilling a wing to put the struts on when the drill snagged, spun the metal wing around my hand and sliced into me. I slowly peeled back the tin to uncover a gaping wound in the top of my hand.

Oh dear. Luckily no arteries severed. I drove to the A&E department at the Royal Hospital and bumped into a blood doctor I'd met before when he bought some of my work. His wife, Christine, had taken their son Julian to the same play-group Ray attended and they now lived (oddly enough) in Ian and Becky Broudie's old house. I sat in his office and had a cup of tea while waiting to get stitched up. Miraculously, my injury wasn't too bad. Five stitches were all it took to patch it up and a couple of weeks later I discovered a scar appearing which looked like a peace pipe. It remains with me to this day.

I loved my tin-sculpting adventures, but incidents like this reminded me that tin cans and guitars make wearisome neighbours and I was often conscious of the damage I could potentially do to my hands. Though the biplane was the only situation which led me to the casualty department, I was constantly cutting myself one way or the other and I have many scars on my hands. It was a dicey business, because you didn't know you'd cut yourself until you saw the red on the silver. I had a method of working which seemed to work, though. I sat on the floor cross-legged and knocked my sculptures together on an old shoe last. I had my tin opener, tin snips, hammer, panel pins and a supply of sticking plasters with me at all times. Many of my sculptures hold specks of my blood. Commitment? ... Or a bloody health and safety nightmare!

******

In the *Guardian*, journalist Robert Clark wrote: 'Mike Badger makes weird little sculptures and automata out of a hybrid mix of exotic fruit cans, cheese graters, Asian joss-stick packaging and plastic Martians. It might sound somewhat naff, but it looks quirkily convincing as a collection of survivalist junkyard fetishism'.

Lost and Found began to open doors for me. Shortly after it wound down, the Bristol City Museum and Art Gallery called me with the intention of booking the exhibition for an as-yet unspecified run during 1998–99. After some more discussion, Christine Jackson from the museum came up to Liverpool for a meeting early in September. She told me she was also in Liverpool to research a possible exhibition on slavery through the ages, but from what she said it sounded like that exhibition would be housed after mine.

She went on to refer to my work as 'charming' and I was delighted she enjoyed it and seemed genuinely enthusiastic. She only had an hour to spare and I felt I talked her leg off, but we left on good terms and she promised to send me a letter to confirm my exhibition was on.

My artwork was taking up an increasing amount of my time as summer morphed into autumn, but The Kachinas were also still rehearsing regularly and working on new songs. During August, we worked up a new track at a session at Martyn Campbell's studio down the road in Aigburth. 'Pick Me Up' would eventually make its way onto my retrospective *Lo-Fi Electric Excursions* album. However, gigs and opportunities outside Merseyside were few and far between.

At the end of September '97, Tommy Scott phoned me and it was really great to have a chat with him. He told me he couldn't make the private viewing that had been set up, so I ended up going to the gallery with him on the Monday instead.

By now, my *Lost and Found* exhibition was on at John Moores University in Liverpool (thanks to Jon Barraclough) and Mersey poet Adrian Henri bought one of my cars. I had made it from a beer can Paul had given me and titled it *Leningrad Cowboy*. I remember the *Batman* theme was playing in the gallery and I had said to Adrian, 'They're playing your tune', to which he laughed. Carl had gotten me into Adrian's poetry when I was a lad and he was my favourite of those Merseybeat poets. He was also a respected artist in his own right and had just bought a piece of my work – life really can be great sometimes. The exhibition would remain on display until 31 October.

Tommy was talking about recording a version of 'Precious Love', which Paul had mentioned he'd been toying with. I was wholly flattered by the idea and told him so. It was an intriguing conversation as he also mentioned he'd be interested in using some of my tinwork for Space's forthcoming record releases. His interest in my work would shortly open a lot more doors for me.

I was glad to get together with him and the following week he told me he'd like to buy my photo-montage *Gorilla in the Midst* for his girlfriend Jill – sweet! I met Tommy in Parr Street Studios and then took him to the gallery to see my exhibition. Tommy also bought a hubcap flying saucer, but he was especially thrilled with *Gorilla in the Midst*. It featured a picture of a picnic scene with a car and a giant gorilla coming out of the rainforest and inspired in a big way by the simple juxtaposition of Berlin artist John Heartfield.

During the *Lost and Found* campaign in Liverpool, I was interviewed on location about my work by Johnny Vegas, who – coincidentally – had also attended the St Helens Art College after me. He liked my work, though was typically challenging when he said to me after I had pointed out an oil can I had mounted on the wall:

'Do you ever get anyone saying "but you haven't done anything to it, you lazy get"?'

'Well, I would agree', I replied. 'I think the less you have to do to something the better.'

After the interview, he showed me a piece of his ceramic work, which was elegant and had an aquiline nature. I knew he was genuinely pleased I liked his work and he was going to buy one of my sculptures for his fiancée, but the next thing I knew he was down in London and had become a TV star.

On the same day I took Tommy Scott to the LJMU, cheques arrived from both Warrington and the BBC. Meanwhile, Chris Willan, who'd previously been in The Twangin' Banjos with Paul, bought another sculpture of mine, called *Space Cadet*.

******

Tommy was as good as his word where getting me on board with Space's record sleeves was concerned. He talked me up to the people from the band's label, Gut Records, and they agreed to come up and see my stuff during November. Tommy arrived with Carolyn, one of the main movers at the label, and they really liked the room full of tinwork and found metal objects. Before I knew it, they were talking about more than just one single sleeve. Further releases, including the band's forthcoming album, were being mooted and they talked of wanting to keep a stylistic continuity. They had no album title as yet, but when Tommy saw the sign written in tin letters on a blackboard I'd made for the film Paul Simpson and I had suggested but never made, he was hooked.

'Tin Planet!' he exclaimed. He loved the concept and felt the idea was perfect for the next Space album title as well, though he had to confirm it with the rest of the band. The upshot was that Carolyn agreed to get in touch again the following day to make an official proposal to use my work on Space's forthcoming releases. I would then be doing a photo shoot the following Tuesday with their designer and photographer for the sleeve of Space's new single, 'Avenging Angel'.

Carolyn did get back to me and once everything was ironed out they agreed to put me on a retainer, which eventually lasted for over five months, taking in the sleeve of the band's forthcoming album (which would officially become *Tin Planet*) and the surrounding singles. I was also commissioned to decorate the club for the resulting album launch, which would feature a display of a giant tin rocket and robots, not to mention tin can disco lights and club signs.

I felt happy the day the agreement from Gut came through. It made me feel vindicated for sticking to my guns and working away at what I loved. To complete a great day, I went to BBC Manchester at the Oxford Road studios to collect some of the sculptures they'd had on display for a couple of months in their foyer area, thanks to an initiative by Viv Tyler in Business in the Arts. They even decided to buy a couple of pieces for their board room.

✳✳✳✳✳✳

1997 had been a great year. *Lost and Found* had put my name on the map as a sculptor and we'd got shut of the Tories at last. Even The

Kachinas got a taste of glory just before Christmas when we supported Space at a triumphant Liverpool show at the L2 on the Winter Solstice, 21 December. The sound check had been great and we managed to maintain the energy when we took to the stage around 8 o'clock. There were about 1000 people there and the buzz of playing to a big crowd gave us all a lift. We had a special guest appearance by Henry Priestman on keyboards and rocked it up. Space were amazing and we all cracked open the champagne in the dressing room afterwards.

SIXTEEN

Lost in Space

BOUGHT A GIANT, SEVEN-FOOT-TALL space rocket in a second-hand shop on Liverpool's Renshaw Street and tin plated it for the band's album release party. I put a light inside and I made some transparencies of portraits of Tommy, Jamie and Franny from the band and fixed them inside each of the rocket's three portholes to make them look like they were travelling in space. I also made signs for the different rooms in the club, including the Disco Dolly room, from which I hung about twenty tin catering cans which housed different coloured lights. I was really pleased with the way it looked and couldn't wait to see it on the night of the *Tin Planet* official launch.

I didn't miss living in London, but still enjoyed the opportunity of checking things out in the capital and this trip was no exception. I took a walk through Covent Garden to Leicester Square and Chinatown. From there, I caught a bus to Brixton to buy some sardine tins for sculpting purposes (a different exotic purchase from my previous trips to Brixton!) and whiled away an enjoyable evening with my sister Ros and her partner Ben.

Back home in Liverpool a few days later, I put on ITV to catch the design segment of *This Morning* to find I was watching myself. It was part of a series they were doing called 'By Design', and in the feature I'd been filmed collecting my source material from the back of Quiggins, then making a space car with a motor from a whisk at the back.

This edition of *This Morning* coincided with the release of Space's single 'Avenging Angel' (this was plugged at the end of the feature), so both Gut Records and Space got some extra coverage off the back of it, which was fine by me. Four million people had just tuned in to watch me making a space car from a tin can tea caddy and an egg whisk!

In March I spent the whole day on an animated TV advert for the album, arriving very early at a studio in Soho and working on creating the set for the *Tin Planet* cityscape. After an hour of looking through the Mitchell 35mm camera, I could see a cityscape I had made from silver cheese graters, bread tins, cans and kitchen utensils and it looked beautiful all lit up. I added more flavour to it by doing some flying saucer shots utilizing a vegetable steamer hanging from a fishing line. After that, the *Tin Planet* robot was animated moving into the city, which was a pleasure to watch with his flashing head and the other robots moving around him.

I was working in tandem with a very talented young director called Gerald McMorrow, who had recently been behind Pulp's brilliant *This Is Hardcore* promo film. He listened with interest to all my ideas and then tried to include as many of them as possible into his animation. His ultimate aim was to make it look like Technicolor and it was going to look fantastic on TV.

Gerald was a graduate of the New York Film Academy and also shot promotional films for many of the Britpop generation, including Catatonia and Ultrasound, before going on to win the 2002 TCM Classic Shorts Film prize at the London Film Festival for *Thespian X*. He would then make his full-length directorial debut with 2008's science fiction epic *Franklyn*.

******

We were invited to Sue Taylor's fiftieth and Hamish Cameron turned up! It was great to see him and also see that he looked exactly as he had in the old days, even though he must have been pushing forty now.

Hamish had always been an enigmatic character. He turned a lot of people on to a lot of things, yet somehow he made a point of swerving away from the limelight or any kind of fame for such an incredibly talented guy.

He told me he'd seen Lee Mavers recently, who had him in stitches talking about his 'Evertone' fixation, and went on to refer to a certain well-known Irish singer/songwriter as 'Fat Morris Van'.

The following week, I was interviewed on live TV by Julia Carling on a satellite TV programme. I had to take a display of my tin can sculptures with me. Psychic medium Derek Acorah was on the show and cornered me in the green room exclaiming that he had gotten a 'great energy' from my work before saying, 'You're going to be so big one day'. That was nice of him to share the enthusiasm he felt from my work. Suppose some people see a 'model' made from a tin can, but to others there's more to it.

****

Space's *Tin Planet* album was launched at last on 8 April. I drove down to the Leisure Lounge with Nettee and she went round Covent Garden while I set up all my stuff. I put all the portraits of the band in the rocket and wired the lights that went on the stage. I took all the tinwork and the rocket. I suspended another tin rocket over the dance floor and the *Tin Planet* robot went on a plinth under glass with the 'press button' light attached. There was also a collection of sculptures behind the bar, which Nettee later arranged on her arrival, and I finished it off with the signposts by the door and the Disco Dolly light in the Disco Dolly room.

Space played a rapturous gig in Camden, where I saw Yorkie and Paul Cavanagh, and the after show party at the Leisure Lounge was equally memorable. Ros and Ben went along to the gig with me and Paul Hemmings, Henry Epstein, Tim Higgins, Steve Appleby, Roger Llewellyn, Danny Dean and Brian Hodge (from the scheme) were all at the party. Boozy night all round. I would have also loved to have worked on some great merchandise for Space to sell at gigs. But that never happened – could have been great for all concerned.

******

That summer in Nice, in the middle of one of our precarious drives along the dual carriageway that runs the length of the promenade, Amber brought out a rubber snake she'd bought and was playing with it as I gamely tried to avoid the cars weaving inside and outside of us.

'What kind of snake is this Daddy?' she said suddenly.

'It's a *viper*!' I exclaimed. It was a name I'd remember and would shortly be returning to.

******

One night, late in June '98, Paul Hemmings called by for a chat. He was still on the road with The Lightning Seeds and they were enjoying the success of their World Cup song 'Three Lions', which was number one in the singles chart.

Paul told me they were staying in what he described as an 'Alan Partridge-type' motel, but the conversation soon turned to my songs. Paul had been listening intently to the new acoustic material that I had been playing round at his and Henry's and suggested that we might think of working on an album of these songs together that could be sold via the Internet, the new and latest thing!

I was well into the idea. We would have to come up with a label of our own here, I thought. Just the idea of it made me feel good and Paul told me he was keen to sit down and seriously talk about it once he was back from playing the Glastonbury Festival that coming weekend.

I got excited about the idea of making a solo record. As I had always been in bands this would be a fresh start, and I had amassed a lot of darker, more brooding material in the late nights after the family had gone to bed. With Paul's help, it became a reality sooner rather than later.

Paul is always very organized and it was great working with him creatively again. By July, I'd decided the record would probably be called *Silent Secrets* (after the song of the same name I had and because the songs had been both secret and silent for long enough) and I was in agreement with Paul's suggestion that it should be sparse and understated.

He would back me with additional acoustic guitar with maybe Henry Priestman to play organ and/or piano on some of the tracks.

※ ※ ※ ※ ※ ※

I'd been practising my songs with Paul on acoustic guitars and with his guidance and demo-ing sessions on a porta-studio. I was ready to record much sooner than I'd imagined – the first in such a long time. As early as 29 July we entered the Music House studio for the first of two days of sessions.

Lance Thomas, the engineer, was very diligent and did a great job and almost before we knew it Louis Johnson had come down to record layers of cello. Paul and I had agreed some strings would sound good on the record. I was delighted we could use Louis. He instinctively knew what to do on my songs. It came as no surprise to hear he'd later work with everyone from The Coral to the Liverpool Royal Philharmonic.

The following day's recording became something of an epic. Paul and I finished off our acoustic guitar parts and we put down all the lead guitar embellishments. After that, I did the backing vocal parts and tidied up my lead vocals. Then Tommy Scott came down around tea time and I went through the songs with him. I'd really wanted to use his voice on the record and he responded by doing some wonderful vocals on the tracks 'Where Love Is' and 'Poverty of the Heart'. His performances were stunning – he sang like a bird.

We were on a roll at this stage and began mixing straight away. The mixing carried on into the night, but as we began mixing the last track on the album, an eight-minute soundscape called 'Twilight in D', Lance started to freak out because the desk started to react very strangely as if from nowhere. Lights began flashing where they shouldn't have on the desk and he seemed perplexed as to what was happening.

He was certainly convinced it was an important take and did everything in his power to get it exactly right, which – to my ears – he did perfectly. Maybe it was something about the song itself. It had caught Lance's attention from the off and he'd even referred to it as a 'Celtic calling song'. The end results suggested he wasn't wrong. With 'Twilight in D' I wanted to make a song in a shape of a pyramid in that it started quietly and slowly built to a peak in the middle and then tailed out like the night entering the day.

It was after 2:30 in the morning by the time we'd finally got it all done and dusted and we were all exhausted – but exhilarated – by getting a whole LP done in only two days.

Danny Dean and I had a low-key acoustic show booked at Stamps in Crosby the following night, so I went around to Danny's place to work out a set. It would mostly be Onset songs – 'Cowboy and His Wife', 'Too Proud to Start', 'Precious Love', 'Rhapsody' – and a dip into The Kachinas' song-book ('Pick Me Up'), although I was toying with having a go at 'James Earl Ray' from the new acoustic album. James Earl Ray was the man convicted of the assassination of Martin Luther King, Jr. I had seen a documentary on him where he was interviewed in prison and I had no doubt that he was innocent of the crime. Even the King family thought him innocent. He was no angel, a small-time criminal who'd been stitched up. I had just heard about his death in prison and was inspired to tell his story in a song:

He shot no King, the gun's still smoking,
Held in the hand of the invisible man.

The practice was a lot of fun and was helped along by a first listen to the new Half Man Half Biscuit album *Four Lads Who Shook the Wirral*, which I thought was their best yet. That was saying something. The good vibe transferred over to the next night and the show itself (one of a long-running series of acoustic shows called 'The Acoustic Engine' initiated by Danny and Steve Roberts from The Tambourines) was the first of a string of shows I would end up doing post-Kachinas at the venue.

******

I had just been commissioned to be the installation artist for Manchester's First Festival of Food at Castlefield. There had been some talk of ITV Granada wanting to film me in relation to the festival, but nothing definite, so I got a shock one day early in September 1998 when Maggie Clarke called me out of the blue to say they wanted to do it that day!

The film was shown that same evening, I think the editor may have been having a laugh at my expense because at one point I appeared on the TV screen above a caption that read 'Mike Badger – Rubbish Artist'. (Josh Dean, Danny's son, got plenty of mileage out of this!) Still, I was pleased with it, although the backing track had to be by The La's. I was proud of what I'd done with the band, but it did my head in that I was always associated with just those songs from the past when I had made so much since. Still, at least they'd used 'Doledrum' this time, which had an intro guitar part I'd had a hand in. It wasn't 'There She Goes' as was usually played when I did TV or radio.

I guess I was chosen to be the installation artist for the First Festival of Food because basically I used tin cans, graters, whisks, etc. They were all food-related materials when you think of it. The venue was Castlefield Arena, where a number of canals converged underneath some spectacular iron bridges. I figured that the main sculpture would be set-off best if I could make it float in some way on the water and be seen easily by the crowds.

In the end I came up with the idea of the *Giant Tin Fish* and it took me the best part of September to assemble it. I made the fish's body by attaching a metal sheet onto the top side of a canoe I had bought from Loot, then every morning – after taking Amber to school – I would drop by the studio to spend hours attaching the scales, which were tin lids cut in half.

It was painstaking work overlapping the scales from the tail right over the body to the head, twelve feet away, plus making the fins and facial features – but it was worth it when I saw the results. It gradually became very ornate and looked like something you'd have seen in a fairground during the Victorian era. It also reminded me of the fish in *The Singing Ringing Tree* and made me realize I'd love to see that again. The *Giant Tin Fish* went on to be a big hit at the festival and ended up touring the whole country in one guise or another. It was my first major commission and turned out to be the magic fish that just kept on giving. You can still see it at its home in the National Wildflower Centre, Bowring Park Road in Liverpool.

******

I'd changed the name of my forthcoming solo album to *Volume* since I'd completed the recording. In the same way the word 'onset' had captured me, I really liked the word 'volume' and its relation to sound and a body of work. Penny Kiley had kindly agreed to help work some PR and came around to the studio to work on a press release to accompany the album's release.

When the album finally arrived from manufacture, there had been a mistake with the printing – two of the plates had been mixed up. However, it worked as a finished article. We mentioned this to Paul's Mum, Angela, and she said something so true:

'Nothing is perfect, only a tree.'

Paul had always been great when it came to putting things in order and was very methodical. It was due to this and his enthusiasm that *Volume* became the very first release on our new Viper Label. The name harked back to Amber asking what that snake was on our fraught journey down the busy carriageway in Nice. It would prove to be a learning curve, but after we'd done the first album the rest just happened organically. It was also Paul who started me thinking about all those early La's recordings that I had in a large cassette box gathering late '80s and '90s dust. Maybe they deserved a place in the wider world.

Public interest in the real story of The La's' early days seemed to be growing too. During the summer of 1998, I'd been contacted by *Record Collector* about doing a feature on what all the ex-La's had been doing. Admittedly, they probably contacted me first because Lee apparently wouldn't be interviewed about it, but they still came to me and I was happy to be involved because – with the exception of Fred Dellar's small pieces on the La's – it was the first occasion when anyone out of the national press wanted to do a full, extensive feature that included me and my role in the band.

I was pleased they took me seriously, but even more so when they printed everything I said and made no attempt to cut things out. I was entirely honest and also mentioned for the first time my contention in regard to the writing of 'Callin' All'.

They printed a photo of me with John Power from when we were on the scheme in 1986 and a brief resume of what I'd done since leaving The La's:

> After leaving The La's, their founder member created the (country-folk-ish) Onset, with ex-La's Paul Hemmings and Tony Russell, described by Pete Frame as 'the most arresting group in captivity'. Mike now splits his time between his current band The Kachinas and his critically acclaimed *Lost and Found* metal sculptures, exhibiting in Bristol later this year. These inspired the title of the new Space LP, *Tin Planet*: indeed, Mike designed the artwork.

By the beginning of October, both my debut solo album and the Viper Label were getting close to becoming reality. On a Friday early in the month, Paul and I put the LP brochures together for Southern Record Distributors to send to the retailers. Penny Kiley brought in the finished biographies and the final draft of her press release. We'd recently acquired an official Viper 'stamp' and we stamped all the copies of the PR sheets. We were almost ready to go.

★★★★★★

A whole lot of great stuff had gone down since my initial *Lost and Found* exhibition in Warrington, but it was hard to believe that anything could top either the Space campaign or the Castlefield Festival of Food commission. Before 1998 ended, however, *Lost and Found* had gone on to the Bristol City Museum and Art Gallery and had become my biggest exhibition to date.

I had a lot of direct involvement with the Bristol *Lost and Found*. I went down to stay with the curator, Christine Jackson, while I was setting it all up and also did a sculpting workshop to launch it. I was impressed with the Bristol Museum. It sat at the top of a hill and the foyer area was very spacious and grand. The great thing was that everyone who visited the museum had to go through my exhibition to get elsewhere in the building, meaning that tens of thousands of people checked my work out in a place where it couldn't have been shown in a better light.

Because of the size of the foyer, my *Telegraph Totem Pole* could be included, while there were at least fifteen glass cabinets housing my sculptures. The museum even found some examples of reclaimed artefacts from Africa to place in a separate case to complement the show. The best fun of all, though, was carrying *Giant Tin Fish* down the road on our shoulders and placing it in the harbour to advertise the exhibition. This was filmed for ITV. There again, it also helped that the person doing the design for the project (a guy called Steven) had done a fantastic job of covering the notice boards. He'd even taken the time to copy the lettering Jon Barraclough had manipulated from an Indian packet to form the initial Warrington *Lost and Found* brochure and covered an entire wall to complement the show.[14] It was a real kick for me to see my work shown with such respect and on such a grand scale.

✳ ✳ ✳ ✳ ✳ ✳

This coincided with the release of my debut solo album, *Volume*. Although it wouldn't officially be released until January, advance copies of the album had been sent out to writers during November and early in December. And I was in Bristol when I read the *Guardian*'s review of *Volume*: 'Badger has staked out classic singer-songwriter territory with these gentle, inquisitive songs which occasionally seem to be about to break into a flurry of La's-style strummery before settling down again, abashed … as if fame is the last thing he wants'.

---

14 The lettering was extracted by Jon Barraclough from an Indian packet of unknown origin. We were very interested in the old printing techniques still used in India and the misregistration of the plates forming secondary colours.

SEVENTEEN

La, a Note to Follow So

EARLY IN JANUARY 1999, I received a call from Brendan Pickavance from the *Sunday Mirror*. He wanted to know if I had a contact number for Lee Mavers. I said I hadn't and that I wasn't aware of Lee choosing to do interviews, so he said he might just call round to his house. Well, 'Good luck', I said, rather sarcastically.

Next day, I received another call from Brendan saying he'd been round to Lee Mavers' house and spent two hours with him and it had been great. Brendan went on to say that Lee had said he loved me like a brother. He also left me Lee's current phone number. I was touched.

A couple of days later, after much contemplation, I thought it might be an idea to call Lee up and see how he'd been getting on. I hadn't seen him since he called with his partner, Nevada Christian, and Ellis, their son, when Amber was a toddler. In fact, he'd called on me more than a few times since the La's days, so maybe I shouldn't be so stuck in the mud.

When I phoned, he was surprised to hear my voice but said that the timing had been impeccable. He was just on his way out the door to where he did not know. He wanted to come over straight away, so that's what he did. When he walked into the flat (now my studio space in Aigburth) he stood in the doorway, took a deep breath, his shoulders slumped and, seemingly exhausted, said one word: 'Home!'

We were both very happy to see each other and hugged. The air was filled with a deep emotion. He was looking good too, very healthy. I think this had been another factor in me getting in touch. I knew he'd struggled with drug addiction for years but I'd heard on the grapevine that he'd been clean for some time. He seemed calm and made no secret of his admiration and affection for me, which I reciprocated.

We had a couple of joints and a cup of tea, then took a walk to the river. The sky was very blue and the water was as still as could be with the sun shining lazily across it. We talked a lot more and Lee told me he'd been feeling at rock bottom just before I called. He thought he'd never see me again. I was touched by his openness and sincerity. Lee had come a long way and neither of us could really believe that we were talking and laughing so easily, like the firm friends we had once been.

Afterwards, we returned to the flat and played each other a few songs. It was obvious Lee hadn't lost any of his talent. We ended up waxing lyrical about The La's in 1986 and it felt like a piece of me I wasn't even aware of – or wouldn't allow myself to be aware of – had returned right out of the blue of a sky like the one we'd seen hanging over the river. I ran Lee home later to see his and Vada's kids but they weren't there, so instead I looked around his house and had a cup of tea. Lee asked when he could call and I said he was welcome to whenever. He said, 'No, I'll call tomorrow' and I said I'd call him within the week and I did too.

******

1999 was already building up to be a great year. Paul and I spoke to Harry at Southern Record Distributors and gave him the OK to put *Volume* on the listening posts in Virgin. Just to put the icing on the cake, Paul phoned to say the album had been given a good review in *Mojo* magazine, wherein journalist Paul Du Noyer wrote, 'At least half of the songs have classic potential'.

I also spoke to a journalist called John Bennett, who wanted a La's photo for a full-page article he'd written for the *Newcastle Journal*. I felt happy and phoned Lee, arranging for him to come round at 1 o'clock the following Monday afternoon. I said that there was good medicine happening.

'Yeah, white buffalo magic!' he replied.

I met Lee again as arranged at the studio the following Monday. We chatted and enjoyed each other's company once more. I put a tape on of some La's demos I had. Lee was knocked out by most of them, sitting there with a contented smile on his face that broadened especially when he heard 'Moonlight', which he had completely forgotten had existed.

Danny Dean popped in to pick up a porta-studio and ended up staying with us for a cup of tea. Then we listened to the rest of the tape.

Then Lee said something I hadn't expected.

'I can't do this without you', he said casually. 'Let's get back together or my bones will just turn to chalk and blow away. How about it?'

He wanted to work with me again in a new version of The La's. I was touched, but the history of what had happened previously still weighed heavy on me. I considered it for a while, but in the end I figured I'd be a mean-spirited bastard if I didn't give this another go.

I would only do it, I said, it if everything was on a 50/50 basis, right down the line: the way it had started out. Lee said he wouldn't want it any other way. No other parties would be involved for the foreseeable future either. He completely agreed, so the idea was that his studio would be set up in Aigburth shortly. However, I told him I wanted to clear the decks of The La's recordings we had done in the '80s also. Lee had always said in the press that the first recordings were the best.

'Let's get 'em all out at last', Lee exclaimed enthusiastically.

We decided to go through the fabled demo tapes in more detail the next Thursday. It was all getting really exciting and then I found out that night that I was due to go on *Blue Peter* with my tin sculptures in March. I saw Paul that night and filled him in on what had been a momentous seven days.

I saw Lee again soon after that. On 21 January, he called round just after mid-day in his battered old space cruiser filled with battered drums, amps and guitars – they'd all been round the block. We had a good old talk again and even though he'd just been hit with a large tax bill and Everton had lost 3–0, he was still made up. We filled in more gaps and confirmed again our need for each other when it came to music. Lee said he needed my guidance. I agreed.

We talked a little about the day and night we'd split up. Then we started talking about Chinese astrological stuff. I said we were both Tigers, but that he was Fire and I was Water. He had evaporated me, but then I'd drenched him. He agreed. Then he said we had to 'get the kettle back on the boil!'

We both laughed at that. Lee played around getting his 'sound tone pulse vibration' – he did this by tuning the guitar to the hum of the amp, which he claimed was the Earth's energy. This was a bit confusing for me, but I trusted him as an artist. He told me he just wanted a vehicle for the sounds we would write and perform.

We went up to the studio to compile some more tapes for the epic La's project we were determined to put together. It was fascinating going through all the tapes and we found even more alternate versions of some of the tracks.

I had to go and pick up my exhibition from Bristol Museum and asked if Lee would like to come along, which he did – and he brought along ex-La's bass man Jasper too! We had a great day down in Bristol packing up my exhibition, returning home late in the evening.

Ever since 'There She Goes' – Lee's most famous song – had become a hit and been used in too many films to recall, a rumour had started that it was about heroin use. I knew the lyric 'pulsing through my veins' but was unaware of any 'smack' being around when it was written. I can remember a very embryonic version in late '86 before he finalized the arrangement with Paul Hemmings in the Stables a few months after I had left in '87. I asked Lee if it was true: 'Is there any relation to heroin?' 'No', he said emphatically.

I thought not. Just goes to show how a journalist can mention or surmise something and how it can then become currency. It had always upset me that – because of this – one of the first words people said after hearing the name 'The La's' was 'heroin'. I thought of that horrible phrase 'heroin chic' and how some young music journalists should be more responsible when bandying about false truths when heroin has fucked up so much – especially in Liverpool during the early Thatcher years. Nothing very 'chic' about that!

Heroin/opiates exist as a God-given gift to take away our pain. Take it when you are not suffering in agony and you soon will be.

✱✱✱✱✱✱

Volume was continuing to perform well on the back of the good reviews it had received. Paul had phoned to tell me the distributor needed more CDs because the thousand they'd originally taken had all gone out. It looked as though we'd have to take another 500 down for them.

I was made up with both my reunion with Lee and the way the critics and public alike had responded so positively to my first venture as a solo performer, but I was equally thrilled my sculpting seemed to be taking on a life of its own. On the back of the hugely successful Bristol show, *Lost and Found* moved on to the Leicester City Gallery early in 1999.

Reviews of *Volume* weren't uniformly positive. In *Q*'s review of the LP, their writer, Peter Kane, had dismissed it outright and even questioned my motive in releasing the album. Huh! But then Nettee cheered me up by bringing me a copy of *Bigmouth* magazine, which had just reviewed the album. Their review turned out to be the ultimate anyone could have asked for. Their writer, Ian Salmon, was totally on it and it really gave me a lift. He felt it was 'delicate, beautiful, dizzying and dreamlike ... packed with gorgeously fragile songs' and concluded that 'this is one hell of a debut'.

Things were moving. We set up the Viper Label account at the bank and paid in the first £20. It was provided by my Dad (he insisted) for the four CD copies of *Volume* he wanted to pass on, while we'd already received two cheques for two CDs to send out to individual customers. Suddenly, we had to start thinking about business – whether we wanted to or not. We didn't know where it would all lead, but it felt natural to both Paul and me, so we took the plunge. I'd been self-managed for most of my musical career anyway, so what the hell.

Even allowing for the Leicester *Lost and Found* exhibition, musical stuff dominated the immediate future. On 30 January, I saw *Volume* on the listening post in the Virgin store in town, as promised. *Select* magazine had picked up on the album too and their album review spoke of how '"Silent Secrets" [is] like the '70s *Magpie* theme crossed with The La's rockin' out in a taverna ... proof positive Lee Mavers wasn't the sole custodian of song-writing gold'. A few other publications also weighed in with appraisals of the album. Another very positive one was John Bennett's in *The Journal*, which suggested *Volume* 'is a quiet, beautiful album made in the spirit of *Astral Weeks* which grows with every listen and sounds as if it were made for dark evenings or the quiet of Sunday morning'.

******

I started to work on new stuff with Lee. Early in February, I practised the lead guitar parts to 'Mind Field' and it was sounding boss. I also played around with a new arrangement of The Kachinas song 'Pick Me Up'. The new rehearsal room was taking shape. I moved my tin sculpting stuff up to the studio and hoovered the place, straightening it out. We were both buzzing when we saw how well it was coming on. Somehow, only The La's could possibly have had an experience like ours. Twelve years apart and back working again? It was incredible to think we could resolve it. It was such a positive and powerful signal for the future.

Later on in February, Lee came down with his Dad, 'Jim Bob'. It was a pleasure to meet him again and he turned out to be very likeable and chatty. He spoke of putting a false ceiling in the practice room for us. We ended up talking about jazz and Lee's grandfather, who was a jazz guitarist. Lee's Dad had caught the guitar-playing bug off Lee and told me how he'd started learning on a Gibson Lee had given him.

Lee had wanted me to start learning the guitar parts for his new material and encouraged me to spend a lot more time practising guitar again. On 25 February, I spent most of the day running through new songs 'Human Race', 'Robber Man', 'Mind Field', 'Ladies and Gentlemen' and 'Travellin' On'. It was a great buzz to play such crafted, flowing lead lines and Lee seemed to love the way I was playing them too. I could feel it all sparking at this time and we obviously thought the world of each other. Lee seemed to be happier each time we met, especially since the guitars started to come out on a regular basis.

My musical partnership with Lee continued to grow. Jasper came down with Lee. He'd played on the first La's recordings fourteen years earlier, in February '85, at the Attic: 'Reindeer', 'Sweet 35' and 'Red Deer Stalk', to name a few. We played 'Mind Field' and 'Human Race', then later had a go at a song I had written called 'Road to Ruin'. Jasper played bass well and was really happy to be with us.

Blue Peter confirmed the date for filming and also requested I take all my large-scale sculptures with me to the BBC Studios, so all of a sudden I had preparation and transport to sort out as it was short notice. In the end, the *Blue Peter* people sent their guys up to Leicester for my work, so on Thursday I'd been down to round up everything I wanted them to take, including the *Tin Planet* robot that had featured on Space's album.

I found the time for music that day despite everything. I practised more at the studio, this time working through 'Timeless Melody' and making sure I had it down. Lee's method was to write all the songs down in red ink and then write over the titles again in black when it had been learnt to his satisfaction.

We discussed three La's albums we wanted to put out, which would entail releasing all the original demos that we had so dearly loved once and for all. These would be the first two albums: an album of tracks that featured me on vocals and an album of Lee's songs that was ostensibly the original versions of *The La's* album tracks. The third album was to be an album of all new La's material featuring new songs by Lee and myself.

★★★★★★★

On Monday, 15 March, I caught the train to London as planned. Then a car collected me from Euston to take me to the BBC Television Centre in Shepherd's Bush. They had done a great job of displaying my work all over Studio 4.

The whole *Blue Peter* experience was something. I was well looked after and the team were wonderful to work with. I really liked Konnie Huq, the interviewer, and she was even more gorgeous in real life. They casually told me that they had six million viewers and I couldn't get that out of my head when that red light appeared on the camera. It all went off great though – good TV for young people, simple as that. I even got *Blue Peter* badges for Amber and Ray and I was awarded a special green *Blue Peter* badge for being an environmentally friendly artist. The cameraman came up to me after the interview, looked at my work and noted, 'You must take some funky drugs!' (Turned out he was from Huyton...)

Amber's teacher in Dovedale School had got wind that I was on *Blue Peter*, recorded the programme and showed it to the class the next day. That meant a lot to me and to Amber.

Like Bristol, the Leicester *Lost and Found* had its memorable moments. I went down to do a talk and a sculpting demonstration at the gallery after I'd been on *Blue Peter* and met a guy from Grimsby who told me he'd been to the Leicester exhibition twice a week since it had opened. The Leicester exhibition wasn't anything like as big a show as the Bristol one (more of a well-presented space with my *Tin Rocket* in the window), so I was amazed my work could inspire this devotion.

I said one of the gallery staff, 'See that guy over there?' pointing to the fella with shades on, dressed all in black. 'Has he been in the gallery a lot?' She confirmed the Grimsby bloke had been there regularly each week. I was dumbstruck. Grimsby must be as far from Leicester as Liverpool, but the logistics of the travelling hadn't dampened this guy's enthusiasm one bit. I was touched but a bit spooked. I didn't know whether to be flattered or scared by that depth of commitment.

Back in Liverpool I went over to Burrows Lane with Lee and Jasper. My Mum and Dad were away and we had a practice in the kitchen during the evening. On the way in through my Mum and Dad's door, Lee said to Jasper in typical disdain, 'Wipe your face on the way in.'

We played more songs including 'There She Goes', which was magical. The version of it we'd worked up even impressed Lee, who suggested it had never sounded so good. It was a hell of a riff to learn, with more subtle nuances than I could ever have imagined. It was a personal achievement to nail that song, which no one could deny by this time had become a standard.

Lee spent a while waxing lyrical about the majesty of The La's and how perfect it all was now. He was on a real high and we were all really on the trip with him. We wanted to do it in a really low-key, 'no publicity' way this time. The idea of there being no La's albums for a decade and then three in a row was just fantastic and – at this stage – still plausible.

Lee was also very un-impressionable. Madonna could have walked in the room and he wouldn't have bothered looking up from his Everton programme. The only music he said to me he liked at this time was 'Female of the Species' by Space (I think because there was a bit of Sinatra in there). He also loved the version of 'Girl from the North Country' by Link Wray I had played him. We listened to the old 1954 Lightnin' Slim recordings in the car.

One day he was in a rage and started on Manchester, saying how all that music scene was full of shit and how irrelevant it all was, superficial and inconsequential. Jasper and I just sat quiet letting him vent. After he seemed to calm down I said, trying to bring a little perspective on things, 'Well, not everything is sweetness and light here in Liverpool music y'know is it?' ... to which he launched into a new tirade:

'That lot! They're worse than any damn Manc!'

... Oh dear.

We were working hard on the first demo-album project, which we had fittingly titled *Breakloose*. I had suggested that we separate the material I sang from the material that Lee sang. I was aware that many people thinking of The La's would be familiar with Lee as the lead singer, and I hadn't wanted to shuffle the set of songs into one body of work even though we had played them all mixed up live in 1986.

The second collection of original recordings we had decided to call *Callin' All*. Lee had said he could change the credit and it would put an end once and for all to that stupid debacle. Then, on the third album we could present newly written songs sung by both of us.

A few days after the session at Burrows Lane, I invited Paul down to the studio we had fashioned in Aigburth and met with Lee and Jasper. We boxed off all the artwork for the album sleeve, working out the colours, photos and design in detail. We all left feeling very excited and I celebrated by heading over to Stamps in Crosby with Martyn Campbell for another of my series of low-key acoustic shows.

******

Shortly after this, I took Lee and Jasper down to Wiltshire to visit the Megalithic sites in Wiltshire in my old 5 Series BMW. As we pulled up in the car by Silbury Hill, there was a helicopter hovering next to it that looked as though it could be military because it was all black and ominous-looking, though it had no markings on at all .Weird! In the end, it moved away and we climbed Silbury Hill. When we got to the top we ran into a guy who visited crop circles from West Derby in Liverpool!

We discovered that a huge solar-winged disc had appeared in the crops between Silbury and Avebury – you could see it from the top. Then we visited the West Kennet Long Barrow and marvelled at the stones in Avebury, walking the whole circle and feeling a deep sense of awe. After checking out a further crop circle, we took a trip to the beautiful village of Castle Combe, where *Doctor Doolittle* was filmed with yet another Huytonian, Rex Harrison. It had been such a memorable day.

Lee had mostly been a positive force to be around since we'd rekindled our friendship, but one day around this time he was a lot more depressed. I'd called to pick him up but we ended up talking for a long time before we went to get Jasper. Lee spoke in some detail about the anguish he was feeling inside. He told me he felt incomplete, clogged up and fractured within himself. I did my best to help him rally, giving him all the positives I could and he did respond to them, but his self-esteem had been damaged over the years and sometimes it came across as arrogance, I suppose.

He understood this but felt he couldn't match up to the positives I had been giving him. It wasn't true at all, because I felt he had been a very positive force since he'd come back into my life and I couldn't believe someone so brutally honest and passionate could feel so bad about himself. I tried to coax him out of the place he was in, saying he'd just painted himself into a corner and he could get out of there if he wanted to. It was an ongoing process, but I felt we'd get there eventually.

We were sure we had a common goal in The La's once again and when we practised later we were convinced. We played 'There She

Goes' again and Lee borrowed the mandolin I'd been given by a relation called Alec. Funnily enough, Alec lived at the end of Dinas Lane in Huyton, where Lee had grown up.

It all felt so exciting, but it was still very embryonic and we needed to be careful with it. That's life, of course. Sometimes all you need to do is a simple line drawing, while at other times you're shackled to the English language trying to grope around in the dark to find the letters to fire your imagination.

Sometimes the rehearsals were easy and fun. One day early in April I'd been listening and singing along to The Ramones before I went to pick up Lee and Jasper. We had a really good day that day, practising for ages and just laughing together. At one stage, I sat on the new bench in Lee's garden with him, just talking in the sun, and it felt magical. The chemistry seemed to be there. Lee was always winding Jasper up but he took it all in stride. He'd known Lee since school and was magnanimous and always a pleasure to be with.

But it was still a fragile situation. For the first time since we'd met up in January, Lee said something that raised serious doubts in my mind about us working together. It threw me in a big way as we'd only just completed what had seemed to be yet another positive rehearsal session.

I had been working my butt off learning all the parts to about a dozen of Lee's songs at his request and I was very happy with what I had achieved. Until this stage, Lee had been very encouraging, telling me that I alone had The La's feel. Then he suddenly said:

'You've learnt nothing, have you?'

It came out of nowhere and it really stung. I felt deflated and insecure. It had all been going so well.

It made me realize I had to be careful, because Lee was so volatile. He could still be negative, but the next minute he'd be gushing about my ability to play saying that no one had the feel I had.

Unfortunately, what he said made me feel I should take our reunion more cautiously. How could I believe someone whose moods swung so dramatically?

I saw Lee the day after he'd made the comment because his daughter Ella was having a birthday party. I sat down on the little bench between the trees with him and tried to sort it all out. I told him what he'd said and that he blows hot and cold. He muttered something about how he could be an uppity little bastard sometimes and it blew away. He went on to say that I would be able to batter him from one end of his garden to the other – in true Huyton style – and it was a big garden too. I could have, and maybe I should have?

He said with obvious honesty that he hadn't meant to upset me. I guessed I shouldn't complain about his bold, brutal statements. Right or wrong, he was being true to his feelings at that particular time. He was a totally mercurial, one-off character. He was very hard to deal with sometimes, but he'd given me more ups than downs at this stage. We settled into talking about all the exciting things that were happening and I tried to keep it upbeat.

* * * * * *

Late in April, Lee had got his mate Donal to set up the Mother Ship (his name for his mixing desk). Paul came over to see and hear the studio for the first time and was greatly impressed with it all.

Lee came over later on as it was their twins' first birthday party and it turned out to be a memorable afternoon, as we listened to some of The La's demos through the desk for the first time. They sounded amazing and it gave me a big boost. I couldn't wait to practise playing 'There She Goes', 'Human Race' and 'Ladies and Gentlemen' later on, and all felt right with the world that evening. I went for a walk through Sefton Park around 7 o'clock and the light was dancing everywhere. It was magic.

Getting together with Lee had helped me to appreciate The La's songs all over again. Later that month, I practised the lead guitar parts to 'Freedom Song' and realized just how absolutely beautiful the melody was. The great version we had of it on tape had been recorded very spontaneously by Lee back in 1986 and it really affected me. Re-learning all the parts had given me a much greater appreciation of all we'd achieved in the band's early days, even allowing for the way it had ended so abruptly and unhappily for me. Despite the one setback we'd had, Lee seemed so different now and he was also proving a good influence on Jasper, whose bass playing was really gaining in confidence.

April turned into May and still Lee and I were getting together and playing. Towards the end of the month, we spent a day running through some of the songs again before taking a walk down to Liverpool's long-abandoned Festival Gardens. We got through a hole in the fence and spent some time sunbathing and getting stoned in the Japanese Gardens on the deck over the water. It was great.

It was a philosophical day. We talked about the miracle of finding things that you are meant to find when you take the initiative to look. Later on, I returned to the new studio and fitted a silver metal splashboard over the sink. It was a lid I'd found in a skip, amazingly enough, yet it looked fantastic in the studio. It was the perfect size and served a dual purpose, sealing in the sink and securing it as the draining board had previously been loose. Love it when that happens!

It all felt like poetry in motion at this stage and it wasn't the only great discovery I'd made. There was also a big piece of metal sheeting I'd discovered that fitted the boarded-up window outside to a T, and the MDF board I'd found in a jigger. That was so perfect I might as well have phoned up and ordered it to the specifications it had arrived with. The studio décor had really taken off. We had a beautiful '30s/'40s-style couch and chairs as well, all in green, along with a desk and carpet, and the great job Jim Bob had done with the false ceiling too. It was incredible the way all these great things had arrived, seemingly by chance to the perfect specifications. And they were all things other people were throwing out. The beauty people discarded never ceased to amaze me.

✷✷✷✷✷✷

With the new studio looking a treat, I went along to see Joe Strummer with his new band, The Mescaleros, play a great show in Liverpool on Sunday, 6 June, at the Lomax (first time I'd been back since being barred). They put on a damn fine show and Strummer's new songs proved he hadn't lost his touch with the passing of time. Of course, most of the crowd were dying for him to delve into his past and the whole place went wild when he played a selection of The Clash classics. I'd never seen The Clash at Eric's, but Lee had. He'd been loitering around in the afternoon with a couple of mates and Mick Jones had got them in through the back door for the matinee. He would have been fourteen at the time.

I was still on a high from Strummer's show, but we still had some work to do down at the new studio. On the Wednesday, Paul and Lee had agreed to meet Donal, who was coming up from London to re-check the new mixing desk he'd installed. He looked over the desk and corrected any technical faults and we were ready to go. The desk was an old London Weekend Television desk dating back to 1971 and apparently it was one of only two still in existence. It looked far out, but while Paul had more of a head for the technicalities of such things, I was just really excited about getting started on new music again.

It was actually two days later, on 10 June, when we finally met up at the studio and started to put The La's' 1986 recordings down onto the reel-to-reel, half-inch 8-track machine. It was going to be a two-step process of elimination in that some versions and also some of the tapes/copies were better than others, so the first thing we needed to do was get them down and hear them. We got eight tracks down during this first session and they sounded amazing. The Mother Ship really added something that let the music reach its full potential and it felt like this was the beginning of something really fruitful.

It didn't last. By the following week, Lee was on a downer. On the Tuesday, he came in saying he couldn't listen to the tapes and was just generally negative and unenthusiastic about the whole project. He perked up a bit when Paul and Jim turned up and we got into chatting about a broad range of things. Sandy also called down out of the blue and popped in to see the room, ending up staying for a few hours. Lee had known Sandy as our friend back in 1986 and was keen to tell her how he'd been feeling over the past years. He got an awful lot out of it, and Jim was listening intently too. Paul was more reserved and spent most of the time fiddling with the equipment. Sandy seemed to understand a lot of what Lee was saying, reassuring him because he was a sensitive character. She talked of his aura and his personal problems. At Lee's request, she was happy to offer him some counselling in the near future. If he so desired.

After Sandy had gone, Lee said he thought she was boss. He said talking to her had helped to centre and balance him and he'd even felt better as soon as she came into the room. I was delighted by

Sandy's apparent stabilizing effect on Lee and hoped she could help him through his discomfort. He would need to be able to focus if we were to make progress musically.

I was still enjoying spending time with Lee, but he remained hard to read. Early in July I went down to the studio and he appeared to have changed tack altogether in that he wanted to work on new stuff and forget about the early demos – the thing which had fired his enthusiasm so much when we'd first met. I was fine about it in that I actually wanted to record new stuff with Lee, but I also had to consider whether putting my name on a contract for the studio space was a wise move. It would mean paying £1,800 for a year with no guarantee of an income because of the way Lee continually chopped and changed his mind. Meanwhile Lee had no money concerns: 'There She Goes' was a seemingly endless fount of revenue.

He was now becoming much more volatile and hot and cold the whole time. Yeah, the times he was on a high could be amazing, but I wanted to be sure I could at least get our album (*Breakloose: Lost La's 1984–1986*) out. Unlike Lee, I had no regular income. I'd been spending so much time on The La's Mk 2 that I had not been pursuing my artwork to the extent I was able to previously, and was basically skint.

When I put this dilemma to Lee, it seemed he didn't have the capacity or empathy to understand my situation. In addition to this, he was constantly changing his mind as to putting our demos out and a question mark that was drawn on the head of his favourite guitar (known as The Coffin) appeared over his head in my mind's eye. He just couldn't decide on anything. It was baffling and exhausting in equal measures. To me, it just seemed so damn simple. It seemed Lee was now solely committed to make reasons *not* to be productive. Whether this was/is a safety valve on his behalf that prevents failure only he can answer.

But I was sick of being pulled around by the nose and forced into dealing with someone else's mess like a Henry vacuum cleaner!

Things had to come to a head about all this. I was completely at a loss about what to do except stand my ground. It was then I was forced to realize that the new La's is – and will probably remain – a labouring, unproductive and stagnant project. There would need to be a seismic shift in Lee for it to break free and re-define itself as a force to be reckoned with a second time.

... He was like a kite caught in a tree.

Eventually, I said to Lee that I'd invested too much time and energy in this project not to see it through. When I start something, I finish it. That's the way it is with me and I had far greater financial constraints. I could have actually gone right ahead and released the tapes that I owned legally at any time since I had left The La's originally, and many others would have. But I hadn't even considered doing that without Lee's input – his inability to commit had now turned into a huge anchor.

I put my foot down and said we're going to release these tapes. We even knew how to do it all independently too, having already released an album on our Viper Label.

A couple of days later, I went to the studio again and this time Lee phoned to suggest he'd like to take the practice room on (which had previously been my studio) and pay the rent himself. I thought this could be a great idea. I certainly didn't want to see him high and dry. I had been helping him and would do so as much as possible to get him motivated once more.

Just when I was getting used to that idea, Lee kicked off with a load of bullshit the next night I went down the studio. He went into a real rant. According to him, Paul was smarmy; Paul and I had always been out to get him and all this other bullshit. It was clearly payback time. I had 'money in my talk' in doing the *Breakloose* LP and had apparently never intended anything other than making a profit for myself. I was stunned. What was the matter with him? It was like he had to block anything good happening and there was no method in his madness at all! I tried to take it all with a pinch of salt but it was really hurtful regardless.

Thinking about the way Lee had changed since January put my head in a spin. We'd agreed to a total 50/50 split in everything when we'd started The La's for a second time but that had all gone by the board. I suppose I should have seen the warning signs when Lee had suggested I learn his stuff and then he'd look at the ideas for new songs I had, which he had subsequently *never* done. The La's had never been like that in the '80s. It had originally been very natural and organic. We used to pitch ideas together and take them where we felt they needed to go. I guess I'd gotten too hung up trying to show both Lee and myself I could manage his guitar parts to realize I was falling for it all a second time.

After all the to-ing and fro-ing, though, I felt it was time to make a break. It didn't need to be permanent but maybe Lee needed a wake-up call if he wanted to really work with me. It wasn't that I was glad not to be working musically with Lee – I respected him deeply and hoped he got help for his compulsive indecisiveness and volatile manner – and I firmly believed that, deep down, he did want to make great music, but whether it would be enough for him to do anything concrete remained to be seen. I really hoped he could win his battle. The world deserved his immense talent; there was no getting away from that.

'My head, La! It's like Einstein's' office ... bits of paper stuck everywhere.' – Lee Mavers

Aside from his writing credits, Lee told me he wanted nothing in terms of sales from *Breakloose: Lost La's 1984–1986.* He said he had an income already and I should take the lot as I had a family to take care of. I had originally suggested we halve the profits, but I didn't intend to argue the toss. He was right: I did have a family to look after and had never received anything from The La's.

But for all that, I would ensure he got his appropriate credits on the songs he had helped me with and any songwriting royalties. I wished him well for the release of his self-compiled *Callin' All*: his own 'Lost La's' album. And I made sure that he had copies of all the tapes that I had of all The La's material from 1984 to 1986 to do with as he wished.

The following week, I went along to Rainhill Tapes and picked up the finished *Breakloose* master. It was that simple! I called over to see Paul and we listened to the finished CD, which we both really liked. We decided the album would be the second release on our fledgling Viper Label, following on from my solo debut. We'd be doing the album completely analogue for the vinyl and getting CDs done, too, because we needed to finance the vinyl.

I phoned Lee again, this time to give him the landlord's number in relation to him taking on the room for the studio. I briefed him on what to say and he rang me back ten minutes later to say he'd got it. I felt very relieved. Even though our time together hadn't worked out, I would have hated him to have had to dismantle all his equipment and leave the room we'd worked on.

It seems to me that when you work with Lee it has to be on his terms, but then he doesn't respect you. Stand up to him and you ain't going to be around, but he will respect you for standing your ground. Whatever the end result of all that is, it causes too much acrimony to deal with in the long run.

BROKELOOSE ONCE MORE.

******

A couple of days later, my journalist friend John Bennett called to ask whether I'd seen that day's copy of the *Daily Star* (like that was going to happen!). In it, Lee had referred to John Power's band Cast as 'crap' and 'spoiled brats'. The half-page article had the headline 'Mavers Breaks His Silence' and went on to say this candid chat was his 'first interview in ten years'.

It was really sad. It made Lee look bitter and twisted and he came off far worse than John Power (or 'Powers', as they called him in the text). Reading this article with Lee mouthing off had made me feel he'd walked into an elephant trap. He had as well. The journalist had phoned up just saying he was a fan and wanted a chat, and taped the whole thing, then printed his rant. When I saw Lee next he said this about it:

'I hold my hands up – I said it – but the *Daily Star*! I wouldn't wipe my arse with it.'

******

Wedding Bells

Looking back on it, I can't really explain exactly why Jeanette and I wanted to get married after living together so happily for twenty years and bringing two beautiful children into the world. It just felt right and there was a mutual understanding, I suppose. Besides, it was the best excuse possible for a party!

We'd set the date for Saturday, 31 July 1999 (twenty years to the day we'd gotten together on holiday in France), and the day couldn't come soon enough. We'd hired a troupe of flamenco dancers for the wedding ceremony and they were practising their routine by the time I reached the Unitarian Church Hall on Ullet Road, where our marriage would take place. By this time I was struggling to contain the strength of emotion I was feeling.

We'd decided on the Unitarian Church Hall (near its inglenook fireplace) for the ceremony partly because of its setting (it featured some truly beautiful sandstone masonry), but mostly because it was as near as we could get to a non-religious wedding ceremony, as the place was apparently all-embracing and tolerant of everyone's views. We'd liked the place for a long time and in fact it was also where both Amber and Ray had been to play-group.

Danny set up the sound for the music after the wedding and the guests started arriving around 4 o'clock. All our nearest and dearest were there and they all looked fantastic. We'd decided on a selection of classical music (John Williams, Caruso, J.S. Bach and some Django Reinhardt) to play in anticipation but words could barely describe the vision of beauty displayed by Jeanette and Amber (as bridesmaid) as they entered the hall for the ceremony. Nettee wore a golden kimono-style dress adorned with oriental patterns, while Amber wore a plain cream dress with a gold and red band on the waist.

A few minutes later we were officially Mr and Mrs Badger. I could hardly take it in – I felt like the luckiest man alive. Some of the 'pomp' was taken out of the ceremony itself when Ray saw fit to shout 'poo!' as loud as possible, much to everyone's delight. Ray looked really dapper too. He wore tartan pants and a traditional Scottish tweed jacket we'd bought in Aberdeen several years before.

Later on, we got into the entertainment provided by La Joya Flemenca, who went down a storm. We'd decided on the Spanish theme for the evening because it was something very unexpected and dynamic. All the stamping and swirling was breath-taking.

Then, more food was provided and our band for the night, Alaska (Danny Dean and Steve Roberts' band) plugged in and played a tremendous set.

Lee and Vada turned up, which was great, but it was interesting because John Power and Belinda were there too, and it was the first time they'd seen each other since the *Daily Star* article. When they eventually crossed paths John let on to Lee but Lee just ignored him ... Crazy damn dude.

Anyhow, we danced all night with our nearest and dearest and enjoyed the best day of our lives!

EIGHTEEN

Freedom Now

PAUL TOLD ME THAT *Uncut* magazine was keen to feature a track from our forthcoming *Breakloose* album on a compilation CD which would be on the cover of their October 1999 edition. We'd also been granted 'Rock Recommendation' status in the Virgin, HMV and Our Price shops in Liverpool. This meant that, for two weeks, Viper CDs would be in the racks and everyone walking into the shops would see them immediately as they entered the premises.

To get the album ready I needed to make a trip to London to have the songs mastered for the vinyl. Late in August, I left Lime Street station early in a train up to the Big Smoke. The place in question, Porky's Studio, was situated in Shaftesbury Avenue and I discovered the proprietor, George, to be a thoroughly decent bloke. It turned out he was from Liverpool (where else?) and was a legendary figure in his own right. He had worked with just about everyone who'd ever made a record in the UK and had long been known as the top man for cutting and mastering recordings in the country.

He retired a few years after our meeting, but I remember the time we spent together very fondly. He always played the tracks loud because his hearing was shot after years of mastering and he was well known for etching little messages into the vinyl's run-out to personalize them. As with most of his work, he etched 'A Porky Prime Cut', while on side one he inscribed 'Go the Whole Hog!' and on side two I asked him to inscribe 'Freedom now – Break loose!'

I really liked George. He intimately understood the whole magnetic vs digital sound issue that Lee and I had so often discussed. He made me realize the cut was still very much a part of the whole creative process. He was pleased I took such an interest and told me the only other guy he'd met in recent times who had wanted to be involved in a similar mastering process was one of the fellas from Cabaret Voltaire when some of his back catalogue had been making the transition from vinyl to CD. As a rule, George told me, musicians just got the master tapes and bunged 'em directly onto CD. If that was the case, it was no wonder they didn't sound as good after their digital mastering 'processes'.

John Bennett, who was now working for *MOJO*, completed a full and extensive feature on The La's, which had taken some doing on his behalf, and it had tied in with the release of *Breakloose*.

******

Finally we let go of the studio at 166B Aigburth Road.

When I thought of the place, so many amazing times flooded into my mind. I thought of all the energy and creativity that had flowed through it. The La's' amazing summer of 1986. John Power coming down to rehearse with us for the first time. Nettee doing her degree at Liverpool Art School. The Onset's whole history. Geoff Davies turning up to ask us if we'd do an album for Probe Plus. The practice room downstairs, all that fun and learning. The Onset's German tours. The cake shop and all the music parties and people gathering. The Kachinas. Amber arriving and lighting up our lives. The whole Tin Top sculpting experience. Ray being conceived and being carried by his Mum. Then, even after we'd moved to live primarily in Addingham Road, I'd still meet there weekly with friends and in recent times it had been a major catalyst in bringing The La's' unreleased material to a place where it would soon be available to the wider public. It would take some time for my soul to let go of the place.

There was also a new Viper Label HQ. This was to be a room on the top floor of Paul's new house in Dovedale Road off Penny Lane. We soon had a phone and fax line installed in there and finished off the furnishings with my little green, 1930s three-piece suite, which had also come from Dinas Lane.

While I was there, we got a call from S.R.D. to tell us that Woolworth's had agreed to stock the album. Maybe we could infiltrate the youth market after all. It was great news and must have had some effect in the end as *Breakloose* would eventually go on to become Viper's biggest seller, though I've always been aware it might not be appreciated as much by La's fans who associated the group entirely with Lee's songs. I know it was greeted with enthusiasm by the many local fans who knew the material on the album from when I had been a playing member in 1986.

✳✳✳✳✳✳

I called over to see Geoff Davies and went across the Pennines with him to see Half Man Half Biscuit play at a college in Todmorden in West Yorkshire.

I hadn't seen HMHB for a while and was keen to go, seeing as Geoff would be driving. The fact it was Todmorden intrigued me. The Onset played near there once and Tony Russell's girlfriend, Katrine from Germany, had seen the name and mentioned with horror that it translated as 'death murder' in German! Also, there had once been a local phenomenon known as the 'Todmorden Lights', where mysterious displays of lights had been seen in the sky that no one could satisfactorily explain. It reminded me of the 'Lubbock Lights', similar strange lights that had been spotted at night in Buddy Holly's Texas hometown during the 1950s.

I saw Nigel Blackwell before the show and he told me about a discussion he'd had with a promoter at another of their gigs. The guy had been in possession of a copy of the *Elegance, Charm and Deadly Danger* compilation and apparently said he was considering bootlegging The La's' two tracks as they were so rare. Nigel told him about our release as a result, but it only confirmed for me that we were right to put *Breakloose* out. If we hadn't addressed the issue of The

La's' early tapes, they would surely have surfaced anyway, but without proper mastering or packaging and design.

******

I had sent the publisher Dick Leahy Music some press and an introductory letter and they'd requested some music in response. I'd sent them *Volume* to check out, and their man Peter Stratton phoned me up to say how much he'd enjoyed the album.

The upshot was that I arranged a meeting with him the following week. I did some research into his background and discovered he had strong links with Merseyside, having previously published both Ian Broudie and Michael Head (Shack's *Waterpistol* album), as well as George Michael. That impressed me, though to be honest I'd initially approached him because his office was situated at 1 Star Street! The name really appealed to me as the ideal address for a publisher.

My meeting with Peter proved amiable enough. His Star Street office had a framed *NME* cover of Michael Head on the wall (saying 'This Man Is Our Greatest Songwriter' – good on you, Mick!). Peter seemed a lovely guy and Dick Leahy Music was certainly in a position to help advance careers for guys like me. He had owned the Bell Record label during the 1970s. However, when I stated that I had never had a publishing deal in my life, Peter looked incredulous. He composed himself and asked me how I'd managed to survive?

'I just have', I said, disarmingly. What else could I say? It was the truth, after all.

NINETEEN

Double Zero

THANKFULLY, THE MOMENTUM IN my sculpting career then showed an upturn. The opportunity of a joint exhibition with fellow Huyton artist Amanda Ralph – herself a very talented sculptor – was about to become reality, with plans for a show in Gostin's building being confirmed for early in 2000. Early in November, I met up with Amanda to discuss the invites for the preliminary private viewing and also the catering, supplying the wine, etc.

The exhibition was a great success. I sold quite a lot of pieces and enjoyed the ambience of the gallery, where I would write a lot of my diary entries in my spare time. Adrian Henri attended in his wheelchair after he had suffered a massive stroke. Catherine, Adrian's girlfriend, had always got him out of the house, though, maintaining a solid interest in the local arts scene. There's a nice photograph of me taken there with Adrian Henri (he had referred to Amanda Ralph as 'a poet of the found object'). Adrian had attended the exhibition and bought another of my sculptures – the *Bella* car – for Catherine. The piece was one of my favourites, too: I'd crafted it from a corned beef can I'd picked up at a supermarket in France some years before.

The same day, I called in to see Steve Hardstaff. He worked in the graphics department of the Liverpool Art School, in the Hahnemann Building on Hope Street. We had a cup of tea and talked about Buddy Holly, Johnny Burnette, reggae and a load more. Knowing Steve to be a great authority where all things 1950s rock 'n' roll were concerned, I told him about an idea that I had also put to Paul about the release of a sci-fi rockabilly compilation (mostly based around early '50s rock 'n' roll recordings) on Viper. The revenue that we had received from the lost La's *Breakloose* album had now given us license to look further afield at other potential releases. Steve was immediately taken with the idea and even suggested he do the cover himself – right answer! Ironically, we might never have had the idea had it not been for the *Jukebox at Eric's* album he had helped compile with Roger Eagle.

It was great news, not least because – with Steve's knowledge – he could help with compiling and writing the sleeve notes as well, though I already had the beginnings of a themed album. Steve had released a couple of collections of obscure country blues on his Pigmeat imprint, and I felt that if this possible project went well Viper could end up doing a lot of work in tandem with him. He really was the Number One Aficionado where early roots-of-rock 'n' roll was concerned.

We'd already been thinking of some possible titles (like *Flying Saucer Boogie, Rocket in My Pocket, Satellite Boogie* and *Flying Saucer Rock 'n' Roll*) but if Steve could round it out with some more discerning choices we were well on our way to making it a reality.

Much as I loved my artwork, music was still my main concern as we headed towards the end of the millennium. Encouraged by the response to *Volume*, I'd also started writing and rehearsing new songs with Paul. They were already sounding a lot brasher and much more in the rock 'n' roll vein. I'd written one called 'Bottom of the Hill', which was one of the hardest rockers I'd ever been involved in and we were really buzzing about it. I was hoping to record the new tracks as soon as possible and I knew the record would be an album that declared itself 'here'. It felt right to do a heavier electric album after the breezy, ethereal *Volume*.

✶✶✶✶✶✶

Steve Hardstaff agreed to help bring the sci-fi rockabilly compilation *The Ultimate 50s Rockin' Sci-Fi Disc* to fruition with us and Paul and I had a number of really positive meetings with him around this time. Steve was a mine of information and a great help in guiding us through the protocol required in releasing other people's recordings. Through him, we discovered it was a lot easier to release work if the source material was over fifty years old. As he'd promised, he'd come up with some other titles he suggested we include, and by the time we'd thrashed it all out we had the makings of what sounded like a great record.

One day, over at Steve's in Tranmere on the Wirral, I was just leaving when I bumped into Chris Sharrock, ex-La's drummer (among many other bands). Chris had lived next door to Steve for years and he was moving house at the time. I hadn't seen him in the flesh for a while, but of course he'd been busy touring with both The Lightning Seeds and – in more recent times – Robbie Williams. He had only recently returned from the States and he told me he had seen copies of our *Breakloose* CD available for sale on import in a Los Angeles record store. Wow. Chris then offered his services to play drums when I told him about my plans to record some new songs.

In the first month of the new millennium I wanted to make a reality of a new solo album titled *Double Zero*. Taking up Chris's offer of drumming, Martyn Campbell's bass skills and Paul playing lead guitar, we set things up and we had a couple of practices as a quartet, working up the arrangements to my new, harder-rocking songs at the Stables at Paul's Mum's place. What a pleasure it was to work with those guys. They were all used to playing with each other and knew each other inside out. The songs came together really quickly. Wham bam, job done.

We all wanted to make a point of making the songs sound as 'live' as possible, so all the bass and drums were recorded live in the studio and even some of Paul and my guitars were put down the same way. I insisted on there not being any acoustic instruments at all in contrast to the wholly acoustic approach on *Volume* and wanted a hard-driving, rock 'n' roll album. Working with Chris, Martyn and Paul was great and it took a while for it to sink in. It felt like a dream and what I really dug was that they all enjoyed being given the freedom of expression to do their own thing. I'd made a point of letting them sort their own parts out and the record benefitted no end from it.

The album was made very much as a four-man unit, but when it came to overdubbing and adding a few more flourishes, I asked Tommy Scott to add his formidable vocals to 'With You' and the wistful 'Autumn in the Mind'. Paul's younger brother Tim also contributed backing vocals to both songs, adding a low register vocal with Paul on 'Autumn in the Mind', while Danny Dean came in to add some blinding lead guitar on both 'Underworld' and during the middle instrumental part of the final track, 'Hear Me Calling You'. Paul then added a picked guitar riff to 'Fashion Victim', and I re-did the twangy guitar parts I'd recorded for my version of Roky Erickson's 'Clear Night for Love'.

I'd wanted to record 'Clear Night for Love' for ages. I'd walked into the Probe shop when it was still in Button Street one day in 1990 and they were playing the track. It hooked me instantly. It was such a beautiful, no-nonsense song full of innocence and love. It was from Roky's *All That May Do My Rhyme* album and it was the song that really got me into him and then the 13th Floor Elevators. It was – as it said on the sleeve – 'Made in Texas by Texans' and it said everything I needed to know. I loved recording the song with the lads and had really got into the twangy lead lines Luther Perkins-style on my new green Burns guitar.

The title *Double Zero* itself was wordplay, in the sense that twice nothing is even more nothing and it was related to being in the first month of the year '00.

✶✶✶✶✶✶

During February 2000, one of what Paul and I believed to be our minor projects suddenly came to fruition in a way neither of us would ever have believed. Paul had a friend called Esther McVey who had been a TV presenter and host on Channel 5. He'd known her on and off for a long time and she was now in a relationship with a guy called Mal Young (from Roby, down the road from Huyton) who was with the BBC. I'd gotten to know Esther too when Paul had taken her along to see my *Lost and Found* exhibition during 1997.

Paul and I had previously put a pitch in for the soundtrack to a short-lived BBC series called *Sunburn*, which had come to nothing, so we didn't have great expectations when Esther told us about a new series Mal (now an executive producer with the Beeb) was commissioning called *Doctors* and that he wanted us to put some music together for it.

We gave it a go. Paul came up with a chord sequence and I finished it off by simply reversing it to round it off, so it didn't take long. We sent it off, expecting nothing and got a reply from Mal saying it was great, when could we record it properly? It all happened so fast, we had no idea at the time that it was actually going to be a long-running BBC drama on BBC 1.

When we came to record it, Mal, to his credit, also turned up at the session to supply enthusiasm and handclaps and we got the whole thing down in a few hours. We drafted Leon from Space in on drums and again called on Martyn Campbell to play bass.

We'd been professional about it, but hardly sweated either. Little did we know when we recorded it that it would be used for all of the 36 episodes that went out during 2000, let alone the hundreds of episodes that have been screened since and continue to be scripted fifteen years on.

Since that time, our *Doctors* theme has gone on to give us a royalty which has helped the Viper Label survive, so that one little session proved its worth in gold. With typical irony the track itself was probably one of the least meaningful pieces of creativity I've been involved with – but the most financially rewarding. It's heard every day by millions of people all over the world. So much for pouring your heartfelt emotions into your songs.

Don't get me wrong, I'm still pleased as punch to have played a part in it, but I suppose it's the fickle nature of the creative industries. A final twist was that they never used the mix we thought they would, which has a guitar line through it by Paul that shouts 'I'm a TV theme tune'. Instead, they opted for the simple chord version. The BBC even nominated it for an Ivor Novello award.

As for Esther – what can you say? This was before she entered those dark corridors of power as a Tory MP and hooked up with Iain Duncan Smith to strip funds from the disabled and most vulnerable in our society.

※ ※ ※ ※ ※ ※

Danny Dean and Steve Roberts had moved their acoustic evening to Liverpool at the Zanzibar. The Acoustic Engine was a brilliant platform for emerging singer-songwriters. I played there quite a bit, as did many local luminaries like The Hokum Clones, Nick Saunders, Vinny Peculiar, the magnificent first incarnation of Tramp Attack and simply too many more to mention.

It made for some memorable evenings. There was generally a very reverent atmosphere with most people coming in, being respectful and really listening to the songs, but the Zanzibar had originally been a dance venue, so occasionally you got strays coming in wanting to party. On one occasion, a couple of girls came in and wanted to let loose. What was going on here? One of them got on stage during Vinny Peculiar's set and lifted her top to show the whole crowd a most exquisite pair of breasts. I'm afraid poor old Vinny was never gonna compete with those!

At another Acoustic Engine gig, two older fellas came in and were sitting there trying to be good and listen even though they'd had a good few drinks – you just knew they were really looking for more action. They were sitting opposite Roger and me and after one particularly solemn, deep, reflective song, one knowingly said to the other with a wry smile:

'I never knew the world was in such a state!'

Roger and I ended up rolling around the benches in laughter. These two guys had, with perfect Liverpool timing, just hit the nail on the head at that moment.

The Acoustic Engine spread its wings a little after a while and began doing some out-of-town venues, including a little wine bar in Maghull called Bar Du Fey. During April, Dan and Steve told me about this girl called Lizzie Nunnery they were putting on there. She was only sixteen, but Steve was enthusing about her. She'd already knocked the audience out the first time she'd played at the little venue and when I went along to see her with Martyn Campbell she blew us away too. This girl was writing these songs with the most profound lyrics that had such depth, and she could really turn a tune too. We thought she was amazing.

Paul and I would go on to record some tracks with Lizzie a few months later, but nothing came out in the end. It was a good project for all concerned and I think she was grateful of the chance to get these first versions of her songs down.

******

Another great old friend of mine re-entered my life. Jonee Mellor now opened the Magnet with Eddie O'Callaghan. Jonee and Eddie had the right idea. They wanted to create something really worthwhile for Liverpool. The decor in the Magnet was great – deep red and sultry, flock wallpaper with gorgeous signs on glass with lights behind them. Ollo, an old mate from Huyton and The La's days, had done all the upholstery and between them they had it looking like a kind of American speakeasy/diner.

Jonee asked me if I would install an assemblage cabinet I had previously exhibited. It consisted of thirty small boxed shelves I had found. Over time, I had filled the shelves with curios: tins, model people, exotic packets, weird ceramics and a range of unusual found objects – and Jonee was well into it. He wanted it at the foot of the stairs in the club and once he had installed it I wired a small light into each box, five across in six layers, before painting each box a different colour.

Then I put a variety of objects in and we placed a piece of Perspex over the top of it to stop people taking stuff. It looked amazing and I was given a fee to change the contents three times a year to keep it interesting for the regulars, and that carried on for about six years. I ended up scouring car boot sales for all nature of unlikely things, but I was indebted to Jonee and Eddie, who were true patrons of the arts.

******

My *Double Zero* album was finally released in June 2000. There wasn't a big fanfare, although *Mojo* rang requesting a picture of me to run with their review, which turned out to be very positive. Journalist Steve Rippon wrote it and said some nice things:

> Tracks like 'Bottom of the Hill' and 'Fashion Victim' sound like refugees from a lost Buzzcocks album. The John Barry-esque bass motif of 'Shadow of the Real World' and sitar-like guitars of 'Field of Heartache' hark back effectively to different Sixties pop traditions. Had The La's been able to accommodate both Badger and Lee Mavers, could world domination have been far away?

Much later, the album would also receive some unexpected praise from the US, courtesy of a review in *Goldmine* by Jo-Ann Greene, who proclaimed: '*Double Zero* is a tight, joyously melodic collection of a dozen absolutely effervescent guitar-driven pop songs and storming garage-psych rockers'.

In terms of promotion and playing shows to support the record's release, it was all very low-key. I did one great support show for The Clint Boon Experience at the Zanzibar, which was just me with my new Marquee Burns guitar, but I also did a few shows as a duo with Paul. I believe they were good, but I can remember playing a pub room on the banks of the Mersey in Rock Ferry and Paul complaining, 'God … from Glastonbury to this!' I loved playing with him as always, but felt at that particular time he'd forgotten how lucky he'd been to have played the main stage at Glastonbury.

******

Danny Dean told me about a new band who played one of his nights called Tramp Attack. I got to see them playing at the Hanover Hotel on Hanover Street with Dave Jackson, who I'd just met in town. What a treat. Every song was brilliant. What a bunch of scoundrels. I remember clearly Matt Barton's 'Barrel of Fun', Dave McCabe's 'Broken Man' and Jay Redmond's 'Ladybird'. Ian Lane played a solid beat behind them all and Kristian Healey on lead vocals shouting out 'Please let there be a double-decker bus'. It was like watching The Strawberry Alarm Clock mixed with The Creation gone Merseybeat.

As a result of this, Paul and I went down to their practice room in view of putting them in the studio. We also took a bunch of discs down for them, which they seemed very pleased with.

The next time we went down to the practice room to see them, I was flattered when I walked in and Dave McCabe was going through the chords of my old La's song 'Moonlight'. Not long after, Sean Payne came in for a chat and mentioned a benefit gig that was to be held at the Zanzibar for a local guy who'd recently been shot. He said that Lee was going to be getting up and playing 'In My Life', to which Paul added sharply, 'I've done nothing in the last ten years.'

It didn't take us long before we got Tramp Attack into the Lab studio and witnessed them laying down five ace recordings. You never would have believed that they'd never been in a studio before. Kristian Healey howled out like a man possessed. When I saw Dave McCabe put down the lead guitar to 'Broken Man' in one take, I remember thinking, 'My God, this nineteen-year-old kid's got it.'

TWENTY

In a Viper Style

BACK IN THE MUSICAL universe, one of Viper's most important historical releases came to fruition during the summer of 2000. Legends don't come much larger than Arthur Lee from the influential late-'60s outfit Love – not in Liverpool anyhow – and through Paul's persistence we managed to get clearance to release Arthur's live show with Shack backing him from their show at the Liverpool Academy in May 1992.

Like the album itself, how Arthur Lee came to play with Shack in the UK is convoluted to say the least. Promoter Keith Curtis' sleeve notes probably supply the most coherent version of events:

> At the time, we worked with a group called Dr. Phibes and the House of Wax Equations who played regularly at the Locomotive Club in Paris along with several other bands. Through these French contacts, we met Stephane Bismuth who we found out was managing Arthur Lee. A deal was struck – Arthur was to play London and Liverpool, backed by Shack, who were part of the Liverpool/Paris axis as well as being massive Love aficionados.

The gig itself found Arthur and Shack (featuring Mick and John Head and then-Rain man Martyn Campbell on bass) playing songs from Love's classic trio of early albums, and immediately passed into legend. Paul had the tape of the gig, as his good friend Keith Curtis had promoted the show, and he took it upon himself to write to Arthur Lee in prison in California – diligence. At the time, Arthur was incarcerated on drugs and firearms charges because of the 'three strikes and you're out' laws they had in California and we didn't really expect an answer.

We could hardly believe it when we heard back from Arthur's lawyer. We had wanted to know if he would be into the tape of the show being released – he was enthusiastic about the idea and we got clearance immediately. Well, almost immediately – we did have to draw up a contract for him in jail via his lawyer, but we soon sorted it out. Probably the fact that Arthur had enjoyed the shows so much playing with the Head brothers and company helped our cause.

The record itself was not the greatest quality recording Viper ever released, but it's certainly one of the most spirited and it's a very important record of a great night in Liverpool on both CD and vinyl. We always put the spirit of the performance as paramount. Typically crazily, we asked Arthur himself to supply some sleeve notes to sit along Bernie Connor's appraisal of the band Love and the Liverpool show. However, because of the protracted mail process with the prison system we didn't get them and had the sleeve all designed and ready to go when, to our surprise, his notes finally arrived – literally the same morning the sleeves were going to print! So we could include them after all. In these notes Arthur was full of praise and even described the gig in Liverpool as 'the most memorable of my life'.

✱✱✱✱✱✱

With the Viper Label, eclecticism was the key. We were keen to get archival stuff out there, but also to release great local artists. During the summer of 2000, I'd bumped into Dave Jackson again, former frontman of The Room and Benny Profane. He'd told me about his new project, a band called Dead Cowboys, and had given me a tape of their songs.

Dave was and remains a great wordsmith. The La's' very first gig in St Helens was with was Benny Profane and I'd later played with them in The Onset. Another thing in Dead Cowboys' favour was that their guitarist, Greg Milton, had been in another great Liverpool band called Barbel, whom I loved. Both Paul and I liked their tape a lot and I believed it to be among the best things the guys had ever done. It seemed like we were on the same path, so we were well up for doing the first album with them.

Elsewhere, there was a typically convoluted story behind how we came to release our Captain Beefheart and His Magic Band's live album. I had a tape of the band's live show from Liverpool's Rotters Club in 1980, which I'd originally got via Roger Eagle. Much as I loved Beefheart, I hadn't actually listened to it for years, but it sounded great and we were keen to release it as Roger would have approved of it and he wasn't with us anymore. I was keen to do it as a tribute to Roger as much as anything.

We tried to get in touch with Don Van Vliet himself, hoping he would give his blessing, but it was no great surprise when we didn't hear back. We knew he had completely distanced himself from the machinations of the music business since his last album, *Ice Cream for Crow*, in 1982 and hadn't expected miracles. Still, we thought we would go ahead with the release anyway, the plan being to make a donation to Greenpeace (a big deal with the animal-loving, environmentally conscious Captain) from the profits.

On the morning we went in to master the tape, though, again in perfect timing we got a right shock. We discovered that a label called Ozit Records was literally about to release the same show on CD. So what to do? Well, we realized there was a lot more Beefheart material out there and decided to make our release into a *Live in the UK* album instead and include the better tracks from the Liverpool recording.

It became a comedy of errors. Chris Hewitt from Ozit phoned Viper's number and tried to have it out with Paul for us allegedly nicking his tape. Ironic, bearing in mind the tape had been in circulation in all the right Liverpool circles for years. The phone call was a red rag for Paul, who had taken the call by chance.

Mr Ozit claimed his office in LA had been talking to Beefheart himself, which was a hilarious notion. No way would he have had any contact with Ozit or any other labels, as we'd recently found out the hard way. The guy was talking nonsense and Paul shot him down in flames.

In the end, our Captain Beefheart album (*Magnetic Hands: Captain Beefheart and His Magic Bands, Live in the UK 72–80*) was released with tracks also taken from Magic Band performances in Portsmouth and the 1972 Bickershaw Festival – Bernie Connor again delivering resplendent sleeve notes ... albeit at gunpoint!

We later tried to make a donation to Greenpeace on account of Don but the cheque was returned to us with a note telling us they didn't accept donations from businesses!

Our remit with such 'recording quality' limits has always been a case of if a great performance merits its release, then we would try to do the best we could with the recording during the mastering process. At Viper, we've always felt it shouldn't be a case of production over content. Just because technology has moved on and people expect a new clarity to the sound of records, that doesn't over-ride a band's or musician's performance. If you wanted to go on sound quality alone, would you have ever discovered Robert Johnson, Charley Patton, Jimmie Rodgers and the Carter Family? Didn't those early recordings have all the ingredients to thrill our very souls?

✱✱✱✱✱✱

Just prior to Christmas came the news of Adrian Henri's death. He'd passed away after a long illness at the age of 68 on 20 December 2000 and I lit a candle in his honour.

In the way that music and art went hand in hand for me, for Adrian it was art and poetry. Collaborating with Roger McGough and Brian Patten as the Mersey Poets, Adrian would be a big part of the best-selling *The Mersey Sound* anthology and could count the likes of jazz legend George Melly, playwright Willy Russell and beat poet Allen Ginsberg among his circle of friends. His verse was influenced by both surrealist art and the French symbolist school of poetry, but he was always a firm believer in the importance of live poetry reading, hence our first meeting that memorable first time in King's Cross in 1984.

When I had taken his purchase of the *Leningrad Cowboy* car to his house after my exhibition in 1997, the experience turned out to be amazing. His house was full of paintings and sculptures and one in particular of a woman's head with spikes coming from the top made a real impression on me. We had a good talk that afternoon and I got to know his girlfriend Catherine too. They were both really happy to have the car, which they then parked on the mantelpiece. Adrian showed me a copy of a Frida Kahlo book he had gotten from a bargain bookshop in town. It was a printed copy of her notes and sketchbooks and it was beautiful. I went straight there and bought a copy for Jeanette.

Sadly, after that Adrian had suffered a huge stroke. A little while later at one of the Mersey Festivals of Street Art in Williamson Square, I was making a yellow submarine from Coleman's mustard tins for the Beatles-themed event and people would occasionally stop and have a word. Suddenly, I noticed this bloke in a wheelchair watching me. I smiled at him and carried on, later Phil Battle from the Festival of Street Art said to me, 'Have you seen Adrian?' I replied, truthfully, that I hadn't. Phil told me the bloke I'd seen in the wheelchair had been Adrian and I felt my heart sink. I felt so crap I hadn't recognized him. I had heard he'd had a massive stroke, but from once being so big, Adrian had become so emaciated he looked like a different guy altogether. It was upsetting knowing that he realized I hadn't recognized him and it ate away at me. Later that day I made a point of saying 'Hi Adrian' to him, trying to redeem myself, but it was so sad trying to converse with him discovering his speech had also been so badly affected. And this for one of Liverpool's most articulate sons.

Adrian's girlfriend, Catherine, was an angel with him though. From then on he was often to be seen at the openings of exhibitions and he attended all the Festival of Street Art events. Catherine even got him back painting at the Bridewell and was an incredible carer for him. God only knows what would have happened to the poor man without her. Wonderfully, Adrian's speech improved and I remember seeing a late period photograph of him actually standing up in an article from the *Sunday Times* magazine.

It was ironic that it would be in these last few years of his life that I would actually get to know him best.

The last time I saw Adrian was shortly after the Gostin's exhibition, at a huge retrospective the Walker Art Gallery had put on. I was pleased this had happened and the timing was perfect, to see all his paintings in one place and in Liverpool's grandest gallery of all. It seemed entirely fitting. The last thing he said to me was about the *Bella* tin car. He'd quietly reminded me about it behind Catherine's back, as it was intended as a surprise for her. I replied that I had it there for her.

'Keep it dark, it's a black pudding', I said to him. He laughed. It was a nice way to remember him.

Adrian's funeral service took place on 3 January 2001 at Liverpool's enormous Anglican Cathedral.

TWENTY-ONE

Callin' All:
Lost La's 1986–1987

I N THE EARLY PART of 2001, Paul and I were determined to bring to fruition an idea which had been germinating in our heads for a while. Because we'd both been involved in the Liverpool scene for a long time, it dawned on us that there was a load of great locally recorded stuff out there which merited either re-release or the chance to see the light of day at last.

I suppose the whole *Nuggets* compilation mentality and the fact I'd loved Roger Eagle's *Jukebox at Eric's* compilation made us all the more determined to release a collection of great under-rated local recordings. It turned out to be a real labour of love because the more we looked, the more we found and it soon became apparent that we'd have to do more than just one collection in our *Unearthed* series. I approached the ever knowledgeable Bernie Connor to help with the sleeve notes again for the CD booklet (he submitted a great essay called 'Once Upon a Time in the West' as an introduction) and he also pointed us towards more great tracks, like lost psychedelic rock classic 'Run of the Dove' by The Last Chant.

Compiling the tracks proved remarkably easy. Almost all the artists involved were either friends or associates, but then Liverpool was intimate that way – *Big enough to be a city, yet still small enough to be a village.*

There were few exceptions and even anyone we didn't know well enough to approach personally came into the equation through friends of friends.

In the end, *Unearthed: Liverpool Cult Classics Volume 1* was released in March 2001, housed in a sleeve featuring an old tin globe I had. I liked the fact it gave the record an aspect of global importance, which of course Liverpool has.

The compilation featured wonderful, often out-of-print or hard-to-find tracks (spanning the late '70s to the early '90s) by The Wild Swans, The Stairs, Space, It's Immaterial, Benny Profane, The Tambourines and Barbel, among others. Paul and I were really proud of it and even more gratified when the reviews were almost universally positive.

The *Big Issue in the North* set the ball rolling almost straight away, commenting that 'It's not just '70s bands, this worthy compilation spans Liverpool's music scene up to the early '90s. Roll on Volume 2!'

Mojo and *Uncut* both weighed in behind with glowing critiques during April. *Mojo* noted, 'The Mancs had eclipsed the Scousers by the end of the '80s but this collection of rare and unreleased tracks regains some ground', while *Uncut* were moved enough to describe the album as a 'storming collection of Scouse nuggets – local heroes by the bucket load'.

Sales were quite decent and we were encouraged enough to collate a second volume, which would be released in October 2001. In retrospect, that was a mistake because reviewers saw the title and generally passed on it, the feeling being that they'd already covered it. Also, getting a second volume together quickly ate up the small profit we'd made from the first, so with hindsight we should have waited a while. But Viper remained a learning curve for us, so we accepted the knocks and later did a third volume. I'm really proud of the trilogy now, because I feel we did a service to a great number of Liverpool musicians who could quite easily have slipped into oblivion.

✱✱✱✱✱✱

Pam Young called me to say *Q* magazine wanted to interview me about The La's. Pam was a darling and she'd pitched in trying to work my *Double Zero* album off her own bat. She'd been involved in the industry for years, having worked for The Bunnymen, Julian Cope, The Pale Fountains, Sun Ra and many more, and she was working for The Big Kids at the time (even though she'd split with Edgar in her personal life). I had my reservations about the *Q* interview because there were times when the whole La's thing just felt like an albatross, but Pam convinced me to do it not least to promote my new album.

'The thing is, if you don't contribute, they're gonna write it anyway', she said very wisely, 'and probably get it wrong'. So off I went and met the journalist at the Penny Lane Wine Bar. He seemed like a decent guy and we spoke for quite some time.

A little time elapsed and then the article appeared. In it, I had a line or two referring to Lee and that was that. I wasn't happy, but it was becoming predictable. To be fair to him, the journalist called me personally to apologize for the content of the piece. He told me quite frankly that he'd included most of what I'd said only for it to be edited out before publication and that was the way it was.

I pretty much decided there and then never to do any more interviews relating to The La's period, but I did relent for the massive American magazine *Sports Illustrated* because the writer in question called me personally and it was obvious he was a massive La's fan. I got such a genuine email from him that I agreed to do it against my better judgement and in the wild hope they might actually be interested in some of the things I'd done since. That was naive. Even in that case, the article became a eulogy about Lee Mavers being Liverpool's Syd Barrett or Brian Wilson and the scissors came out when it came to what I'd been doing in the interim. It did my head in sometimes.

Still, whether I liked it or not, interest in The La's remained as keen as ever years after the fact and sometimes it seemed to shadow both Paul and myself. Around this time, we discovered that Mick Moss had sold his original multi-track demos of The La's he'd recorded at the Picket in May 1987. This meant that whoever bought them could – theoretically – release them as the fabled 'original' La's demos, even though they actually weren't, as the proper 'original' La's demos (with the exception of 'Way Out') were the ones Lee and I, along with John Power and several drummers, had recorded across 1985–86.

These were the versions of the songs that held the magic, something that Lee himself had admitted often enough since. After all, it was in an attempt to recapture the magic of those 1986 recordings that Lee had forced the band and record company through all the abandoned sessions and false starts which would finally lead to the 'official' 1990 La's album, which he then so pointedly disowned.

But I still had all the original recordings. They were my master tapes and all great quality. I had given Lee copies of them all a couple of years before in 1999 when we had been going through what tapes existed but he had chosen not to do anything with them since.

Prompted by the news that the Picket reels from 1987 had been sold, Paul and I believed it was the right time for the release of those original 1986 La's recordings, coupled with a great live recording Paul had acquired from Martyn Campbell of a spectacular May 1987 La's gig at the Picket where the band played 'There She Goes' live for the very first time with Paul on lead guitar.

Consequently, what shortly became the second 'Lost La's' album, *Callin' All*, was born. This time, the emphasis was very much on the songs Lee wrote (with the exception of the title track – the fabled 'Callin' All' – which would at last get the chance to shine). We were all unanimous on which were the best versions of the songs available. If we didn't do it now it was only going to be a matter of time before an inferior set of 'original' recordings surfaced, quite possibly under the title *The Fabled Demos*, so we needed to do it officially – and quickly.

Neither myself or Paul wanted this to come as a surprise to Lee so I let him know our intentions, telling him about the sale of the 1987 demos (the Mick Moss Picket sessions) and telling him exactly what our plans were for what would become *Callin' All: Lost La's 1986–1987.* Even though they were our tapes, I still felt I should give Lee the opportunity to stop them coming out if he wished. As it turned out, Lee raised no objection and he has since acknowledged that we did a good job. We did.

I was – and remain – genuinely glad he felt that way because I had a motivation to try and help Lee get that monkey off his back re: the tapes he really loved being released. I truly felt it might also give him the opportunity to move on in his life and it seemed absolutely the right thing to do. It had been no surprise to us really that he had just sat on the recordings I'd given him.

That feeling only intensified when we took the tapes to One Stop in Prescot (formerly RTS) to have them mastered properly. They sounded amazing. The first side had great versions of 'Son of a Gun', 'Doledrum', 'Liberty Ship', 'Freedom Song', 'Clean Prophet', 'IOU', an acoustic Lee version of 'Tears in the Rain' and our epic track 'Callin' All'. The tracks making up the second side of the vinyl version would have selected highlights from The La's' riotous gig from the Picket in May 1987, featuring Paul on lead guitar.

The first-ever live recording of 'There She Goes' would be included – complete with a totally different middle-eight section – and a version of 'Timeless Melody' featuring a section from my 'Open Your Heart'. It concluded with what sounded like flying saucers taking off at the end of a frenzied version of 'Failure', and I knew there and then that the album would make some serious waves.

We realized that Lee was right all along in that the official La's album was a pale reflection of these magical recordings, but I also found along the way in the production of the album that I was proud to recall my own contributions, many of which I had forgotten in my reluctance to go there. This was turning into a cathartic event for me too. These were mostly Lee's songs, yes, but I had brought in guitar parts, harmonies, backing vocals and helped with the arrangements. I had tended to dismiss my contributions to these songs in the past, but now I could see them as being incomplete without what I'd brought to the table.

I also realized this was very much the case where Paul's time in The La's was concerned. His guitar work really shone on the 1987 live recording and he too brought his own character to Lee's songs, not least 'There She Goes', on which Paul had helped Lee with the guitar arrangement in the Stables. In fact I can honestly say if we hadn't taken the bull by the horns those particular recordings would never officially have surfaced and the world would have been worse without them.

Sleeve notes for *Callin' All* were supplied by John Bennett, someone who had previously painstakingly researched the early La's story for *Mojo*, and a sterling job he did.

Danny and Steve's Acoustic Engine evenings, which I'd been enjoying (and performing at), continued to be a vital showcase for great local talent. It was at one of these nights (at the Zanzibar) that I first ran across Robby Stevenson and Danny Roberts. Together, they were The Hokum Clones and I caught them playing an amazing version of the old murder ballad 'Stagger Lee'. It knocked me out. I can remember the first time sitting down with Robby, I rolled a joint with some Gold Seal Hashish. 'Bet you never got that in Huyton', he sniggered, and I was happy to hear that he was another Roby Lad.

Soon after, Robby came over to my place to hang out and before long Viper began recording The Hokum Clones in a variety of different ways. They had a remarkable acoustic take of old blues sounds, so we wanted to preserve that raw and ancient feel of theirs, which was still somehow totally contemporary in its own way. We tried all kinds of things, before finally settling upon a tiny Dictaphone! It had the perfect sound when we spun it back through the mixing desk we had set up in my attic in Croydon Avenue.

One night, The Hokum Clones were playing up there and were just finishing a stunning take of the old Robert Johnson tune 'If I Had Possession Over Judgement Day' with Robby hollerin' like a man possessed. It woke Amber up and she stuck her head in the hole leading up to the attic to find out what the hell was going on. She was confused, but intrigued as well. I remember thinking 'I hope she remembers that moment', because she was witnessing history in my book and I would rather wake the kids up with something as charged as that than anything else I could imagine – even if it was a school night. In the end, this recording would feature on the Viper compilation *The Great Liverpool Acoustic Experiment* and – sure enough – it was the track John Peel chose to air on his radio show.

The attic proved to be a place of great creativity for a while. We had temporarily moved to ours because Paul's wife Rachael was now pregnant and didn't need a load of musicians traipsing through the house all the time. When Matt Barton and Ian Laney had split from the first version of Tramp Attack (Dave McCabe had started working with Boyan Chowdhury in what would become The Zutons), we recorded their new project, The Mother Lovers, in the Viper attic studio.

At the time, Matt had just finished his course at LIPA and met Paul McCartney at the leaving ceremony. He'd apparently asked Paul whether he liked the name Tramp Attack or The Mother Lovers more as a band name. When Paul suggested The Mother Lovers was better, they went with that for a while. They recorded 'Rex' in our attic around the same time Edgar Jones came over to record 'Hey Mister', and I recorded my blues montage 'Memphis Egypt' … Talk about having your own post code!

******

Paul and I had sent copies of *Callin' All* out well before its release date and it had created a lot of press interest. It wasn't officially released until July 2001, but as early as the end of May it was voted number one in the *Mojo* chart and we were getting a lot of good feedback.

When the reviews started rolling in, they were very enthusiastic. *Mojo* followed through on their positive vibe, suggesting these versions of the songs had 'an endearing humanity' and were 'spine-tingling'. *Record Collector* also weighed in with words of praise: 'one of those great lost bands, it's as if you're in on a secret before it's even been told'. Perhaps the most satisfying notice, though, came from producer Mike Hedges, one of several big names who'd overseen failed sessions for The La's' eventual 'official' album. In *Q*, he went so far as to say that the 'demos from 1986 are the definitive La's recordings. They are absolutely stunning'.

Going on the critical appraisal alone, you'd have thought *Callin' All* would have gone on to be a smash hit of sorts, yet strangely enough – while it performed well enough – it was actually less commercially successful than the *Breakloose* La's album had been. Maybe that was because a lot of would-be buyers saw the titles and thought, 'Oh, I have them already'. It was hard to credit. The fact that they were essential tracks that had assumed mythical status due to Lee's insistence that they were the best La's recordings probably didn't mean a great deal to most fans in the cold light of day. And there was also the issue of CD sales being in general decline. Even in the three years Viper had then been operating we'd noticed a tail-off in sales overall. It was yet another indication of the unhealthy state of the music industry.

Lee undoubtedly had some fantastic songs ready to go should he have so desired. In fact, I had learnt most of them myself during our time together in '99. I remembered him playing 'Fishing Net' (for me, the greatest of his unreleased songs) – he was in his front room in Roby and he just launched into it and was incredible. There we were back in Roby and all those familiar landmarks were in sight, not least just up the road the little farm my Aunt and Uncle had next to Roby Station where I had spent so much time growing up.

******

The *Lost and Found* exhibition was now at the Atkinson Gallery on Southport's lush boulevard Lord Street. The Hokum Clones had played the preview night and I had sold a few sculptures. The gallery had asked me to mount my *Giant Tin Space Rocket* above the entrance way to the Town Hall next door to help advertise the show. I did so and it looked spectacular – very Tin Tin!

But it was great that there was a load of real talent still coming through in Liverpool. The Acoustic Engine nights which had been firing me up and now the acoustic night that The Hokum Clones had made a regular event at the Masque made us realize what a huge pool of unsigned talent was out there, with so many artists deserving much wider exposure.

With this in mind, Paul and I felt we needed to record this chapter in the ever-evolving history of Liverpool's music scene, and thus Viper's *Great Liverpool Acoustic Experiment* compilation album was born. The idea was to include some of the more established local artists to help draw some attention to the newer ones. Jonathan Ross championed Space's acoustic version of their hit 'Female of the Species', playing it on his Saturday morning show on Radio 2.

I got a call from Dave McCabe asking if Viper might like to do some recording with his new project, the then-fledgling Zutons, but Alan Wills from Deltasonic got there before us and the rest as they say is history. (Anyhow, can't say we would have been able to give them the push they got on Deltasonic.)

Paul and I genuinely believed the *Acoustic Experiment* album would help to herald a new renaissance and bring Liverpool to the fore as the home of the great British singer-songwriter, but its commercial performance just blew away on the Mersey wind. It's still a relatively unknown treasure and we still believe Liverpool will ride the crest of the wave in music again.

Viper's second *Unearthed: Liverpool Cult Classics* volume hit the shops in the late summer of 2001. It was launched by a Viper Records bash at the Magnet early in September, where I was the DJ for the night. It was also a retro night in celebration of it being the thirtieth anniversary of Eric's club closing (including its reprise as Brady's) and I had a great time rounding up some vinyl for the occasion in my attic and then spinning it all on the night. I played some perennial punk, new wave, garage and reggae favourites like Wire's 'I Am the Fly', Dillinger's 'Cokane in My Brain', The Cramps' 'Human Fly' and Honey Bane's 'Girl on the Run'. It was like my very own *Jukebox at Eric's* that night.

People always say they remember where they were on the days JFK and John Lennon were assassinated. In recent history, though, the date everyone remembers is 11 September 2001, or simply 9/11, as it's usually called. In my case, I was at home, more precisely in the attic at Croydon Avenue, chatting with my old pal John Hodgkinson when Jeanette shouted up, urging us to put on the portable telly that we had up there. We watched agog as one tower of the World Trade Center smoked, sending plumes all over Manhattan island. We could barely speak as it was, but then we saw the second plane fly into the other tower. By then we were drained, utterly speechless. Drawn towards the flame, we watched the collapse in a terrible silence. Everyone alive remembers exactly where they were during those moments on that horrific day.

Ironically, a day or so later – while the world was still in a state of shock and in fear of further atrocities – I got a call from Jo Jones at the Atkinson in Southport. She explained that the rear of my *Giant Tin Space Rocket* (which was still suspended above the entrance way outside Southport's splendid Town Hall) had slipped down one of the suspension wires and come to rest pointing directly at the Town Hall building. In the light of what had just happened in New York, she was keen for me to come up immediately and help with its removal.

TWENTY-TWO

Growing Up Is a Killer

PAUL AND I STARTED more recording with The Hokum Clones at
Viper HQ. It had been going so well that we'd hoped to do a full
LP for Viper, but they stalled when they got a new manager who was
keen to hook bigger fish for her boys. Sadly, they ended up being too
raw and meaty for the delicate palate of a conservative music industry
that (as we had all accepted by this stage) required less challenging
fare to market successfully.

I loved the sessions with Danny and Robby, though. The cream of
the tracks ended up on Viper's *21st Century Liverpool Underground*
compilation, along with tracks from The Big Kids and the original
Tramp Attack. We also got The Hokums to put the finishing touch
to the third *Unearthed: Liverpool Cult Classics* volume with their
stunning version of 'Rock Island Line', the song Leadbelly had
popularized and which Lonnie Donegan had brought to the masses
during the 1950s skiffle boom. It would in turn influence John Lennon
and Paul McCartney's pre-Beatles outfit The Quarrymen and help
kick-start the whole Merseybeat era. The Hokums' version brought

the tradition home in fine style and it seemed the perfect epitaph for the *Unearthed* trilogy: i.e., where it had all started.

✷✷✷✷✷✷

I started teaching guitar to young students at St Margaret Mary's Primary School in Huyton's Pilch Lane. Another La's connection was no surprise. The previous guitar teacher there, who was moving away from Liverpool, was a guy called Boo (real name John Byrne) who had gone to school with Lee and was the actual player of the 'There She Goes' riff on the official single release: crazy world again! Jeanette had started working at the school doing therapy with the kids. John had said he was leaving and got in touch with me on Jeanette's recommendation. La la land!

It turned out to be fascinating but intense work. I worked with Year 3–6 students, doing half-hour sessions with small groups of between two and six in each class. I began with simple guitar tuning, but gradually got to a stage where they'd grasped the rudiments and I could teach them chords and then songs like Elvis Presley's 'Suspicious Minds', Dylan's 'Blowin' in the Wind', The Ramones' 'Rockaway Beach' (I was proud of that one) and the inevitable 'Yellow Submarine'.

It was a lot of work, but very rewarding. The pupils had a great time, which – to me – was the most important thing, but I even got into doing compositions with some of the keener ones. I got to give a Christmas performance, where I played '2022 Blues' to all my students' parents. That was nerve-wracking!

✷✷✷✷✷✷

It all brought my life full circle in that I had lived up the road from Pilch Lane East when I was growing up. My then best mate, Carl Davies, his brother Ian and fellow actor David Morrissey had all been pupils at St Margaret Mary's as kids and I had walked past that school so many times on my way to Carl's place when I was a teenager. I now ended up back there, starting the job literally days after I attended Carl's funeral in October 2002.

What had happened to Carl? So many of our formative years had been shared together and it was so sad that alcohol had become the major influence in his life. I had lost all contact with him in recent years because his behaviour had become so erratic and volatile when he got drunk, but it didn't stop me thinking of him and even in his darkest days I'd continued to respect him as an artist.

I had actually been out for a drink with Ian Davies (aka Ian Hart) only a couple of months before Carl's death. Ian told me Carl had got what he referred to as 'wet brain'. Carl's kidneys basically couldn't cope anymore, so I wasn't too surprised when Ian called a short while later to tell me Carl had passed away. He'd been in London for years but eventually returned home to Woodford Road, seemingly to die. His Mum, Peggy, had woken up one morning and found her son dead on their living room carpet.

Carl's funeral took place in Allerton and I placed a few photocopied sheets of *A Secret Liverpool* adverts in the grave in memoriam, including the one with The Beatles with blank faces from the *City Limits* magazine. *A Secret Liverpool* had been our baby and I would always love it because it was the first time I'd ever appeared on a record.

It was good to see our old mate David Evans after so long too, not the best of circumstances, but he'd been a good mate to Carl. Then, after the funeral, I saw Carl's ex, Gill. She reminded me of the note Kevin, David and I had put under their door asking her to leave our flat in Lawrence Road so we could carry on our dream of being in a band. It brought it all flooding back to me: the way Carl had cut all his hair off in chunks and started wearing white gloves. We'd hardly seen Carl in the flat after Gill had moved in, they just stayed locked in their room. It all seemed so funny and yet all so sad now. Gill seemed apologetic after all these years.

I remember Carl had once told me that he wanted to call his first child Splash, but in the end he and Gill had gone on to have a daughter called Lorrie. It was lovely to finally meet her, even under such tragic circumstances, as it was to see Carl's younger sister, Julie. Pure Liverpool. She could tear a strip off you in an instant without seeming to have to try and she did it many a time when we were teenagers and trying too hard to be out there. 'Just look at the kip of yer!' she'd say.

Gill had gotten a load of huge photocopies of pictures of Carl blown up to put in the bar after the service. They were all Sellotaped together because she'd previously ripped them in half during one of their many rows when they were young lovers.

Ian showed me a crumpled piece of paper he had in his hand. It was a poem he had written about his elder brother and I just remember reading the phrase 'pockets of loose change'. I couldn't help smiling because it instantly reminded me of Carl with his pocket full of jangling busking money, usually just enough to get him his next bottle and some fags. Ian had written it specially, but had been rendered unable to read it at the service.

Ian's next acting job was in the Lebanon playing the former hostage Brian Keenan in *Blind Fight* which – for me – is still his finest hour in front of camera. It was a truly staggering performance and no doubt very cathartic for him at the time.

I also met with a whole bunch of buskers and friends of Carl's from his London years. I was pleasantly surprised to discover they'd heard all about me and it felt good to know I'd still been in Carl's thoughts after so long. I sat and talked with them and heard some astounding stories of Carl nearly burning the house down in the squats where they had lived. Carl had frequently lit cigarettes and fell asleep drunk with them still burning at night time. It was sad to think he'd ended up drifting after he'd moved down to London (our old flat in 211 Camden Road in 1984 with Ian eventually taking a room upstairs) and, because of the transient world Carl lived in, so many people had lost contact with him.

His friends from London rightly believed a load more people would have turned out for his funeral if only they'd known. One of these buskers' friends was a guy called Arthur and he was a lovely chap. I was saying about how Carl was incredibly generous, about how he always adopted a 'what's mine is yours' attitude and went on to say how he would give you the shirt off his back. I'd meant it figuratively, but Arthur said, 'Well, yeah, he did to me.'

It turned out Arthur had once been busking and was playing an REM song when Carl happened to walk past wearing an REM T-shirt. Carl heard the song, took the shirt off, threw it at Arthur and kept going. Never even broke his stride.

Another couple told me they had moved into a squat in Camden and Carl had been set on painting his room. He'd gotten as far as buying a big tub of white emulsion, but two months later it still sat unopened in the middle of the room where he'd put it down. One night the couple were ribbing Carl about it, calling him a lazy bastard because he still hadn't started on the decorating. In response to this, Carl suddenly whipped the top off the tub and in one movement sent the entire load of paint over the ceiling and down one of the walls of his room. Once it had settled, most of it ended up in one huge puddle on the floor. If that wasn't crazy enough, he never cleaned any of it up. As a result, his footprints went through it every day. They would lead out of his room when he got up, down the communal stairs, along the pavement to the off-licence where he got his vodka and ciggies and then all the way back from the offy to his room. The footprints would then lead from the front door of the house in the other direction as he left the house again, this time to Camden Tube station where they would stop when he boarded the train and start again when he got off onto the platform at his busking pitch, usually by Tottenham Court Road station. (Jonathan Richman's 'Ice Cream Man' was one of his regular tunes.)

My mind boggled when I heard his story. On the one hand there was something incredibly poetic (and hilarious!) about it in the sense that those footprints literally mapped out the man's life in such a graphic way, yet at the same time the idea of having to try and live with someone so impossible to deal with was enough to make my stomach churn. I felt so sad that my old friend should have come to such an end. Genius knows no constraints.

The one really special thing that came from Carl's funeral was the chance to get re-acquainted with his Mum, Peggy, once again. She'd been so kind to me as a teenager and when I started at St Margaret Mary's in Pilch Lane. I would go and sit with her for half an hour during my lunch break once a week from then on. We'd talk about Everton and all the local news and it was wonderful to get to know her again. Sometimes Ian would phone from the middle of an American desert set somewhere to get the footie results and I'd have a natter with him.

✻✻✻✻✻✻

22 December 2002. Joe Strummer (aka John Mellor) also left this world for a new rock art and X-ray world in punk rockabilly heaven. I remembered Hamish telling me when he had seen Joe play the Royal Court, he had said over the mic, 'Hey, what's happening with The La's then?' I also remember seeing a photograph of him once in what I thought was a La's T-Shirt – then I realized that his motorcycle jacket was just hiding the C and the H.

TWENTY-THREE

New York State of Mind

I CAME UP WITH THE idea of what would become my *Lo-Fi Acoustic Excursions* album. The process of compiling it involved grouping these disparate acoustic recordings together as a kind of audio diary of two decades, spanning the years 1983–2003.

Compiling it, I was again staggered to think that I'd survived in the music 'industry' in one form or other for twenty years without a manager or even a regular record label in the traditional sense of either term. But there it was. I formed my own independent Generator label to release my songs. It might have been a little indulgent of me to have gone through Viper – say the album took a while to recoup?

I described the record as 'lo-fi, high-flying, inter-planetary, previously unreleased ballads, rockers and laments' and the songs included everything from outtakes, alternate and stripped-down versions of Onset tunes like 'Walking Tall' (from an early Spencer Leigh BBC Radio Merseyside session) through to an early version of *Double Zero*'s 'Autumn in the Mind' recorded at the Gossamer Dome, Ynys Mon (Anglesey) with Paul and Henry Priestman in support.

I also included the acoustic, Hank Williams-style version of the classic country ballad 'Cool Water' recorded by Lee and myself in 1986. Listening to it again made me smile and reminded me of when Lee and I were meeting up every day, playing guitars and writing songs – being open to all kinds of music before the nonsense kicked in.

****

For years, I'd dreamed of playing in America and had often felt that if The Onset had made it over there the sky would have been the limit. We'd been close to getting there for the Woodstock '94, but it never happened.

Finally, the chance of a stateside trip presented itself and it came through music, though not the way I'd imagined it. The opportunity came my way via a trade mission that Viper were eligible for, which provided the funding for return flights and a hotel. (This was the first time I had received external funding for anything, some people make very good careers out of it ... thank you very much.) The trip took place in October 2003 and (typically) provided no new trade at all for Viper. However, some very interesting incidents took place on the periphery and several chance meetings would end up opening doors for me for the future.

I flew over to New York with Pete Wylie and Bez (from The Happy Mondays) of all people. It was totally crazy at the check-in at Manchester Airport and the flight seemed to last forever, although I could barely contain my excitement at the thought of seeing New York for the first time. I didn't know Bez at all, but he seemed like straight-up, decent guy. Where he went after we landed I really couldn't say, though the immigration people seemed to be very interested in him.

On the evening of our arrival, we went to a reception at the Hotel Chelsea. People from the music industry milled around in the basement bar. I got talking to one guy who asked me where I was from. I said, 'Liverpool' and he mentioned the name 'Mike Badger'.

'I am Mike Badger', I said.

'No, you're not', he said.

'I should know.'

'You can't be!' he insisted.

Eventually, Pete Wylie came over and confirmed who I was, much to the dismay of the guy.

I was introduced to a guy called Howard Thompson, an ex-Brit who had been involved in the industry for many years. I soon got to talking to him about Captain Beefheart with enthusiasm. As the events came to a close, he invited Pete and me to his apartment next door to the hotel for a drink and to show me some original Don Van Vliet (aka Captain Beefheart) artwork. In his apartment he had works by the great man, also by Suicide's Alan Vega and John Lydon. Welcome to America. He even had a collection of original Betty Page stills in his bathroom.

Finally, Howard completely blew what was left of my jet-lagged mind when he produced Buddy Holly's actual birth certificate. Buddy is just about my main man. How the hell did I end up holding his birth certificate on my first-ever night in America?

I loved the scale and energy of NYC. I was so into it that I went around photographing the fireplugs that arose from the sidewalks like dragons. (I didn't know it at the time, but apparently Oldenburg did the same thing years before)

It was also nice to get to meet Dave Pichilingi, who was there, and Pete Wylie a little more. After I'd been there a couple of nights, Pete's mate Josh had a few exhibits showing in a hip-hop exhibition in Chelsea, and I was invited. There were loads of serious-looking hip-hop dudes. Among them I saw this huge American Indian guy there and thought, 'Whoo ... look at *him*' – actually he looked like a native version of Marlon Brando in plaits and bone-choker. It was remarkable to me because the first thing I'd done when the plane had touched down in America was to clench my fists and silently exclaim, 'Indians!' It was a personal acknowledgement of where I was, I had always loved everything to do with Native Americans/Indians, maybe as far back as drawing tribal marks with my Mum's lipstick on her old teddy bear's face when I was a toddler.

I went outside the photographic gallery to smoke a roll-up, but it started to rain so I stepped under the scaffolding covering the facade of the shop next door. Then, like it had been scripted, the Indian guy I had seen inside the show also stepped out into the rain. He looked at the sky and stepped under the scaffolding next to me. I felt I just had to say something to him.

'What part of the country are you from?' I asked.

'I'm from here, but we're from everywhere!' he answered. That was the start. Encouraged, I told him I was into Indian poet and activist John Trudell's work.

'You know John?' he asked, amazed.

'Yeah!' I said. '"Rant and Roll"!'

I was about to expand on that when two cool-looking black guys emerged from the gallery on their way home.

'Hey, you think you're so fucking cool! How come YOU don't know who John Trudell is?' my new friend said to them. I felt like I was in a cartoon.

The guy told me his name was Ernie Paniccioli. He showed me a copy of his book and asked me to buy it and read it. (New York directness...) He also gave me his card and told me to phone him. If John Trudell was in town, he'd introduce me.

I phoned Ernie a couple of days later from the Maritime Hotel (the hard sell had worked) and told him I'd read his book. He'd had an incredible life: after living on the New York streets from the age of twelve he'd gone on to live with singer-songwriter Richie Havens, befriended jazz legend Cecil Taylor for a couch to sleep on and lived seemingly many lives along the way.

Ernie answered his phone as bold as brass and told me to be in the lobby at the Maritime at 11am the following morning. I was there on the dot and so was he. I followed him out of the lobby to his Pathfinder jeep. I sat in the passenger seat and he gave me a signed photograph he had taken of John Trudell and an Indian dancer in full blue face make-up. Ernie played a track by Public Enemy's Chuck D who was referring vociferously to the proliferation of Common Sense Deficiency Syndrome.

Ernie told me he was going to introduce me to the most beautiful woman I had ever met. Not just beautiful on the outside, but beautiful in every possible way. He then drove me across the Brooklyn Bridge and into Queens, stopping to take photographs of graffiti along the way. This had been Ernie's staple work for years, even before he was photographing hip-hop artists he was photographing graffiti.

Eventually we parked. I had absolutely no idea where we were going, but Ernie made some calls and we got access to an apartment, where we removed our shoes on entry.

Inside the apartment, I heard and felt a sound from the kitchen. It was definitely someone singing. Then, as if from nowhere, this beautiful Tibetan lady called Yungchen Lhamo came out with some food for us. It was an incredible moment. I couldn't get over the sight of this woman with long black hair past her knees!

Yungchen's friend (and fellow musician) Jodan was also in the apartment and asked if I had ever heard any of Yungchen's music. I had to admit I hadn't, so Jodan put on a VHS tape of her singing in front of an audience. I was spellbound by the purity and beauty of her singing and my eyes just started to stream with tears. I was filled with such a surge of emotion and well-being.

We all talked for a long time and eventually Yungchen suggested we do some recording in the next room. Jodan (originally from Chester of all places!) played an African drum, while I improvised on guitar. Yungchen sang and harmonized with an intuitive skill that astounded me, notes clear as a bell emerged effortlessly and swam about the room. We recorded eight spontaneous pieces of music there and then. It was not like anything I had ever experienced before (or since!). The ninth was a monologue recited by Ernie about giving thanks for every day. It was so perfect and free. I looked at Ernie afterwards and even he was filling up. He couldn't believe *he'd* just recorded with Yungchen Lhamo, never mind me. So far, it appeared to me that New York truly was the place where miracles happened.

Yungchen's story was awe-inspiring. She had escaped occupied Tibet travelling across the Himalayas with a three-year-old son on her back to be with the Dalai Lama in northern India. She had been signed to Peter Gabriel's Real World Records label, after singing traditional Tibetan prayers and songs around the world taught to her by her grandmother after she had been removed from her parents by the Chinese.

Feeling purified and cleansed on leaving Yungchen's apartment, on the way back towards the jeep with Ernie I bent down to pick up a leaf from the ground for posterity. At that very moment, an oriental-looking man who had been walking ahead of us bent down and picked up a leaf, then carried on, walking away from us.

'Did you see that? You bent down and picked up a leaf, that guy in front hadn't seen you do it but did exactly the same!' exclaimed Ernie.

Not the only 'leaf' incident: I had picked up a leaf before leaving Liverpool from the ancient oak in Calderstones Park to drop outside the Dakota Building.

Henry Epstein had flown over for a few days and we went to see John Power play at the Bitter End in Greenwich Village. After the gig we went to an all-night café with Wylie and Paul – everyone had been passing around 'business cards' at events and Henry trumped us all when he gave Wylie his card: the Joker!

TWENTY-FOUR

More Unearthing

ALL THREE OF VIPER'S *Unearthed: Liverpool Cult Classics* albums had taken a lot of putting together, but with the third one we felt we could round the series off by acknowledging some of the more recent unsung Merseyside heroes, for example Pontoon and The Hokum Clones as well as the likes of Shack, the pre-Clinic outfit Pure Morning and some classic 'lost' singles like Those Naughty Lumps' legendary 1978 release 'Iggy Pop's Jacket' and 'British Refugee' by the short-lived Spitfire Boys (possibly Liverpool's only true punk band). They featured Frankie Goes to Hollywood man Paul Rutherford and future Siouxsie and The Banshees' drummer Budgie, both of whom were at St Helen's art school with my sister Ros before I attended the school.

One regret Paul and I both had was that we didn't manage to get 'Big in Japan' by Big in Japan on any of the three volumes, but we just couldn't get clearance from anybody. Bearing in mind the band's stellar line-up (Jayne Casey, Budgie, Bill Drummond, Holly Johnson and Ian Broudie), it was a real hot potato, but – with hindsight – we should probably have just included it and – if anyone had had any problem with it – told them it was too important to omit. I know that's probably what Roger Eagle would have done.

Around the time the third volume was released, I did a radio interview with DJ Dave Monks on KCR, a local station that was broadcast all over Huyton and Prescot. Dave was an absolute gent and the slot gave me a chance to bring Danny Dean in to join me for a couple of acoustic tunes, plug my *Lo-Fi Acoustic Excursions* album and let people know I was still around and doing stuff.

******

A family holiday in Majorca coincided with the untimely death of John Peel. In my case, I was out walking with Ray and saw a British newspaper from the day before. There was John Peel on the cover and the sad story of his passing in Peru. I got really choked up when I tried to tell Ray who he was. I don't recall sounding too articulate, but I feebly tried to explain the enormity of who he was and what he was responsible for.

However, with the exception of The Hokum Clones' excellent 'If I Had Possession over Judgement Day', John only really got behind one Viper album, probably the most outlandish and uncharacteristic album we released – an electronica album by Otaku No Denki that featured Joey Cannon, Dean Salleyman and Chris (brother of Dave) McCabe. John Peel had gone on to play every single track from that one. He was a champion of what was different, I suppose.

Paul and I came across these guys when Joey and then Dean worked on our website. We would go to Dean and Dave's flat situated in the old 1930s block near town where *Violent Playground* had been filmed in the '60s. Strange noises emanated from the bedrooms as the guys constantly worked on their futuristic-sounding sonic forms. On top of this, there was the metallic echoes and booms of trains slowly taxi-ing into Lime Street. It was like something from David Lynch's movie *Eraserhead*. Paul and I loved the idea of doing an album with Otaku No Denki because it would certainly throw a spanner in the works to anyone thinking they had a handle on the label. Both Jeanette and I had photographs included on the sleeve.

Edgar Jones, formerly Edgar Summertyme of The Stairs, was a legendary character in Liverpool and I'd had the pleasure of getting to know him a bit when we were picking our kids up from Dovedale School. One day, in the playground, I gave him a couple of copies of our 1950s Sci Fi and Horror B Movie Rock n Roll compilation albums *The Ultimate 50s Rockin' Sci-Fi Disc* and *The Ultimate '50s & '60s Rockin' Horror Disc*. The next time I saw him, he gave me a cassette tape with some music on it. When I got home, I put it on and thought these must be tracks Edgar wishes Viper to consider for any future 1950s US comps. However, on second listening, I realized to my shock and delight that these were Edgar's current recordings he'd been working on at home in Princes Park.

Paul agreed that this was something very special and I approached Edgar on our next meeting, asking him if he'd like to release them on Viper. He said 'absolutely' he would. Then I heard nothing for months until we went for a walk in the park (with the new member of the family, our dog Megan) and he happened to mention, 'Oh, I've got that album done if you're still up for it?' Fabulous!

The album would be released as *Soothing Music for Stray Cats* by Edgar Jones and The Joneses and we were very proud to be releasing it on our label. The record ended up getting quite a kick commercially: it was released in November 2004 and almost immediately Noel Gallagher from Oasis named it as his album of the year, which was a big thumbs-up for us and certainly helped with sales.[15]

Paul and I love its authenticity and the fact it's so different to virtually any other music ever heard coming out of Liverpool. It's a fine piece of work that includes Blue Note jazz sounds, doo-wop, authentic R & B and a whole lot of soul – all the more astonishing for having been handmade by Edgar at home.

✶✶✶✶✶✶

Robby Stevenson had relocated up to Perthshire in Scotland, so I decided to go and play a one-off gig up in Edinburgh at the Backpackers

---

15 Early in 2011, the *NME* gave it the number one slot on its 'Greatest Albums You've Never Heard' list.

club, organized by local lad Steven Lucas. He was in a band called The Alchemists of Pop who sounded like *The Wicker Man* soundtrack crossed with that *Electric Mud* album Muddy Waters released later on in his career.

Curiously enough, I remember The Alchemists telling me a new version of The La's, with Lee and John joined by two new musicians, were playing a gig at the Savoy in Cork, Ireland, that very same night I was at the Backpackers. Who'd have believed that? My only gig in a 'bleam' had coincided with the new La's in an even much, much longer time – even more synchronicity. Robby, on hearing that, rather generously interjected with:

'Maybe they are – but this is the place to be tonight!'

Robby had done lots of touring with his partner Danny Roberts as The Hokum Clones. They had supported The Coral and The Zutons on numerous jaunts around the UK and beyond. They were the ideal support band in so many ways, just the two of them and minimal equipment – they could just kip on the tour bus, hence no expensive hotels.

They'd really made a name for themselves in Liverpool, supported Richard Ashcroft (who Martyn Campbell was then playing with) and had also supported the hotly tipped Canadian troupe The Polyphonic Spree, led by the magnificently named Tim DeLaughter. I saw them play Liverpool University's Mountford Hall. They had Edgar Jones guesting on double bass and they were *red hot* that night. Later on, we hung out with Tim DeLaughter and talked about psychedelic music, Kaleidoscope and the original Charlatans: roots-y blues heads singing about 'Codine'.

Shortly afterwards, The Hokum Clones disbanded as things had apparently run their course. Another 'mad one', Danny Roberts, came over to our place in Croydon Avenue and I gave him a cassette I'd put together made up of my purest 1950s rock 'n' roll and rockabilly. Simply because it featured the song of the same name, I'd called the compilation *16 Tonnes Rock 'n' Roll* after the brilliant Jimmy Murphy tune and when I gave it to Danny he just marvelled.

'You do know, don't you?' he said, astonished.

'Know what?' I replied.

'My new band is called 16 Tonnes.'

I genuinely had no idea of this fact at the time, but Danny just stared at me confused. It turned out he'd got the name after the song had been his granddad's party piece at family get-togethers.

****

I was interviewed by Spencer Leigh – BBC Radio Merseyside presenter, author and Merseybeat expert – for the release of Viper's *Unearthed: Liverpool Cult Classics Volume 1* and, during the interview, he mentioned he had the biggest collection of unreleased Merseybeat recordings that existed.

I remember rather patronizingly dismissing his comment as if to say 'what would we want to do with those?' However, Paul and I eventually went up to his house in Ainsdale and listened to what he had to offer. I ended up with egg on my face at the astounding amount of great unreleased music that had been corralled by Spencer.

No less than the first-ever rock 'n' roll created in the UK had been made in Liverpool because of its geographical position and its relationship with America and the sea. Spencer was more than pleased to assist in researching sleeve notes and helping Paul track down people and all for the sheer pleasure to see the music that appeared on dusty old tapes and acetates eventually see the light of day. This would run into three volumes of 1960s *Unearthed Merseybeat*.

Although I had been aware of Liverpool's short-lived band The 23rd Turnoff, the project also revealed a larger body of work by one of the band's members and one of Liverpool's great unsung heroes, Jimmy Campbell. Jimmy had fronted The Kirkbys and then turned to psych-pop with The 23rd Turnoff (the trippy name actually came from the turning to Liverpool from the M6 as it was then). Campbell would later record three fantastically poetic solo albums for the Fontana and Phillips labels between 1969 and 1972. Paul and I felt the alternate take of his magnificent single 'Michaelangelo' was the perfect way to bring the third *Unearthed Merseybeat* volume to a close.

Jimmy sadly passed away from emphysema in 2007 (I was asked to write his obituary for *Mojo*) but at least he was around to receive copies of the three Viper albums via his good friend Billy Kinsley, whose contribution I would also make sure to mention in *Mojo*. Bernie

Connor's eulogizing sleeve notes quite probably made him blush! Having said that, I personally insisted on the heading in the notes relating to Jimmy – 'Liverpool's own little Michelangelo'.

Again, like our *Unearthed: Liverpool Cult Classics* series, I felt Paul and I had done a good job in providing a platform and preserving some important (and often overlooked) pieces of music for posterity. Many were tracks that would otherwise have slipped through the cracks in Liverpool's ever older paving stones.

When Jimmy Campbell died I was asked by someone from the forward-thinking Liverpool Sound City festival to curate a night as tribute to Jimmy's life as a songwriter. I gathered a fine cast of Liverpool singer-songwriters together to play a Jimmy song each. I would be hosting the night too, in conjunction with Spencer Leigh. I played along with Lizzie Nunnery, Danny Roberts, Paul Cavanagh, Una Quinn and Lucas O'Heyze. All of Jimmy's family were there and it was great to meet them. In fact it was like I'd known them for years – but that's Liverpool.

Viper also produced some new songs for the latest version of the very talented Tramp Attack. The band now consisted of Matt Barton (vocals/acoustic guitar), Chris Marshall (bass), Barry Southern (guitar) and original drummer Ian Lane. Barry and Chris had appeared as The Mother Lovers on Viper's *Great Liverpool Acoustic Experiment* compilation.

Paul and I really dug this version of the band and were well into the sounds they laid down at this session. It had a very distinctive acoustic-driven country-pop vibe with some great Scouse wit in the lyrics. Eventually these songs would appear on the second Tramp Attack album, titled *Call in Sick*. Tunes such as 'Write a Letter', 'Late Night Shopping' and Ian Lane's personal masterpiece, 'Learn To Swim', ensured it was another Viper release to be proud of.

Matt Barton had written the tune called 'Double Decker Bus', which would soon find its way onto the Viper compilation *21st Century Liverpool Underground*. It was one of many Mersey-related tunes celebrating the much-maligned form of public transport. One of the *Unearthed Merseybeat* albums had featured Jason Eddie's brilliant 'Mr Bus Driver', while The La's' 'Doledrum' featured the hook 'get on the bus, get out' and The Stairs brought it full-circle with their catchy, ganja-inspired 'Weed Bus'. In future years, I too would be moved to write a song called 'Routemaster '59' about the trips I used to take on them while living in London. These songs were another reason I was proud of my Liverpool heritage and they were quintessentially English – even if it was far less glamorous than the hot rods and Cadillac cars our rockin' American cousins sang of with such affection.

I lost another old mate – Kevin, who I had made friends with all those years ago at St Helens Art College (he was Paul Simpson's younger cousin), who had helped with the early La's and Onset recordings. He had finally lost his battle with cancer. He was only in his early forties and I had so many happy memories of him – not least beach fires in Anglesey when Jeanette and I would stay with Kevin and his long-term girlfriend, Julie McGrail. We had also met Don Van Vliet together. Life can be awfully cruel.

TWENTY-FIVE

Shangri-La

IN APRIL 2006, I was given the opportunity to put more bread on our kitchen table when I was contacted by Paul Smith (from the Manchester-based Business in the Arts), who had recommended me to Susan Woodward OBE (another Huytonian done good) and Jane Lucas from ITV Granada in Manchester as someone who could help them fulfil their objective to create an arts residency that would celebrate ITV Granada's fiftieth year of broadcast.

The Beatles' first-ever TV appearances took place in those hallowed studios and the *Johnny Cash at San Quentin* documentary was even a Granada production.

The work at ITV Granada ended up continuing for eighteen months! While working with the staff on artwork for the Quay Street studios, one of the many highlights was working with Denise Ambery on the logo for *World in Action*, a programme that had helped secure the release of the Birmingham Six.

* * * * * *

During 2006, we also compiled and released two albums I feel are among the very best things Viper have ever done. I got the title *Protest!* from a Radio 1 programme presented by John Peel in the mid-1980s about protest music – when Radio 1 still did that kind of thing! It was this show that got us thinking about compiling an album of tracks all related to the great struggle people have endured to better themselves and the lives of others. With tracks ranging from 1928 through to the mid-1950s, the subject matter ranged from civil rights, the threat of the A-bomb, unemployment, prostitution and war, and we managed to get tracks as diverse and brilliant as Billie Holliday's 'Strange Fruit' through to Woody Guthrie's '1913 Massacre'. Actually, Steve Hardstaff's visionary cover montage of the waves of justice lapping at the base of a reconstituted Statue of Liberty is worth the price of admission alone.

Paul had the brainwave for our *Song before the Song* collection. The remit there was to dig out the early, unfamiliar versions of songs that would later achieve mass success when covered by later artists. Again, the songs ranged from the late '20s through to the mid-'50s and the track listing featured things like Big Mama Thornton's original version of 'Hound Dog' (later popularized by Elvis Presley), Josh White's 'House of the Rising Sun' (which The Animals would later take to the top of the charts) and Emmett Miller's majestic version of 'Lovesick Blues' (later recorded by the great Hank Williams). This one also proved to be a popular and intriguing collection that completes a lot of missing pieces in the jigsaw puzzle when it comes to the history of rock 'n' roll.

✳✳✳✳✳✳

After I'd released my *Lo-Fi Acoustic Excursions* collection and an album of unreleased Onset studio recordings, the natural thing to do was sift through the rest of the material I had at home, this time concentrating on recordings for a sister album called *Lo-Fi Electric Excursions*, which I released in 2006. *Whisperin' & Hollerin'* posed one very good question in their review of the album: 'Since when did rock 'n' roll start getting equated with 500 takes (of songs) and 96-track recording studios?' I didn't care about how many copies the album sold – it was necessary for me to get those songs out for me to be able to move on. I was the only person who knew what existed on which tapes and when they dated from. I also liked the way the songs had different textures and recording qualities and I liked the way the record sounded, despite the lack of record company input of any kind.

******

I had been amassing a bunch of songs and decided to ask Martyn Campbell whether he would produce a new album with me, something he was happy to do. I had recently sound-proofed my garage when we had moved to Wavertree and turned it into studio space in time-honoured tradition and was ready to do some recording as spring threatened to turn into summer.

I loved the intimate, live vibe we got working with Martyn and drummer Tony Mac and before I knew it we had takes of 'Empathize', 'Big Boots', 'More Time than We Know', 'Don't Leave Me Standing', 'Low Down in a High Town' and 'Platform 9' done and dusted.

The casual pace suited everyone and the sessions continued on into September when guitarist Barry Southern and bassist Chris Marshall from Tramp Attack came down to record three country-style songs. They brought Paddy Frost from The Loose Moose String Band along with them to play on 'Ashtrays and Tables and Barstools', while Martyn and Tony stuck around for 'Some Things' and the rockabilly-flavoured 'Dig It!' (a long time staple of my live set).

Working with the Tramp Attack guys was liberating. It was literally a case of play the song to them, have a run through it as a band and then – thanks to Martyn – record it. Totally that easy. Although I was already aware of how talented they were from the recording of their *Call in Sick* album, it was the first time we'd worked together as a recording unit. It was a pivotal moment in that these recordings laid down the blueprint for the new band I would eventually start with Barry Southern, Chris Marshall and drummer Ian Lane: Mike Badger and The Shady Trio.

Recording for my next solo album had pretty much been wrapped up after the Tramp Attack boys had been down and we'd got 'Ashtrays and Tables and Barstools' and 'Some Things' completed, but – on Leap Year Day – I recorded the final few backing tracks with Martyn Campbell, this time getting 'Don't Leave Me Standing' and 'Being Wrong' (aka 'Moving On') on tape.

I did know Martyn wouldn't have much more time for the foreseeable future, as he was about to join up with Mick and John Head as Shack's full-time bassist, but as always he was a pleasure to work with. I can say without hesitation that Martyn is quietly one of Liverpool's greatest songwriters. But who's going to know if you don't release anything?

Of the three country tracks, 'Ashtrays' came out particularly well and subsequently became something of a theme tune. Although I'd written the song in the third person, there are definite lyrical pointers to how my life could have gone if it hadn't been for the support of Jeanette and my family.

The lyrics opened with the line 'I've sung to the barmaid when nobody else was around'. That referred directly to the time The Onset did a gig at Liverpool's Pink Parrot in Duke Street one night in the mid-'90's. There was literally no one there, save the barmaid, so I sang to her and we played.

The three songs from the Tramp Attack sessions would later find their way onto my 2008 release *Mike Badger's Country Side*, but the rest of the songs I recorded with Martyn and Tony would wait on the shelf for a while until their eventual release on *Rogue State*.

******

I must put a little pamphlet together sometime called *Graveyard Japes* based on visits to graveyards I have had on rambles with Nigel Blackwell. When we saw a grave in Frodsham covered in brambles and ivy he said, 'That's where the man who invented camouflage is buried.'

Another time in Hale, on seeing the date 1755: 'Look at that: five to six.'

Best though was in Woolton cemetery: when I had shown him the Eleanor Rigby grave stone he immediately started to memorize other names on adjacent graves as potential song titles.

✳✳✳✳✳✳

I had a lot of reservations about Liverpool being the 'Capital of Culture' – how was it going to be expressed? Well, one good thing to come out of it was the *Beat Goes On* exhibition that was set up in Liverpool's World Museum. During January 2008, some of the folks behind it collected twenty-odd of my music-related artefacts for inclusion. Of these, I was pleased they chose Jeanette's great photo of Lee and me practising with our semi-acoustic guitars (see the book cover) during The La's' early heyday in the backyard at 20 Falkner Street, as well as hand-written lyrics to the band's songs 'Moonlight' and 'Liberty Ship.' My artwork also got a look in: they showed the *Tin Planet* sculptures that featured in Space's 'Avenging Angel' video and the *Tin Planet* robot.

✳✳✳✳✳✳

It's another world when corporations get involved. Yes, Liverpool is a cultural capital and always has been, but for all my workings in the creative industries in the city for years and with so many, I didn't know anyone who had been included in the 'celebrations' really. Ironically, with the exception of some paid work with the *Superlambanana* sculptures, I had a very lean year in 2008 while the fanfare was all going on.[16]

Not wanting to be too down on the whole Capital of Culture event, but so much of these things result in people who 'have' having a whole lot more at the end of it while most others have to just crack on with things. Reminds me of that brilliant quote from *Rab C. Nesbitt* when Glasgow had been awarded the accolade years before: 'Can you spare ten pence for a cappuccino?' Now, after the circus had left town there was a ring of straw left at the start of 2009.

✳✳✳✳✳✳

16 The original *Superlambanana* was fabricated by another St Margaret Mary's boy, Andrew Small.

I have a philosophy I suppose it's 'to do' – it really is that simple. When you act instinctively on something you feel passionately about there's a small chance that something might come about as a result of that action. The alternative 'not to do' absolutely guarantees that nothing will happen, so I choose 'to do'.

Another musical venture I embarked on was *Mike Badger's Country Side* for my sister label Generator. I figured a collection of songs that had a country leaning would do well in the roots field, a genre that was seemingly becoming ever more respected by the critics in recent years, as the gap between commercially released 'music' and everything else widened.

The cover image for the *Country Side* CD is a picture of an old French threshing machine in a field that I had photographed in Cognac. When I was on the way to Nonconform to work on the design I had a piece of tinwork all ready to go for the cover, but I bumped into Dave McCabe and we had a pint in Ye Cracke. He insisted I should make the threshing machine the cover. 'And that's where you recorded it!' he laughed. I duly obliged.

Although the songs came from a variety of sources, I felt it hung together as an album in its own right. It was that thing of either being too roots for the mainstream or else not country enough for a lot of the 'square hole' country music that's prevalent. I was shocked then when it got play listed on country music radio in the US. I can truly say I have never released a record with sales in mind. I release them to represent as accurately as possible who I am or was at any given time and how I want to express myself.

******

On holiday in Scotland we were driving over the Skye Bridge when The Lightning Seeds' single 'Lucky You' came on the radio. Once again, the song's knack for bringing good fortune kicked in. On our return to Liverpool I had been invited to showcase at the 2009 South by Southwest Festival in Austin. I was on my way to Texas. Lucky me!

******

In the February of 2009 I did something I had done so many times before, to walk up the steps of the main stand into the grand arena of Goodison Park. Only this time it was different: it was an evening kick-off and a song I had written, 'Born a Blue', was being blasted out and reverberated around the stadium. Opposite, the Bullens Road Stand was *all* red – Everton were about to play Liverpool in the FA Cup quarterfinal. I stood at the top of the steps, arms fixed firmly in the air opposite the Liverpool supporters as I, along with Danny Roberts and Matt Dean (William Ralph 'Dixie' Dean's grandson), sang to the crowd through the PA system. That's something I will never forget, and the feeling was only topped by Dan Gosling's winning goal two minutes before the end of extra time. Get in!

******

It was also now the tenth anniversary of The La's' *Breakloose* release and I had discovered more tracks on various tapes over the past few years, so this seemed like the time to give it the expanded, remastered makeover it deserved. New technology for cleaning and enhancing clarity on tracks had developed over the past decade too.

Breakloose was re-issued with an option to download the tracks as well as buy them on CD. There wasn't the same fanfare as the first time the album came out, but the expanded edition received an especially nice review from Jamie Bowman in *The Word*: 'Timeless and instantly evocative, the earliest La's material shows they were onto something special from the start'.

How could I sum up what The La's achieved as a band? We brought back driving acoustic guitars to Liverpool and reminded people what a good tune and riff can do for you. Some stars shine forever dim in the night sky; some shine so bright the wattage just blows the fuse. The Onset never had the hit record, but forged ahead anyhow. I suppose I've always played roots music – and at a grassroots level!

There's a parallel universe someplace, I'm sure, where The La's are the biggest thing since sliced bread, having released a dozen albums and defined a generation.

The trouble is, in that universe Freddy and The Dreamers were bigger than The Beatles.

Roll Call

Ros Badger – Moved to London 1979. Formed the beloved children's knitwear company Little Badger. Creator and author of books themed on homemade arts and crafts.

Carl Davies – Released the *A Secret Liverpool* compilation in 1984, which featured the first release by The La's. Relocated to London in 1984. A second volume titled *The Best Kept Secret Liverpool* never appeared. Busked most days on Tottenham Court Road. Moved on 2002.

Ian Davies (Hart) – Brother of Carl Davies. Helped finance *A Secret Liverpool*. A respected actor of film and TV, playing John Lennon in *The Hours and Times* and *Backbeat*. He's had an illustrious career on stage and screen – probably best known for his role as Quirinus Quirrell in *Harry Potter and the Philosopher's Stone*.

Jeanette Badger (née Handler) – Married 1999. BA in Fashion and Textiles from Liverpool Polytechnic. Now works as a holistic therapist.

Kevin Wright – Continued to make music with different groups. Recorded Janice Long session in the mid-'80s with Esprit. Moved to Anglesey in the late '80s to become a fisherman. Moved on 2005.

David Evans – Played with The Riotous Hues and The Tractors. Compiled *Elegance, Charm and Deadly Danger* compilation LP in 1985, containing two La's tracks (the first Badger/Mavers compositions to be released): 'My Girl Sits Like a Reindeer' and 'Sweet 35'. David was entertainment manager at Central College of Lancashire and now has his own promotions agency, The Sounds that History Saved, and Selective Management.

Lee Mavers – Surfaces from time to time choosing to play impromptu sets in small environments rather than taking to the main stage. Still lives in Huyton, playing and writing for himself and taking care of his family.

Jonee Mellor – Became road manager for many well-known artists, including Paul Weller. Opened the Magnet Club (Liverpool) in the late '90s, now works in film and TV as a set decorator.

Michael (Mick) Head – Formed Shack with brother John after The Pale Fountains and released the seminal album *The Magical World of The Strands*. Continues to release critically acclaimed albums and plays live with The Red Elastic Band.

Chris (Biffa) McCaffrey – Bass player with The Pale Fountains. Moved on 1989.

Hamish Cameron – Boogie woogie piano player, cosmic rockabilly, poet and astrologer. Moved on 2014.

Nick Walker – Is now an artist living in Manchester and has his own garden design business, www.GardenEscapes.co.uk.

Geoff Davies – Founder of Probe Records shop in 1971 and Probe Plus Records label in 1982. Released The Onset's debut LP, *The Pool of Life*, in 1988. Continues to release albums by Half Man Half Biscuit and an array of left-field music mainly from the North West of England.

Sam Davies (aka Eric Shark) – A member of pre-punk art maestros Deaf School. Produced The Onset with Geoff Davies and continued to perform whenever Deaf School resurfaced. Moved on 2010.

Simon Cousins – Bass player with The Onset. Works for St Helens council and performs acoustically. In 2014 released his solo debut album, *Given Songs*.

Danny Dean – Lead guitar with The Onset went on to host the Acoustic Engine with Steve Roberts. Now plays solo and has his own gardening business in north Liverpool.

Tony Russell – Former La's and Onset drummer. Has a newspaper distribution company and teaches drums in Formby.

Paul Hemmings – Played with The Twangin' Banjos. Signed to Go! Discs as La's guitarist in 1987, joined The Onset in 1988 and The Lightning Seeds in 1994. Releases his own sonic experimentation albums under the name The Floatation Project. Now a partner in the Viper Label and guitarist with Tommy Scott (Space).

Tommy Scott – After Hello Sunset and The Australians formed chart-toppers Space. The Drellas followed, and he now performs festivals with Space and plays acoustic shows.

Amber Badger – A self-employed illustrator based in Liverpool.

Bernie Nolan – First live bass player with The La's (and bass player with The Onset in the early '90s). Is a songwriting postman.

Jim 'Jasper' Fearon – Bass player with The La's Attic Sessions in 1985 and drummer on their world tour of 2005. Plays drums with Una Quinn's Threads.

John Timson – First drummer with The La's. Married Lee Mavers' sister Lisa. He is an engineer who also buys and sells classic American cars.

Paul Rhodes – Drummer on The La's' track 'Freedom Song'. Comedic activist and writer. Moved on 2004.

Phil Butcher – Bass player on the first La's recordings in 1984. Is now a dog trainer in Los Angeles.

Barry Walsh – Drummer on The La's Attic Sessions, September 1986. Lives in north Liverpool.

Tony Clarke – First live drummer with The La's. Went on to play drums with Back From Nam. Now has a painting/decorating business in Aintree.

John Power – After The La's, he formed hit-makers Cast. Plays live and releases acoustic-driven folk/blues under his own name. Played John Lennon in *Lennon* at the Royal Court Theatre in Liverpool. Still performs with the original line-up of Cast.

Paul Simpson – Conceptualist. Founding member of Teardrop Explodes. Went on to form seminal Liverpool band The Wild Swans before further ambient expression with Skyray. Now a playwright.

Ray Badger – Plays guitar in Liverpool band The Probes.

Bernie Connor – DJ, music historian and writer of Viper sleeve notes. Hosts eclectic online music podcast *The Sound of Music*.

Steve Hardstaff – Illustrator and sleeve designer. After retiring from Liverpool Art School continues to work with Probe Plus on Half Man Half Biscuit album covers and with Viper compiling American archive albums.

Martyn Campbell – Formerly of Rain, has since played with Richard Ashcroft, Shack and Arthur Lee. Still plays bass with The Lightning Seeds.

Edgar 'Summertyme' Jones – Founder of The Stairs, The Isrites and The Big Kids. Continues to write, play and record his own compositions in Liverpool.

Alan Wills – From Anglesey originally, played drums with The Wild Swans, The Room and Shack before forming Top. Created the Deltasonic record label, releasing hit albums by The Coral and The Zutons among others. Moved on 2014.

Where to See Mike Badger's Art

Huyton Railway Station Mosaic
Celebrating the station's 170th anniversary, the mosaic (which is wall mounted in the subway) was created from broken tiles, crockery and metal and inspired by competition-winner Rebecca McGrory's design.

National Wildflower Centre (Court Hey Park, Roby)
The giant tin-can fish, which has been exhibited around the country, is permanently on display in the pond at the entrance to the Centre.

Bluecoat Display Centre (Liverpool City Centre)
The donation box at the counter was created to help raise funds for the centre. Made from recycled tin boxes with a nautical theme.

Cavern Walks Shopping Centre (Mathew Street, Liverpool)
Situated at the site of the original Cavern Club. The suspended sculpture situated above the staircase is titled *A Musical Composition*. Made from reclaimed musical instruments that reflect songs by The Beatles (commissioned to celebrate what would have been John Lennon's seventieth birthday).

Museum of Liverpool (Pier Head, Liverpool)

The *Tin Planet Robot* commissioned by the band Space for their hit album *Tin Planet* is on permanent display in the museum's music section, along with other artefacts associated with Liverpool popular music.

The Sorting House (Newton Street, Manchester)

Suspended sculpture of a globe reflecting the building's history in the sorting and distribution of Royal Mail.

Discography

A Secret Liverpool – Roy G. Biv (one-sided compilation LP) (Davies Records) 1984

A Secret Liverpool – The La's (two-sided compilation LP) (Davies Records) 1985

Elegance, Charm and Deadly Danger – The La's (compilation LP) (PUSH Records) 1985

The Pool of Life –The Onset (Probe Plus 19) 1988

The What Say You – The Onset (12-inch EP) (Furious Fish) 1990

The Pool of Life Revisited – The Onset (Probe Plus 40) 1994

Volume – Mike Badger (Viper 001) 1999

Breakloose: Lost La's 1984–1986 (Viper CD/vinyl 002) 1999

Double Zero – Mike Badger (Viper 004) 2000

Unearthed: Liverpool Cult Classics Volume 2 – The Onset (Viper 009) 2001

Callin' All: Lost La's 1986–1987 – The La's (Viper CD/Vinyl 008) 2001

The Great Liverpool Acoustic Experiment – Mike Badger (Viper 10) 2002

Unearthed: Liverpool Cult Classics Volume 2 – The Kachinas (Viper 23) 2002

Lo-Fi Acoustic Excursions – Mike Badger/Onset/La's (Generator Label) (Gen 09) 2003

Lo-Fi Electric Excursions – Mike Badger/Kachinas/Onset/La's (Gen 11) 2004

The Onset – The Onset (previously unreleased studio recordings) (Gen10) 2005

Mike Badger's Country Side – Mike Badger/Onset (Gen 12) 2009

Breakloose: Lost La's 1984–1986 (remastered and expanded) (Viper 52) 2009

Callin' All: Lost La's 1986–1987 (deluxe edition, remastered and expanded) (Viper 062) 2010

Rogue State – Mike Badger (Viper 83) 2011

Lucky 13 – Mike Badger and The Shady Trio (Gen 13) 2013

Viper 100 compilation – Mike Badger (Viper 100) 2014

Badger Tracks – The La's/The Onset/Mike Badger/Roy G. Biv (Gen 14) 2014

John Got Shot – Mike Badger and The Shady Trio (7-inch vinyl) Eighties Vinyl (EVR020) 2014

Mellowtone (ten-year compilation) – Mike Badger and The Shady Trio (Mellowtone) 2014

Honky-Tonk Angels on Motorbikes – Mike Badger and The Shady Trio (Gen 15) 2016

www.mikebadger.co.uk/store

www.The-Viper-Label.co.uk

Art Biography

An Exhibition of Modern Art (collage, The Pilgrim Gallery, Liverpool 1984)

Merseyside Unknowns (Liverpool 1991)

British Craft Room, Liberty (London 1996)

Tin Can Alley (exhibition for Art Reach, 1996–97)

Lost and Found (solo Exhibition, Warrington Museum 1997)

Manchester's Festival of Food (installation artist 1998, 14-foot long floating tin fish, toured UK waters)

Lost and Found (exhibition, Tubal Cain Gallery, Harrogate 1998)

Tin Planet (album cover for Space, national billboards)

'Avenging Angel' (video/animated TV advert 1998)

Lost and Found (exhibition, Bristol Museum 1998–99)

Lost and Found (exhibition, Leicester City Gallery 1999)

This Morning (ITV, *By Design* 1999)

Blue Peter (BBC, *Lost and Found* 1999)

Gostins Gallery (joint exhibition with Amanda Ralph, Liverpool 2000)

Transformations (Pitt Rivers Museum, Oxford 2000)

Lost and Found (exhibition, Atkinson Gallery, Southport 2001)

The Sorting House (installation, Newton Street, Manchester 2002)

Installation Artist for Mersey River Festivals (2000–4)

Festival of Street Art (Merseyside 1996–2004)

Memory Block English Heritage (Liverpool Community Art projects 2004)

ITV Granada Artist in Residence (*Celebrating Fifty Years of Broadcasting*, 2006–7)

The Beat Goes On (Liverpool music exhibition, Liverpool World Museum 2008–9)

Superlambananas (ITV Granada, competition winner 2008)

Go! Penguins (ITV Granada, competition winner 2009–10)

Go! Penguins (design, Mab Lane Youth Centre, Huyton 2009)

Mike Badger's Reclaimed World (The Vitreum, Merchant Taylor's School for Girls, January–February 2010)

A Musical Composition (suspended sculpture, Cavern Walks, Liverpool, July 2010)

Huyton Station underpass mosaic (with Knowsley Community Radio, competition winner, November 2010)

Honky Tonk (country music exhibition, the Bluecoat Gallery, Liverpool 2011)

Tin Planet Robot (Museum of Liverpool, July 2011)

In the Window (the Bluecoat Gallery display centre, Liverpool 2013–14)

Mike Badger's Post Pop Art Show (music posters and memorabilia, The Vitreum, Merchant Taylor's School for Girls 2014)

The Pen Factory (window installation, Hope Street, Liverpool 2015)

Recycled Art Workshops (NW schools and colleges, 2001–15)

www.mikebadger.co.uk

Index